REPRESENTING FUTURE GENERATIONS

The impact of climate change on young people and future generations has become a key issue globally, and current international law-making processes insufficiently represent the interests of these groups. While ideally the interests of future generations would be mainstreamed, the authors argue that proxy-style mechanisms for representing future generations should urgently be pursued as a parallel strategy. This book analyses existing institutions in the UN which indirectly represent vulnerable groups and uses a novel combination of legal and philosophical methods based in the tradition of John Dewey's pragmatism and international legal realism. The chapters include case studies of climate change cases brought before international courts, tribunals, and the UN envoy to demonstrate how representation of future generations can be implemented to bring about institutional reforms. Written in accessible language, it will make a useful reference for researchers, graduate students, and policymakers in international environmental law, global environmental governance, and environmental philosophy.

PETER LAWRENCE is Adjunct Senior Researcher in the Faculty of Law at the University of Tasmania, Australia. Peter holds a PhD in international law from Tilburg University, The Netherlands. He works closely with philosophers and has been a visiting scholar at the Munich School of Philosophy, Germany, the Ethics Institute, Utecht University, The Netherlands, and the Australian National University (ANU) College of Law, Canberra, Australia. He is the author of *Justice for Future Generations: Climate Change and International Law* (2014), a co-editor of *Giving Future Generations a Voice: Normative Frameworks, Institutions and Practice* (2021), and a contributor to the *Oxford Handbook of International Environmental Law* (2021).

MICHAEL REDER is Professor of Practical Philosophy with a focus on social and political philosophy at the Munich School of Philosophy. He earned his doctorate in 2006 with a dissertation on the global governance paradigm and completed his habilitation in 2011 at Ludwig Maximilian University, Munich. He has conceived and led numerous research collaborations on topics such as representation and democracy, climate change and justice, and politics and transnational solidarity. He has been a visiting scholar at Ateneo de Manila University, the University of Cambridge, Fordham University at New York, and Georgetown University at Washington, DC. He is also the author of numerous books, including *Climate Change, Justice and Sustainability* (2012) together with Edenhofer et al., *Philosophie pluraler Gesellschaften* (2018) and Tamoudi and Faets, *Politik der Zukunft* and *Zukünftig Generationen als Leerstelle der Demokratie* (2020).

Additional Contribution

Nicky van Dijk did a PhD at the University of Tasmania, Australia, researching how to represent future generations and young people in climate law-making. They now work at Friends of the Earth – the Netherlands as a project lead and researcher on a climate court case against the bank ING.

The **Earth System Governance Project** was established in 2009 as a core project of the International Human Dimensions Programme on Global Environmental Change. Since then, the Project has evolved into the largest social science research network in the area of sustainability and governance. The Earth System Governance Project explores political solutions and novel, more effective governance mechanisms to cope with the current transitions in the socio-ecological systems of our planet. The normative context of this research is sustainable development; earth system governance is not only a question of institutional effectiveness, but also of political legitimacy and social justice.

The **Earth System Governance series** with Cambridge University Press publishes the main research findings and synthesis volumes from the Project's first ten years of operation.

Series Editor

Frank Biermann, Utrecht University, The Netherlands

Titles in print in this series

Biermann and Lövbrand (eds.), *Anthropocene Encounters: New Directions in Green Political Thinking*

van der Heijden, Bulkeley and Certomà (eds.), *Urban Climate Politics: Agency and Empowerment*

Linnér and Wibeck, *Sustainability Transformations: Agents and Drivers across Societies*

Betsill, Benney and Gerlak (eds.), *Agency in Earth System Governance*

Biermann and Kim (eds.), *Architectures of Earth System Governance: Institutional Complexity and Structural Transformation*

Baber and Bartlett (eds.), *Democratic Norms of Earth System Governance*

Djalante, Siebenhüner (eds.), *Adaptiveness: Changing Earth System Governance*

Behrman and Kent (eds.), *Climate Refugees*

Visseren-Hamakers and Kok (eds.), *Transforming Biodiversity Governance*

Biermann, Hickmann and Sénit (eds.), *The Political Impact of the Sustainable Development Goals*

Lamalle and Stoett (eds.), *Representations and Rights of the Environment*

Jörgens, Kolleck and Well (eds.), *International Public Administrations in Environmental Governance*

Bäckstrand et al. (eds.), *The Politics and Governance of Decarbonization*

REPRESENTING FUTURE GENERATIONS

Climate Change and the Global Legal Order

PETER LAWRENCE
University of Tasmania

MICHAEL REDER
Munich School of Philosophy

with guest chapter by NICKY VAN DIJK
Lead researcher climate case ING Milieudefensie – Friends of the Earth the Netherlands

CAMBRIDGE
UNIVERSITY PRESS

CAMBRIDGE
UNIVERSITY PRESS

Shaftesbury Road, Cambridge CB2 8EA, United Kingdom

One Liberty Plaza, 20th Floor, New York, NY 10006, USA

477 Williamstown Road, Port Melbourne, VIC 3207, Australia

314–321, 3rd Floor, Plot 3, Splendor Forum, Jasola District Centre, New Delhi – 110025, India

103 Penang Road, #05–06/07, Visioncrest Commercial, Singapore 238467

Cambridge University Press is part of Cambridge University Press & Assessment, a department of the University of Cambridge.

We share the University's mission to contribute to society through the pursuit of education, learning and research at the highest international levels of excellence.

www.cambridge.org
Information on this title: www.cambridge.org/9781009655866

DOI: 10.1017/9781009655859

When citing this work, please include a reference to the DOI 10.1017/9781009655859

First published 2026

Cover image: © Marco Bottigelli / Moment / Getty Images

A catalogue record for this publication is available from the British Library

A Cataloging-in-Publication data record for this book is available from the Library of Congress

ISBN 978-1-009-65586-6 Hardback

Contents

Preface

All chapters in this book involved input from both authors and were written together, with the exception of Chapter 7 written by Nicky van Dijk, for which we are grateful. Over the course of three years, we developed the arguments together through many joint online and in-person meetings, discussions, and workshops, collaboratively writing, debating, and constantly refining the chapters. We are both grateful for this collaboration that transcended usual disciplinary boundaries and continents.

We wish to thank staff at Cambridge University Press (CUP), particularly Emma Kiddle and her team, for their enthusiasm and hard work in bringing this project to fruition. We also extend our thanks to the Earth System Governance (ESG) book series editor Frank Biermann for supporting our book.

Research on which this book is based was made possible by a grant under the Australia–Germany Joint Research Cooperation Scheme ('Representation of future generations: the global legal order and climate change').

The writing of this book was made possible by generous support from our families, friends, colleagues, and respective host institutions; if we have missed anyone in the following, please forgive us.

We acknowledge the generous support received from colleagues at the University of Tasmania (UTAS) Faculty of Law, Hobart, and in particular the Dean Gino Dal Pont. We would also like to thank Rachael Ormerod for administrative assistance and the Law Librarian Angie Richards who supported research related to the book with great skill.

The following colleagues gave generous feedback on drafts and/or engaged in stimulating exchanges of ideas related to the book: anonymous reviewers at CUP, Jonathan Pickering, Jan Linehan (who sadly passed away June 2022), Matthias Hartwig, Nicky van Dijk, Bridget Lewis, Yvette Maker, Jonathan Verschuuren, Jonathan Boston, Simon Faets, Ana Honnacker, and Danilo Gajic.

We received invaluable feedback from audiences who heard presentations of parts of the book at: the Conference of the Society for Intercultural Philosophy

(Tübingen, June 2021); the ESG Conference (Toronto, October 2022); the ESG Conference (Radboud, October 2022); Tilburg Law School, seminar series 'Constitutionalizing in the Anthropocene' (December 2022 and February 2024); Max Planck Institute for Comparative Public Law and International Law, seminar series 'Law, Climate Change and the Environment' (Heidelberg, October 2023); Munich School of Philosophy (October 2022 and June 2023); UTAS Faculty of School (Hobart, February 2024); and the Department of Philosophy at Fordham University (New York, March 2024).

We would like to thank the team of the Chair of Practical Philosophy at the Munich School of Philosophy for their highly dedicated and meticulous editing of the texts, as well as the adjustment and review of the references and bibliographies, namely Anne Meuche, Laura Silvestro, Sophie Wax, and Alwin Frings. Thanks also to Jacqueline Fox for her excellent proofreading and editing of the manuscript.

We wish to thank our children Hannah, Sylvia, Margaret, Franz, and Carla for their support and inspiration in writing this book. Talking with children about questions of representing the future is such an inspiring and important way to refine and expand arguments. Thank you also to Clare Wilkinson for technical support.

Above all, we extend our thanks to our partners Anja Hilkemeijer and Lia Saile who made this book possible in so many ways.

1

Introduction

1.1 Aim of the Book

The aim of this book is to examine the question of whether future generations ought to be represented in the global legal order and institutions to address the climate change challenge and, assuming a positive answer to this, how best such representation should occur. 'Future generations' is defined as persons born in the future.[1] In light of the recent legal claims by young persons on behalf of future generations, and the recent School Strikes for Climate campaign, one might question whether it makes sense to consider representation of future generations as distinct from representation of young people. Without doubt, the interests of young people (loosely defined as people under 18 years of age) overlap significantly with those of future generations, in terms of being subject to climate impacts. Moreover, young people who are denied the vote have limited opportunities to have their views reflected in decisions by governments. But, in distinction to future generations, young people can articulate their interests. Owing to this factor – as well as empirical evidence that questions the extent to which young people in fact act more favourably than other parts of the population in relation to long-term interests[2] – the approach taken in this book is to limit the analysis to representation of future generations defined as persons born in the future. However, it is recognised that young people may act as proxies for future generations and that future generations do not constitute a discrete group; the group of living human beings is constantly expanding and, in this sense, generations are multiple and overlapping (Barry 1977: 271).

If the interests of future generations were already effectively incorporated in international and national law and policy-making on climate change, then proxy representation of their interests would be unnecessary – as would the writing of

[1] cf. other definitions of future generations in Tremmel (2009: 19–20).

[2] The empirical evidence as to whether young people *are* more concerned about the future than older people is mixed. See discussion of the literature in Gonzalez-Ricoy and Rey (2019: 7).

this book. However, it is clear that in the context of climate change, current international law rules, and national laws – including treaties, legislation, and judicial decisions, are inadequate to meet the threat of climate change, and the interests of future generations are inadequately reflected in these laws, rules, and decisions.

Extensive evidence demonstrates that contemporary global law and institutions are proving inadequate to prevent ever-worsening anthropogenic ecological impacts, and climate change impacts in particular. For example, the 2019 sixth Global Environment Outlook report (GEO-6) of the United Nations Environment Program (UNEP)[3] points to the unfolding of a major species extinction event that compromises planetary integrity and Earth's capacity to meet human needs; declining genetic diversity in turn threatens food security and ecosystem resilience (UN Environment 2019: 325). This is intimately intertwined with climate change, which is a global driver of an array of environmental, social, health, and economic impacts, as well as heightened, society-wide risks (UN Environment 2019: 04). The Intergovernmental Panel on Climate Change (IPCC), which brings together the world's climate scientists, paints a grim picture in its 2023 report of the gap between what scientists state is required to bring down greenhouse gas emissions and the action taken by governments to do so.[4] The IPCC report also concludes that global warming will continue to increase in the near term due to increased cumulative CO_2 emissions, even in low-emission scenarios.[5] Scientists have elaborated a concept of planetary boundaries that conceptualises certain thresholds related to

[3] As of July 2024, UNEP had taken action to coordinate meetings of experts to draft a seventh Global Environment Outlook (GEO-7) report pursuant to a UN Environment Assembly resolution of 2 March 2022 (UNEP/EA.5/Rev. 1) to be released not earlier than 2025. UNEP stated, *inter alia*, that:

> GEO-7 proposes to build on key findings from GEO-6 and those of other major assessments which are:
>
> - Current policies cannot keep pace with the rate of environmental degradation we face today.
> - With current policies none of the environmental SDGs [Sustainable Development Goals] of the main internationally agreed environmental goals (e.g. Paris Agreement, Aichi Targets, etc.) will be achieved.
> - Because of this we face a triple planetary crisis of climate change, biodiversity loss and pollution.

Available at: www.unep.org/geo/global-environment-outlook-7.

[4] See IPCC (2023). This report makes clear that, while the UN climate regime 'is supporting rising levels of national ambition' (A.4: 10),

> a substantial 'emissions gap' exists between global GHG [greenhouse gas] emissions in 2030 associated with the implementation of NDCs [Nationally Determined Contributions] announced prior to COP26 and those associated with modelled mitigation pathways that limit warming to 1.5°C (>50%) with no or limited overshoot or limit warming to 2°C (>67%) assuming immediate action (high confidence). This would make it *likely* that warming will exceed 1.5°C during the 21st century (high confidence)

(footnotes omitted) (A.4.3: 11). While '[m]any countries have signalled an intention to achieve net zero GHG or net zero CO_2 by around mid-century … pledges differ across countries in terms of scope and specificity, and limited policies are to date in place to deliver on them' (A.4.3: 11). The report notes that there is a lag in the adoption of low-emission technologies in most developing countries, particularly less-developed countries 'due in part to limited finance, technology development and transfer and capacity' with public and private financial flows from fossil fuels 'still greater than for climate adaptation and mitigation' and climate finance falling short of the levels needed to limit warming to below 2°C or to 1.5°C (A.4.5: 11).

[5] IPCC (2023) B.1.1: 12.

various dimensions of earth systems (including climate, biodiversity, and ocean acidification) which cannot be transgressed without serious risks for human beings continuing to operate within a 'safe operating space' (Lade et al. 2020).

Given human beings' dependence on the continuing functioning of these earth systems, the transgression of a number of these boundaries (including in relation to climate) is already impacting human beings, with developing countries and the poor most affected. In addition, these impacts are projected to continue to become worse, with future generations increasingly impacted. Future generations will be impacted by climate change in highly differentiated ways, depending on a range of vulnerability factors, including economic level, Indigenous status, gender, age, disability status, and geography, with low-lying islands and countries with low-lying coastal areas particularly affected (see Section 3.4.3). Other factors are linked to highly variable levels of adaptability and resilience. For example, whether individuals and communities can afford to install air-conditioning units could affect their ability to survive heat waves, as could their capacity to build storm surge walls to survive a hurricane or systems to lessen the impact of river flooding.

One potential objection to our focus on 'future generations' lies in the fact that individuals and communities will experience differentiated impacts. This has led some to question whether the concept 'future generations' is coherent and to assert that its use necessarily masks these differences (Humphreys 2023: 1063; cf. Lawrence 2023). While it is true that climate impacts will affect future generations in highly differentiated ways, depending on their economic and other statuses, it is also true that *all* future generations are at risk from climate change. Thus, for example, a wildfire or storm surge causally linked to climate change can now – and in the future – decimate a wealthy settlement and cause extensive loss of life. In summary, 'future generations' has heuristic value; its use in this book does not imply that future generations comprise a homogenous group.

A further possible objection to the approach we take in this book is that it could be contended that it rests on an assumption that one can look into a crystal ball and predict the future, which stretches credibility, especially the further into the future one goes. There are good answers to this concern. First, the fact that there could be a groundbreaking technological breakthrough (for example, to remove carbon from the atmosphere) – whether next year or in 2100 – is not relevant in the sense that any proxy representative institutional mechanism can only make assumptions based on *current* knowledge, including in relation to technological capacity, the need for a stable climate, and for adequate food and shelter. Moreover, scientific projections in relation to climate change currently tend not to go beyond 2100. In addition, as a practical matter, any proxy-style institution or mechanism for future generations would likely focus on projected future generations' interests in the short and medium term rather than the exceptionally long term (and not beyond 2100). Indeed, in terms of future generations' interests, the fact that climate impacts are projected to become increasingly harmful illustrates the failure of current international and national law and policy-making to incorporate sufficiently the interests of future generations.

While international environmental law rules – such as the principle of intergenerational equity, which prima facie reflects future generations' interests – do exist, these rules tend to be too vague and/or only weakly implemented at the national level because of vested interests. Law- and policy-making – at both the national and international levels – continue to be heavily biased against the interests of future generations.[6] A range of factors accounts for this, from the prevalence of short-term thinking as a matter of human psychology through to the dominance of discourses and powerful vested economic interests resisting change (Stoddard et al. 2021: 661–2). In particular, the neoliberal discourse of unending economic growth and unfettered resource extraction underpinned by property rights has stymied the necessary regulation required to address climate change (Capra & Mattei 2015: 71).

A key argument in this book is that proxy-style institutions can help remedy this bias against the interests of future generations in current international law-making. While mainstreaming the interests of future generations in law- and policy-making remains 'the main game', proxy-style institutions can and should be utilised as a parallel strategy. In this book, we elaborate a theory of proxy representation which allows for a more nuanced appreciation of the different ways proxy representatives could operate. This theory distinguishes, for example, between a 'proxy representative function', which occurs when the proxy purports to speak or act on behalf of future generations, and a 'proxy compliance function', which occurs when the proxy acts to ensure better compliance with (international) legal rules that protect future generations. However, where such rules are absent or inadequate, stronger rules are required, thereby entailing a 'proxy law reform function' in which the proxy advocates for stronger rules which respect the interests of future generations.

In practical terms, proxy representation of future generations in relation to climate change in the international legal order can include a range of scenarios. First, it could involve a claim by a state before an international tribunal (such as the International Court of Justice (ICJ)) on behalf of future generations; for example, where a Pacific island state brings an action against a major greenhouse gas emitter state, with the island state purporting to bring the claim on behalf of the state's future generations, in addition to its existing citizens.

A similar scenario is presented by the 2023 decision of the United Nations General Assembly (UNGA) to request the ICJ give an advisory opinion on the

6 For a discussion of the concept of bias in this context, see Lawrence (2021).

obligation of states under international law towards both their own citizens and future generations (UNGA 2023). This scenario forms the subject of one of the case studies in this book (Chapter 6). This scenario includes the possibility of an intergovernmental or non-government organisation (NGO) or scientist presenting an *amicus curiae* brief to the ICJ which highlights the interests of future generations, for example, through highlighting future impacts on biodiversity. A further possibility is an international tribunal itself purporting to decide on behalf of future generations, and/or the court itself acting as a proxy or guardian for future generations. Finally, there is the possibility of a claim before an international human rights committee by young persons purporting to speak on behalf of future generations, as discussed in the analysis of the *Sacchi* case brought to the UN Committee on the Rights of the Child (Chapter 7).

The possibilities sketched earlier involve climate change related litigation before international tribunals. This book, however, takes a broader view of 'the global legal order' that comprises international institutions (including international tribunals) and international law. The latter encompasses both 'hard' (binding) and 'soft' (non-binding) international law, including in the form of treaties and resolutions adopted by states meeting as the conference of parties (COP) of the UN climate bodies, as well as resolutions of other UN organs. We acknowledge that burgeoning climate change related rule-making is occurring at levels beyond the traditional state–state paradigm, including by substate and non-state entities, such as subnational governments, cities, corporations, and NGOs captured by the concept of 'transnational law' (Etty et al. 2017, 2018; Cotterell 2012, 2016; Heyvaert 2017; O'Connell & White 2019). To keep the scope of this book manageable, we do not cover this broader field here, but the normative framework of this book provides a strong basis for future research in this direction. While we define 'global legal order' as referring to 'international law', rather than the broader concept of 'transnational law', we acknowledge that international law interacts with national law in a variety of complex ways – and not necessarily in a top-down manner. Thus, for example, non-binding COP resolutions of the UN climate regime ('soft law') may be taken up and given greater weight in national court decisions, which, in turn, influence the content and direction of international legal obligations. In addition, we acknowledge that non-state actors – including, for example, highly organised, corporate fossil fuel interests hostile to action on climate change – influence the form, content, and level of bindingness of international legal rules relating to climate change (Cotterell 2016; Etty et al. 2017, 2018; Heyvaert 2017),[7] as well

[7] McGee and Steffek (2016) trace the rise of voluntary-style approaches to climate change regulation linked to neoliberalism, which then found expression in the rise of 'pledge and review' style mechanisms in the UN climate regime.

as particular discourses, such as the dominant neoliberal discourse which prioritises economic growth (Drysek 2021; Stevenson & Drysek 2014).[8]

This book analyses international law and international institutions and related literature within its scope as of 1 July 2024. In terms of international institutions, this book also explores proxy representation through establishing new institutions in the UN system. These issues have strong contemporary policy relevance. As this book went to press, the United Nations held a Summit of the Future on 22 September 2024 and adopted a *Pact for the Future*, including a non-binding *Declaration on Future Generations*.[9] The Declaration in para 32 noted the proposal by the UN Secretary General to appoint a Special Envoy for Future Generations but did not agree to create one (United Nations General Assembly 2022a: para 3). However, in October 2024 it was reported that a senior UN official had announced at a major international conference that the Secretary-General was intending to proceed to create such an envoy (Day 2024).

Answering the 'ought' part of the research question at the heart of this book – 'Why should future generations be represented in international law-making and related institutions?' – entails drawing on philosophical theories relating to intergenerational justice and theories of representation. Representation of future generations can only be by proxy. This book breaks new ground by elaborating a theory of proxy representation which melds political theory with legal theory.

In this chapter we set out the methodology adopted in the writing of this book (Section 1.2) before discussing connections with the Earth System Governance Project (Section 1.3) and possible critiques (Section 1.4). We conclude with an explanation of the structure of the book (Section 1.5).

1.2 Our Methodology: A Pragmatist Approach

An important impulse of this book is its interdisciplinary approach. We are convinced that combining philosophy and international law provides many significant insights, particularly regarding the justification of proxy representation for future generations. To understand our approach, it is important to explain the book's methodology, which is rooted in the philosophical tradition of pragmatism. This

[8] The relationship between intergenerational justice and the dominant discourses in the UN climate negotiations is analysed in Lawrence (2014: 150–68).

[9] For all outcomes of the UN Summit for the Future, including the *Pact for the Future* and *Declaration for Future Generations*, see United Nations (2024). For the mandate of the Summit see United Nations General Assembly (2022a: para 4). The mandate included considering the appointment of a UN Special Envoy for Future Generations contained in the Secretary-General's report (United Nations Secretary-General 2022). In September 2021, the UN Secretary-General first announced his intention to appoint a Special Envoy for Future Generations and create an Office of Youth affairs. See www.un.org/sg/en/content/sg/speeches/2021-09-21/address-the-76th-session-of-general-assembly.

understanding sets it apart from many other philosophical (and interdisciplinary) approaches. But what exactly does this approach involve?

Many philosophical approaches work with a top-down approach. For example, moral principles are first justified on an abstract level, which are then to be implemented top-down. Abstract arguments may, for example, first claim the universality of democracy in general and its moral principles in particular (for example, freedom). In a second step, these theory-based principles are applied to the apparent 'non-ideal' (globalised) world. The problem with this approach is that every theoretical justification implies multiple presuppositions, which are open to criticism from other views, in global and transcultural terms, from the standpoint of other cultural narratives. Thus, with this strategy, ethics often quickly get caught up in theoretical meta-discussions. These discussions are important but are of limited help in a concrete challenge, such as the ethical consideration of the further development of proxy representation. To address this challenge, it is important to recognise and adapt the range of practices – with their diverse normative underpinnings.

Therefore, we propose a different methodology – inspired by the philosophical pragmatism of John Dewey, a central philosopher of the early twentieth century. Dewey's analysis of many global crises of his time led him to observe that many scientific answers – and ethical reflections – were too ideological; as a result, they could contribute little to shaping social and political reality. Reflecting on the normative foundations of democracy, Dewey adopts a different approach: bottom-up, rather than top-down.

Democracy, he argues, should always begin with an empirical observation of current problems. This method is founded on Dewey's approach to epistemology. He views knowledge – and this also applies to political knowledge – as originating from the processing of experiences. Therefore, inquiry involves a multistage process. In his *Theory of Inquiry*, Dewey (1986) identifies the typical steps that constitute this process: (i) identifying a situation that is experienced as a problem; (ii) creating a hypothesis about the various aspects of the problem; (iii) developing viable solutions; and (iv) undertaking an evaluation aimed at proving the validity of the solution.

To find out which values might help offer solutions in the experimental processes of democracies dealing with concrete global problems, pragmatist approaches follow (more or less) Hegel's interpretation of social life and normativity. Hegel's intention was not to prescribe the adoption of top-down political mechanisms to society but, rather, to develop them out of existing social and political practices, and the values embedded in them. This entails integrating values and ethical life with a focus on the variety of social, political, and cultural practices as the starting point of philosophical reflection. Thus, democracy is not the implementation of abstract moral principles through law and institutions. Instead, philosophers indebted to Hegel emphasise the heterogeneous social and political practices that must be improved over time. Pragmatist theories argue that democracies should recognise these various practices and discourses and their potential to deal with social and political problems practically.

Of course, practices can also contradict or conflict with each other. In pragmatist terms, it is then a matter of a joint evaluative and experimental consideration of which practices are best suited to dealing with the practices at hand, to help all people equally to grow in the sense of a flourishing life (Festenstein 2008). This idea of shared growth can, for example, be translated into normative benchmarks – for example, the threshold concept involving all persons subsisting above a threshold as a minimal requirement of justice – with pragmatist approaches that emphasise the constant experimental verification and dynamic development of such benchmarks. This approach helps to avoid democracies basing their moral principles on abstract reasons. From an ethical viewpoint, the genesis and validity of values underpinning democracies are always connected, which means that the validity of these norms can only be proved by reconstructing social discourses and practices.

Dewey does not provide a clear, universal criterion, but neither do his considerations fall into relativism. Quite the contrary. To assess whether particular social, political, or legal practices are better than others, there are two important approaches. The first is to inquire whether these practices contradict their own implied values; for example, if a political practice promises justice but proves to be unjust in its implementation (for instance, by disregarding the interests of future generations), it becomes self-contradictory and needs further development. In the second approach, Dewey argues, these improvements in practices should always be oriented towards the growth and flourishing of all individuals (Festenstein 2008). In other words, political or legal practices should enable a flourishing life for all people. This demand can then be translated into other values (such as justice or solidarity), as we demonstrate in Chapter 3 in the ethical Section 3.4.

In line with this pragmatist methodology, *Representation of Future Generations* follows a bottom-up approach. This approach is less about developing an ideal form of representation from a normative argument, and more about understanding which normative discourses and practices already shape national and international law and society today; how these can be philosophically conceptualised; and what they can contribute to a further development of proxy representation.

Thus, to address the question of how proxy representation can be ethically justified, it is necessary to look afresh at the political form of government assumed to involve the fair, transparent, and just negotiation of political interests: democracy. In Chapter 2, we elaborate on the normative core of democracy from the perspective of different theoretical traditions and explain how, on this basis, a broader development of representation as a basic mode of democracy can be conceptualised. Our aim is to establish a normative basis for the development of proxy representation to include future generations – not from an ideal or abstract theoretical consideration, but from the reconstruction and discussion of the normative foundations of democracy itself. We argue that this ideal is just as applicable to the international realm as it is to the national.

In this context, a key assumption of this book is that the democratic ideal applies at both the international and national levels. This assumption is controversial. Some argue that the democratic ideal cannot apply at international level because many states are not democratic. However, this argument is unconvincing in that the rationale for democracy – in terms of minimising the risk of abusing public power and increasing the likelihood that the value of justice is maximised – is equally applicable at the international level (Chapter 3). Moreover, democracy is not an all-or-nothing proposition; it can provide an invaluable yardstick for reform – even though some structural features of the international system make such reforms particularly challenging.

Dewey's pragmatism can also help us to understand and analyse global dynamics and problems in a more convincing way than, for example, the current debate on global justice. Dewey's pragmatism invites a focus on the experiences of problematic situations. On this basis, pragmatism seeks social, cultural, and political solutions. Pragmatists are usually open to considering alternatives to ideal theoretical framings in the traditions of (Western) philosophy, thus allowing fresh perspectives on global crises. The potential of pragmatism, then, lies in its ability to fully account for the manifold experiences of global problems and of future generations. Moreover, pragmatism enables political solutions that are not biased in favour of political and legal traditions which are part of the problem in the first place. Additionally, pragmatism also leads to an alternative understanding of normativity. Thinking about normativity in the global age does not mean searching for ultimate normative principles (such as global justice) but rather – in a bottom-up sense – for an (inter) culturally anchored and plural understanding of global normativity. In the current debates on global issues, some scholars have already reflected on the potential benefits of Deweyan pragmatism (see, for example, Bray 2009; Cochran 2010; Festl 2021; Frega 2017; Green 2008; Heilinger 2020). This scholarship is helpful in developing arguments as to why, and in what ways, pragmatism can enable us to rethink and reconstruct the meta-theoretical frameworks for proxy representation in the international legal order.

While Dewey wrote little about the law, his pragmatist approach undoubtedly strongly influenced theorising about international law, particularly the emergence of the Legal Realist approach to international law. *Representation of Future Generations* follows the Legal Realist approach, the core premises of which are set out as follows. First, we must approach international law not only from a doctrinal point of view – which asks questions about the content of particular rules of international law by application of the rules on sources but also from an explanatory point of view – which asks about the meaning and origin of particular rules and how they actually function in the international system. Reflecting the pragmatist tradition of empiricism, determining such functions relies on empirical studies that extend beyond narrow, formal approaches to sources of international law to include private and public–private standard-setting activities, for example (Shaffer 2022). Following this approach, international law is studied in its broader social and political contexts (Shaffer 2015, 2022; Bodansky 2015). In addition, law is conceived in instrumental terms, as a means for solving problems and furthering progressive politics (Bodansky 2015: 271).

Following this approach, international law is not just a reflection of power and ideology, but also reflects struggles between competing conceptions of rights and justice. We accept that, in most cases, the rules of international law are clear. The role of judge or other actors in the system is to first apply the accepted formal sources of law, as this is necessary to ensure stability and predictability in the system (Dewey 1924: 24; Hart et al. 1994). Not doing so would risk undermining the legitimacy of the system: decisions would seem arbitrary, reflecting no more than the individual preferences of the person interpreting the rules. In addition, law would risk becoming an apology for power. However, in cases where applying the accepted rules on sources does not yield a result, we agree with the Legal Realists that extra-legal factors must, and should, come into play, and that this should be made transparent. In this situation, recourse should be had to the overarching purposes of the international legal system and to the underlying community values of the system as a whole (Hart et al. 1994). Some scholars question whether such values can objectively be determined, arguing that actors cannot escape their subjective values (Koskenniemi 2005: 532). However, even if objectivity could be shown to be a myth, there is value in maintaining it: abandoning the myth would create a worse situation, in which international law quickly lost its legitimacy and potential to curb power, as it would be perceived as totally arbitrary (Meier 2017: 528).

Legal Realist approaches eschew the application of overarching ethical principles (or natural law) to the international legal order and take a problem-oriented perspective from which values can be tested in terms of how they operate in the real world – their efficacy in resolving particular problems. Dewey (2005) is clear that it is essential to critically assess both practices and the ends for which practices are being pursued in the light of new social realities. The criteria to be employed in making this evaluation are opaque in Dewey's writing, but the normative goal of democracy is critical in his approach – in his view, it involves the realisation of individuals' full capacities.

Applying these Legal Realist-pragmatist approaches to the subject matter of this book, our methodology involves identifying existing rules and principles of international law – such as the principles of intergenerational equity and solidarity – and then ask how these principles and rules can be applied (and, where necessary, modified or extended) to meet the challenge of the global ecological crisis represented by climate change. These normative heuristics can be the basis for creatively developing innovative solutions. This is undertaken on the basis that the overarching goal of the international legal system includes the promotion of justice (extended to include intergenerational justice) and is defined as ensuring the ability of both current and future generations to enjoy the human rights necessary to lead a decent life (see Section 3.4.1). We argue that international law, whatever other functions it has – such as maintaining stability and peace and avoiding war – ought to further justice (Franck 1995). Justice is defined as the protection of human rights (Ratner 2015; Buchanan 2004). The basis for this normative framework lies in the international legal system itself, including in the consensus support by states of instruments reaffirming these values, such as the Universal Declaration on Human Rights (UDHR) (UNGA 1948). In addition, the President of the ICJ has stated that, 'The Court … has the important and noble role of determining existing law and rendering justice between States' (Couvreur 2012). Consistent with the principle that all persons, regardless of when or where they are born, are entitled to human rights, justice must be extended to include future generations (Lawrence & Köhler 2017: 645). Thus, a core aim or value of the global legal order is securing the human rights of both current and future generations. Given human beings' dependence on the continuing functioning of the global ecosystem – including the climate system – justice requires ensuring the integrity of these systems. This interconnection between human beings and the environment is reflected in the human right to a clean, healthy, and sustainable environment, which has received consensus support from all states following its adoption in a UN General Assembly resolution (UNGA 2022b). Indeed, the right to a healthy environment is implicit in all human rights; without protection of the environment, it is not possible for other human rights to be secured (Inter-American Court of Human Rights 2017).

In summary, then, the approach we adopt is that, where international law rules are unclear, judges and other actors operating in the international system cannot avoid making value-based judgements. Where this occurs, normative principles ought to be made explicit and applied to interpret international law to meet the requirements of these principles and the overarching purpose of the entire system to achieve justice, including intergenerational justice. We are not suggesting that philosophical concepts relating to proxy representation or intergenerational justice and solidarity should be invoked directly as a novel source of treaty interpretation within international law rules relating to, for example, the interpretation treaties.

Rather, our position is that philosophical reasoning related to these concepts can help in making explicit value-based decisions where international law rules are unclear. Moreover, it can sharpen reasoning adopted by judges or other actors in the system when interpreting international legal rules, where the accepted rules on sources do not yield clear-cut answers. In relation to treaties, we accept that application of the international law rules on treaty interpretation set out in the *Vienna Convention on the Law of Treaties* (VCLT) (1969) must be the starting point. But, where application of these rules does not give a clear-cut answer, recourse should be had to the aim of the particular treaty in conjunction with the values underlying the international legal order as a whole. How this approach works in practice is illustrated in our case study of the ICJ advisory opinion on climate change, where the normative framework is applied to interpret several important principles and rules of international law relevant to the climate context (Chapter 6).

In addressing customary international law, we accept that international tribunals have not followed their own pronouncements in requiring extensive and virtually uniform state practice and *opinio juris* (the conviction that a rule is considered binding) as preconditions for finding the existence of a rule of customary international law (Bodansky & van Asselt 2024: 273–93). As Bodansky and van Asselt (2024) point out, it is the general acceptance of a rule by the international community which is determinative of whether a rule is accepted as custom, while international tribunals (such as the International Court of Justice (ICJ)) may speed up this process by pronouncing that the rule has become custom. This means that, while we accept that the formal requirements of custom should be applied, again, where this yields an indeterminate outcome, recourse should be had to the normative values underlying the particular rule in question and the international legal system as a whole.

In addition, we identify existing normative discourses about the international legal order which can provide a blueprint for reform of the relevant international legal rules and institutions – potentially valuable for political advocacy surrounding the reform of international law and related international institutions. These normative discourses are not assumed to have a priori validity; rather, they provide a provisional basis for reform, with their ultimate value only determined in terms of how they work out in practice. Given that the rules and institutions we are talking about are future oriented, this gives rise to challenges in terms of legitimacy and effectiveness (explored in Chapter 5). In general, the Legal Realist approach provides both a valuable reference point for the full gamut of individuals and organisations involved in political advocacy to reform the international legal system and related international institutions; ultimately, the value of reforms is only ascertainable by seeing how they work out in practice. Governance reform at all levels is central to the Earth System Governance Project, to which we now turn.

1.3 Connections with the Earth System Governance Project

The main arguments for the representation of future generations made in this book relate in many ways to the basic ideas of the Earth System Governance (ESG) Project. Five of these arguments play a particularly significant role. First, the book contributes to scholarship on intergenerational justice and democracy, both of which are explicitly identified as research areas in the 'Earth Systems Governance Science and Implementation Plan' (2018).

Second, the book makes a contribution to exploring ways of ensuring better representation of future generations of human beings – squarely within the evolving Earth Systems Law approach, which seeks to include marginalised vulnerable groups (including unborn human beings) and involves law reaching out to other disciplines.[10] While the focus of the book is limited to the representation of human beings, we make clear that this does not imply that representation of non-human nature is unimportant or unjustified. Moreover, there are synergies between arguments for representing future generations and nature (Lawrence 2022). We took the decision that it would be too much to include in one volume both proxy representation of human beings and non-human nature (Lamalle & Stoett 2023).

Third, the elaboration for the first time of a theory of proxy representation linked to international law, including specific proxy-style mechanisms, fits well with the Earth System Governance Project's interest in exploring novel and more effective governance mechanisms to cope with the current transitions in the socio-ecological systems of our planet. We make it clear that proxy representation is not a silver bullet and must be combined with a range of other strategies.

Fourth, the book focuses on international law and global governance, while also acknowledging the interaction between international law and law-making at regional and national levels. While two of the case studies in the book involve tribunals at the international level, there is the potential for the principles clarified by these tribunals at the global level to percolate into regional and national law-making, and into political discourses more generally. This mirrors nicely the ESG approach entailing exploration of interactions between various levels of governance.

Finally, the interdisciplinary character of the book (combining philosophy, international law, and global governance) on the reconstruction, discussion, and further development of global governance mechanisms and international law rules sits in the interdisciplinary research tradition of ESG. These five arguments

[10] '[A] law informed by an earth system perspective would be oriented towards the more egalitarian goal of achieving social-ecological justice, notably at a planetary scale (Biermann & Kalfagianni 2020), by fully embracing all present and future earth system constituents including especially marginalized and unborn humans and the non-human world' (Kotzé, Holley & Kim 2022: 5).

demonstrate that the question of the representation of future generations, and the approach to this issue taken in this book, has strong synergies and fits well with the ESG approach.

1.4 Possible Critiques

Alongside the international legal community, the audience for this book includes scholars from adjacent disciplines (such as the humanities or social sciences) and activists engaged in the debate on how best to respond to the climate crisis. In both communities, a certain ambivalence towards law as proxy representation can be observed. On the one hand, the book shows how scholars and activists of these communities worldwide use law to better anchor future concerns in the political system. The rapid increase in climate litigation at the international, regional, and national levels is indicative of this, as are the diverse efforts worldwide to enshrine the interests of future generations in constitutions. Because law is not only influential in liberal-democratic states but also plays a significant role globally in shaping the political landscape, it is used, in a sense, to overcome the limitations of traditional law, which is often more focused on the present. This applies equally to the interpretation and utilisation of various forms of proxy representation in international law.

On the other hand, these academic and activist communities also evince a certain scepticism towards law or representation in general. Especially in Western societies, law is sometimes interpreted in these communities as a typical instrument of liberal convictions that is inherently present oriented and closely tied to an economic logic. In Germany, for example, Christoph Menke (2020) criticises subjective rights because they involve basic freedoms only in the form of property rights.

Another form of this criticism of law targets the Western-oriented logic of law. The argument is that law, deriving from Western culture, inherently implies a superior attitude towards other cultures. In post-colonial discourses, this argument is made, for example, in relation to human rights. Human rights are a Western idea built on a sovereign (and often male) subject with property – which it seeks to protect. Therefore, the law inherently implies the exclusion of people who have been suppressed or excluded through colonisation. All expansions of human rights (for example, social and cultural rights) are interpreted as illusory, thus making little or no change to this logic of exclusion.

In the pragmatic approach of this book, we take these objections seriously, while simultaneously refuting them. Viewing law as a social experimental process allows for a transformation of exclusion mechanisms in law at a fundamental level. Recognising the freedom and interests of future generations in the constitution (for example, in Brazil and Germany) is not just cosmetic and superficial. Instead, it potentially changes thinking and practice. Law and lawmakers must always consider the future. *Representation of Future Generations* argues that law can be used to improve law, in the sense that values inherent in international law can be used as a springboard for reform, by extending these values to help resolve recent problems.

Moreover, after such a critique of law, it often remains unclear what could be put in its place. The idea and practice of law implies many advantages and potentials, particularly against the backdrop of the outlined normative heuristics, which cannot be replaced by other instruments – at least not currently. This holds equally true for international law, where experimental processes are even more open, and are rapidly evolving. Our case studies show that these changes can lead to fundamentally new legal practices, through which the vulnerability of future generations is recognised and politically addressed.

Some scholars and activists also apply this critique of law to the idea of representation. This criticism involves the idea that representation always entails a new form of exclusion: representation of one group results in the concerns of another group not being considered or the group even being recognised. In this critique, then, representation produces what it seeks to overcome: it aims to enable inclusion and participation but, ironically, entails new forms of exclusion. Thus, research on intersectionality points out that forms of discrimination and social exclusion must be analysed and addressed not individually, but in an interconnected manner. This is because the representation of one disadvantaged group is intricately linked to the situation of another group.

Representation of Future Generations rejects this argument in a comparable way: certainly, every form of proxy representation is at risk of narrowing the political and legal focus. It places one group at the centre, diverting political attention from other groups. In extreme cases, this can lead to exclusion or even disregard. However, this potential limitation does not speak against the instrument of proxy representation as such, only against its misuse or lack of evaluation. Indeed, the idea of proxy representation of future generations aims to give a voice to an excluded group – namely, future living people – in the current political and legal process, to recognise their interests and legally secure them. Of course, this entails the risk that other concerns become less important; for example, the currently living poor populations in the Global South. Therefore, an ongoing evaluation of proxy representations from the viewpoints of *intra* – not just *inter* – generational justice is indispensable and a fundamental part of representation itself. In other words, the fact that something can be developed poorly does not mean it should not be attempted. In our view, the potential benefits of proxy representations far outweigh these drawbacks – always subject to the condition that the new transformations are constantly evaluated and the forms of representation continuously developed.

A final limitation of this book is that the case studies involve international institutions (such as a proposed UN Special Envoy for Future Generations) and international tribunals – including the International Court of Justice (ICJ) and the UN Committee on the Rights of the Child (CRC) – but not climate treaty processes. This omission does not in any way imply that such treaty processes are not important. While the UN climate regime has, to date, been limited in its effectiveness, it nevertheless provides a forum for the representation of future generations' interests in the climate context, which has occurred, not just through governments, but increasingly, also through subnational or non-state actors (Kuyper et al. 2018; Kuyper & Bäckstrand 2016; Angstadt & Betsill 2021). Indeed, in addition to climate treaty processes, there is a need to research proxy representative mechanisms in relation to rule-making by subnational and non-state actors. This is clearly an area where more research is needed.

1.5 Structure of the Book

In broad terms, the book is structured as follows. Part I addresses the question of why we ought to represent future generations in the international legal order and related institutions, sets out a normative framework, and links this to a concept of proxy representation. Part II introduces criteria for evaluating the effectiveness and legitimacy of proxy-style mechanisms for representing future generations. An examination of existing mechanisms in the UN system that involve representation of vulnerable groups helps to indicate which normative arguments are likely to gain traction in supporting new innovative mechanisms to represent future generations. Part III contains a series of case studies that illustrate the value of the normative framework and apply the effectiveness and legitimacy criteria. The case studies also provide a springboard for discussion of reform options more generally (Chapter 9).

We now turn to explaining the structure in more detail. Part I presents a normative framework which forms the basis for both evaluating existing international legal mechanisms and frameworks, and for proposing law reform options (undertaken in Part III). The normative framework involves a theory of proxy representation (Chapter 2), before presenting an argument as to why future generations ought to be represented in the international legal order, which draws on theories of democracy and justice (Chapter 3).

Part II begins by setting out the criteria for evaluating the effectiveness of proxy-style mechanisms for the representation of future generations (Chapter 4). The analysis proceeds on the basis that legitimacy and effectiveness are distinct but interconnected concepts, with effectiveness contributing to legitimacy and legitimacy contributing to effectiveness. Each of the possible modes of proxy representation is evaluated in terms of its democratic legitimacy and effectiveness using criteria derived from Klaus Dingwerth (2014) and Sylvia Karlsson-Vinkhuyzen and Antto Vihma (2009). Legitimacy is particularly crucial here, as previous attempts to establish bodies of this nature (including a proposal for a UN Commissioner for future generations made at the 2014 Rio +20 summit) failed due to lack of support from developing countries (Lawrence 2014: 17). Garnering such support will be essential for any such mechanism to succeed.

We then examine several existing mechanisms established at the international level aimed at representing vulnerable groups (children, disabled persons, women, and people living in poverty) to identify which normative arguments are likely to gain traction in efforts to establish proxy-style representative institutions for future generations in the international legal order (Chapter 5).

The case studies in Part III have been chosen to reflect contexts in which proxy-style representation might offer the greatest potential for progress on climate change. The case studies aim to demonstrate how normative arguments for proxy representation can nourish legal arguments in ways that increase the possibility of factoring in future generations' interests.

The case studies contained in Part III include an assessment of the effectiveness of various modes of proxy representation of future generations using the criteria set out in Chapter 4.

The optimal approach to redressing the bias against future generations in international law and policy-making is the mainstreaming of these interests in such processes. As we have observed, mainstreaming often does not work for a variety of reasons. This book does not present proxy representation as a silver bullet for addressing the failure of mainstreaming to adequately internalise the costs imposed on future generations in the climate change context. Rather, our more modest aim is to demonstrate how proxy representation mechanisms can help put pressure on governments to move in this direction. *Representation of Future Generations* aims to provide a strong normative grounding for such mechanisms. In addition, the case studies demonstrate how, exactly, such mechanisms can work, by delineating the links between normative underpinnings and the structuring of global institutions and international legal rules. We aim to show that cross-fertilisation between philosophical ideas and law can result in innovative approaches that feed into a range of ongoing, important processes, including both climate litigation strategies and grassroots activism.

References

Angstadt, M. & Betsill, M. (2021). Non-state Actors. In Rajamani, L. & Peel, J., eds., *Oxford Handbook of International Environmental Law*. Oxford: Oxford University Press, 666–83.

Barry, B. M. (1977). Justice between Generations. In Hacker, P. & Raz, J., eds., *Law, Morality, and Society*. Oxford: Clarendon Press, 268–84.

Biermann, F., & Kalfagianni, A. (2020). Planetary Justice: A Research Framework. *Earth System Governance*, 6, 100049.
Bodansky, D. (2015). Legal Realism and Its Discontents. *Leiden Journal of International Law*, 28, 267–81.
Bodansky, D., & van Asselt, H. (2024). *The Art and Craft of International Environmental Law*, Oxford: Oxford University Press.
Bray, D. (2009). Pragmatic Cosmopolitanism: A Deweyan Approach to Democracy beyond the Nation-State. *Millennium: Journal of International Studies*, 37(2), 683–719.
Buchanan, A. (2004). *Justice, Legitimacy, and Self-Determination: Moral Foundations for International Law*, Oxford: Oxford University Press.
Capra, F., & Mattei, U. (2015). *The Ecology of Law: Toward a Legal System in Tune with Nature and Community*, Oakland, CA: Berrett-Koehler.
Cochran, M., ed. (2010). *The Cambridge Companion to Dewey*, Cambridge: Cambridge University Press.
Cotterrell, R. (2012). What Is Transnational Law? *Law and Social Inquiry*, 37(2), 500–24.
Cotterrell, R. (2016). *Authority in Transnational Legal Theory. Theorising across Disciplines*, Cheltenham: Edward Elgar.
Couvreur, P. (2012). Upholding the Rule of Law at the International Level: The Role of the International Court of Justice, UN Chronicle (31 December 2012). Available at: www.un.org/en/chronicle/article/upholding-rule-law-international-level-role-international-court-justice
Day, R. (2024). *Coming Soon A UN Envoy for Future Generations*, United Nations University (October 9, 2024). Available at: https://unu.edu/cpr/blog-post/coming-soon-un-envoy-future-generations.
Dewey, J. (1924). Logical Method and Law. *Cornell Law Review*, 10(1), 17–27.
Dewey, J. (1986). *Logic: The Theory of Inquiry*, Carbondale: South Illinois University Press.
Dewey, J. (2005). *Democracy and Education. An Introduction to the Philosophy of Education*, New York: Macmillan.
Dingwerth, K. (2014). Global Democracy and the Democratic Minimum: Why a Procedural Account Alone is Insufficient. *European Journal of International Relations*, 20(4), 1124–47.
Drysek, J. (2021). *The Politics of the Earth*, 4th ed., Oxford: Oxford University Press.
Etty, T., Heyvaert, V., Carlarne, C., et al. (2017). The Maturing of Transnational Environmental Law. *Transnational Environmental Law*, 6(2), 193–203.
Etty, T., Heyvaert, V., Carlarne, C., et al. (2018). Transnational Climate Law. *Transnational Environmental Law*, 7(2), 191–200. doi:10.1017/S2047102518000183.
Festenstein, M. (2008). John Dewey: Inquiry, Ethics, and Democracy. In Misak, C., ed., *The Oxford Handbook of American Philosophy*. Oxford: Oxford University Press, 87–109.
Festl, M. G. (2021). John Dewey. In Festl, M. G., ed., *Handbuch Liberalismus*. Berlin: J.B. Metzler, 99–106.
Franck, T. M. (1995). *Fairness in International Law and Institutions*, Oxford: Oxford University Press.
Frega, R. (2017). The Wide View of Democracy. *Thesis Eleven*, 140(1), 3–21.
Gonzalez-Ricoy, I. & Rey, F. (2019). Enfranchising the Future: Climate Justice and the Representation of Future Generations. *WIREs Climate Change*, 10(4), e598.
Green, J. (2008). *Pragmatism and Social Hope: Deepening Democracy in Global Contexts*, New York: Columbia University Press.
Hart, H. M., Sacks, A., Eskridge, W. N. & Frickey, P. P. (1994). *The Legal Process: Basic Problems in the Making and Application of Law*, New York: Foundation Press.

Heilinger, J.-C. (2020). *Cosmopolitan Responsibility: Global Injustice, Relational Equality, and Individual Agency*, Berlin/Boston: De Gruyter.

Heyvaert, V. (2017). The Transnationalisation of Law: Rethinking Law through Transnational Environmental Regulation. *Transnational Environmental Law*, 6(2), 205–36.

Humphreys, S. (2023). Against Future Generations. *The European Journal of International Law*, 33(4), 1061–92.

Inter-American Court of Human Rights. (2017). *Advisory Opinion on 'The Environment and Human Rights'*, Advisory Opinion OC-23/17 (15 November 2017).

Intergovernmental Panel on Climate Change (IPCC). (2023). *Summary for Policymakers. Climate Change 2023: Synthesis Report.* Contribution of Working Groups I, II and III to the Sixth Assessment Report of the Intergovernmental Panel on Climate Change [Core Writing Team, H. Lee and J. Romero (eds.)], Geneva: IPCC, 1–34.

Karlsson-Vinkhuyzen, S. I. & Vihma, A. (2009). Comparing the Legitimacy and Effectiveness of Global Hard and Soft Law: An Analytical Framework. *Regulation & Governance*, 3(4), 400–20.

Koskenniemi, M. (2005). *From Apology to Utopia, the Structure of International Legal Argument*, Cambridge: Cambridge University Press.

Kotzé, L. J., Holley, C. & Kim, R. E., et al. (2022). Earth System Law: Exploring New Frontiers in Legal Science. *Earth System Governance*, 11(3), 100126.

Kuyper, J. W. & Bäckstrand, K. (2016). Accountability and Representation: Nonstate Actors in UN Climate Diplomacy. *Global Environmental Politics*, 16(2), 61–81.

Kuyper, J. W., Linnér, B.-O. & Schroeder, H. (2018). Nonstate Actors in Hybrid Global Climate Governance: Justice, Legitimacy, and Effectiveness in a Post-Paris Era. *WIREs Climate Change*, 9(1), e497.

Lade, S. J., Steffen, W. & de Vries, W. et al. (2020). Human Impacts on Planetary Boundaries Amplified by Earth System Interactions. *Nature Sustainability*, 3, 119–28.

Lamalle, S. & Stoett, L. (2023). *Representations and Rights of the Environment*, Cambridge: Cambridge University Press.

Lawrence, P. (2014). *Justice for Future Generations: Climate Change and International Law*, Cheltenham: Edward Elgar.

Lawrence, P. (2021). Justifying Institutions for Future Generations Based on the Mitigation of Bias and Intergenerational Justice. In Linehan, J. & Lawrence, P., eds., *Giving Future Generations A Voice: Normative Frameworks, Institutions and Practice*. Cheltenham: Edward Elgar, 21–41.

Lawrence, P. (2022). Justifying Representation of Future Generations and Nature: Contradictory or Mutually Supporting Values? *Transnational Environmental Law*, 11, 553–79.

Lawrence, P. (2023). International Law Must Respond to the Reality of Future Generations: A Reply to Stephen Humphreys. *European Journal of International Law*, 34(3), 669–82.

Lawrence, P. & Köhler, L. (2017). Representation of Future Generations through International Climate Litigation: A Normative Framework. *German Yearbook of International Law*, 60, 639–66.

McGee, J. & Steffek, J. (2016). The Copenhagen Turn in Global Climate Governance and the Contentious History of Differentiation in International Law. *Journal of Environmental Law*, 28, 37–63.

Meier, S. (2017). The Influence of Utopian Projects on the Interpretation of International Law and the Healthy Myth of Objectivity. *German Yearbook of International Law*, 60, 515–38.

Menke, C. (2020). *Critique of Rights* (trans. C. Turner), Cambridge: Polity Press.

O'Connell, M. E. & White, S. (2019). Transnational Legal Process and International Adjudication. *Max Planck Encyclopaedia of International Law*, https://opil.ouplaw.com/display/10.1093/law-mpeipro/e3276.013.3276/law-mpeipro-e3276

Ratner, S. R. (2015). *The Thin Justice of International Law: A Moral Reckoning of the Law of Nations*, Oxford: Oxford University Press.

Shaffer, G. (2015). International Legal Theory, International Law and Its Methodology: The New Legal Realist Approach to International Law. *Leiden Journal of International Law*, 28, 189–210.

Shaffer, G. (2022). Legal Realism and International Law. In Dundoff, J. L. & Pollock, M. A., eds., *International Legal Theory: Foundations and Frontiers*. Cambridge: Cambridge University Press, 82–100.

Stevenson, H. & Drysek, J. (2014). *Democratising Global Governance*, Cambridge: Cambridge University Press.

Stoddard, I., Anderson, K., Capstick, S. et al. (2021). Three Decades of Climate Mitigation: Why Haven't We Bent the Global Emissions Curve? *Annual Review of Environment and Resources*, 46(1), 653–89.

Tremmel, J. C. (2009). *A Theory of Intergenerational Justice*, London: Earthscan.

UN Environment. (2019). *Global Environment Outlook – GEO-6: Healthy Planet, Healthy People*, Cambridge: Cambridge University Press.

United Nations. (2024). *Summit of the Future, Our Common Agenda*. Available at: www.un.org/en/summit-of-the-future/pact-for-the-future.

United Nations General Assembly. (1948). *Universal Declaration of Human Rights*. Resolution adopted by the UN General Assembly, UN Doc. A/RES/217 (III).

United Nations General Assembly. (2022a). *Modalities for the Summit of the Future*. Resolution adopted by the UN General Assembly, UN Doc. A/RES/76/307.

United Nations General Assembly. (2022b). *The Human Right to a Clean, Healthy and Sustainable Environment*. Resolution adopted by the UN General Assembly, UN Doc. United Nations Secretary-General.

United Nations General Assembly. (2023). *Request for An Advisory Opinion of the International Court of Justice on the Obligations of States in Respect of Climate Change*. Resolution adopted by the UN General Assembly, UN Doc. A/77/L. 58.

United Nations Secretary-General. (2021a). Secretary-General's Report, *Our Common Agenda*.

United Nations Secretary-General. (2021b). Secretary-General's Address to the 76th Session of the UN General Assembly. Available at www.un.org/sg/en/node/259283.

United Nations Secretary-General. (2022). *At 'Our Common Agenda' Talks, Secretary-General Says Summits on Future, Sustainable Development Goals 'Last, Best Chance' to Manage, Solve Global Challenges Press Release*, SG/SM/21399 (4 August 2022).

Vienna Convention on the Law of Treaties (VCLT) (1969) (adopted 23 May 1969; entered into force on 27 January 1980) 1155 UNTS 331.

Part I

Normative Framework

Justifying Representation of Future Generations

2

Proxy Representation and the Global Legal Order

Integrating Philosophical and Legal Perspectives

2.1 Introduction

The political discussions of the past two decades show that the medium- and long-term ecological impacts of industrialisation on the planet and human societies represent an enormous challenge for societies worldwide and, indeed, the international community. This is most clearly demonstrated by climate change. It is obvious today that the living conditions of human beings worldwide are – and will be in the future – massively negatively affected by climate change. However, although the impacts of climate change have been very clearly demonstrated by scientists, not least through the regular reports of the Intergovernmental Panel on Climate Change (IPCC), there is still political controversy about how to respond to this crisis.

Given that greenhouse gas emissions do not respect national borders, effective responses to climate change must be both national and international. While many governments have established mechanisms to address climate change, both in terms of mitigation and adaptation, these measures are insufficient. The same applies to the global legal order and its related institutions. While some improvements to the global climate regime – including related conference of parties' (COP) decisions – have been negotiated in recent years, serious doubts remain as to the effectiveness of this regime.

At the heart of the global climate regime is the *Paris Agreement*. This treaty relies on countries making voluntary mitigation commitments in Nationally Determined Contributions (NDCs). To date, states have failed to commit to sufficiently stringent NDCs at the level scientists say is necessary to address climate change. The wealthy states (that cause the problem in the first place) have failed to show leadership in reducing emissions. Moreover, the same wealthy countries have not provided the required finance – essential for both mitigation and adaptation – with only about one-third of what experts say is required having been pledged.[1] In addition, there are concerns that the *Paris Agreement* may be structurally flawed, given its reliance on non-binding (soft law) commitments (Lawrence & Wong 2017) and its lack of an effective compliance mechanism, with non-governmental organisations (NGOs) excluded from playing a vital role in holding states to account (Van Asselt 2016). The consequences of weak climate policy entailing inadequate mitigation and adaptation efforts involve harm to both vulnerable people alive today and harm to future vulnerable people, especially the poor.

This brief description of the current situation suggests that it is important to explore new ways to develop and implement a sustainable climate policy from a global perspective. The distinctive feature of this book is its exploration of sustainable law- and policy-making through establishing new forms of proxy representation of future generations. The idea behind this is that, if future generations are represented in the global legal system, this will help facilitate the pursuit of effective and sustainable climate policy- and law-making. Since future generations cannot determine their own representatives, representation in this context must involve forms of 'proxy representation'.

Proxy representation occurs when a person or thing cannot speak for itself; in other words, it gives a voice to the 'inarticulate'. The proxy representative makes reasonable assumptions about the interests of the person or thing being represented. How can we justify proxy representation? Representation is closely linked to theories of democracy. One strand of the argument justifies proxy representation with reference to the core elements of existing democratic theory, which need to be modified in the face of global ecological threats and the needs of future generations. Put differently, these theories need to be modified to incorporate a new model of proxy representation which can help plug a blind spot in democratic theory. Proxy representatives give a voice to vulnerable groups – and future generations – particularly the future people living in poverty, who arguably constitute the most vulnerable. While highly contested, this book takes the position that the ideal of democracy does, and should, apply at the international level.

If we can find convincing ways to represent future generations in democracies, this can give us a blueprint at the theoretical level to develop and sustainably implement proxy representation of future generations at the international legal level as well. In the following philosophical Chapter 3, we will turn to representation as a key mechanism of democracy and discuss whether and how our understanding of

[1] As Ruth Adler (2024) states in her doctoral dissertation, *The Green Climate Fund: A Case Study in the Legitimacy of Global Climate Finance Governance*: 'In this regard, the Intergovernmental Panel on Climate Change (IPCC) estimates climate policies consistent with a 1.5°C temperature goal would require energy system supply-side investment levels of USD1.6–USD3.8 trillion per year for the period 2016–2050'. See also Rogelj et al. (2018) and IPCC (2023). Recent financial transfers thus represent approximately 36 per cent of what is required to meet the lower end of IPCC estimates of what is needed to achieve the temperature goal.

representation can be further developed to respond to the climate crisis and incorporate the interests of future generations. We will demonstrate which impulses the philosophical discussion might have for these developments. On this basis, we explore how the further development of the idea of proxy representation can be transferred to the international level, including both international legal rules and institutions. Our thesis is that developing new forms of democratic proxy representation can be an important strategy in this reform process, both domestically and internationally.

The remainder of the present chapter is structured as follows. First, we demonstrate that traditional concepts of representation – including agency-based, audience, and surrogacy models – struggle in their application in relation to future generations (Section 2.2). We then propose a definition of representation in the legal context, before moving on to define proxy representation, distinguishing between direct and indirect variants. We then proceed to sketch various modes of proxy representation at the national level, ranging from ombudsman-style mechanisms through to informal representation, through social movements and citizens' assemblies (Section 2.3). Such national mechanisms are relevant because they provide inspiration for proposals at the international level. We then describe a range of existing forms of proxy representation in the international legal order, to demonstrate that proxy representation of future generations represents a modest, rather than radical, reform of international law (Section 2.4). Next, we turn to assessing the extent to which indirect representation of future generations is incorporated in the international legal order in terms of environment-related principles (Section 2.5). A matrix setting out the range of functions which proxy representation may perform is then set out. We argue that, by distinguishing these functions, a more nuanced understanding can be obtained as to the functions of existing modes of proxy representation, as well as reform proposals. Finally, we draw conclusions (Section 2.6).

2.2 Traditional Concepts of Representation and Their Limitations

Representation is one important and basic attribute of democratic institutions. It seems perfectly clear what representation does: namely, it provides a vehicle for expressing or articulating the interests of citizens. In this way, large, differentiated societies can facilitate political action and bring to life the democratic idea of participation by all citizens. On closer examination, however, it becomes clear that it is not so simple. At the outset, it is important to note that there is no single definition of representation. For this reason, we outline three important models of representation – and their limitations – from a philosophically inspired perspective.

First, representation is often described as an agency-based concept which relies on the representative being authorised by citizens to form government and represent their interests through the process of democratic elections. In democracies, representatives are elected in a fair and transparent electoral process to deal with challenges, and political decisions are legitimated through the representative's holding office through the electoral process. On the one hand, these representatives are authorised by the *demos*, traditionally understood as the sum of the citizens of a society or a state. On the other hand, these representatives are accountable to the people for what they decide.

In this mode of representation, political parties often play an important role in democratic procedures. Parties offer different strategies to deal with current challenges, for example, climate change. Representation by politicians of different parties in democracies can be understood as a form of (at least partly) 'unbounded' representation. What is meant by 'unbound' in this context? This can be explained by looking at the concrete actions of representatives. Although representatives are authorised to act by the people who voted them into office, they can – once in office – make decisions independently of the electors and with reference only to the basic ideas of the party to which they belong. This shows that their actions are ultimately relatively 'unbound': they have a relatively significant margin of leeway in their political decision-making. Philosophically, such an understanding of representation is called 'actor-centred' because it focuses on the actions of the politician, authorised by the voters.

Looking at the long-term consequences of this type of political action, we can immediately see some problems inherent to such an understanding: agency-based concepts of representation clearly do not work in relation to future generations because they cannot authorise the representatives in a strict sense. Precisely because future generations cannot authorise the representatives – because they are not yet alive – their interests remain at risk of being neglected on a very basic level. If human beings were hardwired to take the long-term view, then this issue would not arise. But empirical studies in the social sciences (see Boston & Lempp 2011; González-Ricoy & Gosseries 2016; MacKenzie 2016) suggest the opposite: human beings tend to insufficiently consider the long-term impacts of their action on future generations.

Second, in addition to this 'narrow' definition of representation, a much broader concept of representation is possible. According to Andrew Rehfeld's influential definition (Rehfeld 2006: 8), for example, Person or Institution A represents Person or Thing B, where A claims to act or speak on behalf of B with respect to a specified set of issues, and this is accepted by a particular audience.[2] In this broad, audience-based definition, representation is less about direct authorisation and more about ensuring that concerns are heard.

[2] This discussion of Rehfeld's and Saward's definitions of representation is based on Lawrence (2021: 604–605).

Rehfeld's concept of representation can work in relation to future generations if we consider the relevant audience not to be future generations but, rather, contemporaries upon whose support the proxy representative relies. Thus, for example, a United Nations Special Envoy for Future Generations, should one be created (see Chapter 8), could, in the context of the UN climate negotiations, be considered as representing future generations if the participants in those negotiations recognised this Special Envoy as having this function through the applicable rules of procedure. Rehfeld's theory keeps separate the question of whether the act of representation is legitimate, rather than building it into the definition of representation itself. However, as Anja Karnein points out, there are usually at least some background norms shared between the representor and the representee.[3] Of course, if there is no audience who accepts that one is speaking on behalf of future generations, this model also does not work to represent them in political processes (Lawrence 2021: 24).

Third, Michael Saward's surrogacy-based concept of representation constitutes another promising way to conceiving of proxy representation of future generations (Saward 2008; 2009). Saward views representation more as a claim than as a fact arising from elections, thus opening the possibility of legitimate representation outside the electoral context. In Saward's view, someone represents the interests of a specified group where they represent the particular group's interests 'because of X' (Saward 2009), where X can be a range of factors, including, for example, ties to a tradition. Thus, according to this view, the representative can act as a 'surrogacy for wider interests' and this can occur outside the electoral context (Saward 2009: 12). Where there is no formal process to assess the claim of representation by the constituency, Saward uses an 'authenticity' criterion to assess the claim of representation. This involves asking whether the representative appears to speak 'genuinely' on behalf of marginalised persons in a context where a stakeholder has a stake in the decision being made, giving rise to a right to have their interests included in the decision-making process (Saward 2009: 13). Under this approach, then, an assumption is made that an organisation or individual purporting to represent a particular marginalised group is genuine, absent evidence to the contrary. If we apply this model to a proxy claiming to represent future generations – provided we assume that the stakeholders have contingent rights upon being born, giving them a stake in the decision – this test might seem too easy to meet. However, if we combine these criteria for representation with

[3] Karnein (2016: 90) provides as an example of a 'shared background norm', the norm that a representative of a member state to the World Trade Organization (WTO) reflects the concept of sovereignty. Thus, a person in charge of the military in a particular state could be accepted as a representative of the particular country by the WTO members, but not the manager of the local convenience store, a block away from the UN Headquarters in New York.

checks and balances – such as a requirement that the interests of future generations be properly reflected in the mandate of the proxy representative, and NGOs are given power to hold to account a proxy representative in terms of whether they are performing in compliance with the particular mandate involved – these concerns can arguably be addressed (Lawrence 2021).

This brief description of three models of representation – agency-based, audience-based, and surrogacy-based – already shows that it is not easy to develop a collective understanding of representation applicable to future generations. Moreover, it is not easy to develop new forms of representation in the face of the global ecological crisis. The reason for this is that democratic representation necessarily implies some important structural limitations: for example, it is possible that representatives elected by democratic procedures do not care at all about the concerns of future generations. Moreover, democracies' inherent limitation of the *demos* to the *current* citizens in a specific territory (nation) tends not to be questioned, despite the obvious global consequences flowing from national political decisions. Both limitations are obviously highly problematic in view of the ongoing extensive discussions about climate impacts and their political treatment.

So far, the concept of representation has been presented as a political concept. A subcategory of political representation includes representation in the legal context.[4] If we consider an international tribunal's capacity to represent future generations, it is important to note that, under Rehfeld's concept of representation, an international tribunal would represent future generations if the 'rules of recognition' – in this case, constituted by the statute of the particular tribunal as interpreted by that tribunal – allow for representation of future generations by, for example, a state appearing before the tribunal or an NGO or scientist presenting evidence before the tribunal. (For more detail, see the scenarios relating to the International Court of Justice (ICJ) set out in Chapter 6.) Indeed, *legal* concepts of representation follow this approach. Lawrence and Köhler define 'representation' in the legal context as involving,

> a claim by a 'representative' to be acting on behalf of a person or thing being represented (the 'representee') in relation to a particular function, based on a legal foundation which involves an authorisation given either by the representee or directly by law.[5] Authorisation 'directly by law' would include the statute of a tribunal explicitly or implicitly allowing for the representation of future generations (Lawrence & Köhler 2017: 654).

[4] The discussion in this paragraph draws on Lawrence & Köhler (2017).

[5] See on this legal concept of representation the original Art. 389 French Civil Code (*Code civil*) (1804), 21 March 1804, as amended on 3 January 2018. The original version of this provision allowed a father to represent the interests of his children within certain boundaries, with women possessing limited rights; this pattern was subsequently introduced across Continental European (and South American) civil law systems. In the modern context, see Larenz & Wolf (2004: 829).

A further possibility is that an international tribunal indirectly represents future generations by applying or developing international law rules which reflect their interests (see Section 2.3). It is important to consider more deeply the wide spectrum of different forms of proxy representation to which we now turn.

2.3 Proxy Representation

As we have seen, proxy representation occurs when a person or thing is incapable of communicating their or its needs or interests because: (i) they or it does not yet exist, as in the case of future generations, or (ii) is incapable of communicating as in the case of a severely disabled person and in the case of non-human nature or ecosystems (Lawrence & Köhler 2017: 654). In *Representing Future Generations*, 'representation' refers to 'proxy representation', unless otherwise specified.[6]

The representation of future generations may be direct or indirect. In this book, we refer to 'direct representation', where a representative explicitly claims to act on behalf of future generations. By contrast, where the representative does not purport to act on behalf of future generations but, rather, highlights their interests, we use the term 'indirect representation'. Both concepts are strongly linked, given that the objectives of representation in each case will often overlap. This distinction between 'direct' and 'indirect' representation can be explained with an example. Imagine that a biologist, who researches climate impacts under a mandate of the *Convention on Biological Diversity* (CBD) (1992), writes a report highlighting the interests of nature and future generations in terms of climate impacts. The biologist does not claim to speak on behalf of nature or future generations, so writing the report would, strictly speaking, fall outside our definition of 'direct' representation. Yet, the report could still constitute 'indirect' representation. The same biologist may also speak explicitly on behalf of future generations, younger people, or a threatened biological species in a media interview or blog contribution as linked to various political processes, constituting 'direct' representation.

This example demonstrates that, as well as being direct or indirect, representation can operate in various contexts with more than one function, with the legitimacy of representation in each case having a different basis. So, in the context of the biologist writing a report on the impacts of climate change on future biodiversity (upon which future human beings will depend) under the CBD, the legitimacy of this representation may rest on the scientific expertise of the expert and the CBD processes. In contrast, the blog piece for an NGO (for example, Extinction Rebellion) may rest on a different source of legitimacy, linked more to

[6] This section draws on Lawrence (2022).

the expertise of the person as a scientist (independent of the CBD), combined with their voice as a concerned citizen (Lawrence 2022: 4).

This example points to yet another important aspect: proxy representation is usually related to a clearly identifiable actor who speaks on behalf of someone else. In many current debates, such an understanding is assumed when discussing ombudspersons for future generations. In some cases, an institution can also be understood as an actor. In these cases, however, proxy representation also implies an agency connotation, meaning that the institution acts as a quasi-individual actor on behalf of someone else.

In this book, we do not limit ourselves to representation in this narrow sense. This is because entirely different forms of proxies are conceivable. First, we must recognise that collective entities (for example, networks or social movements) are also forms of proxy representation. Such entities are not clearly defined as individual actors; yet, they also purport to speak on behalf of someone else, including future generations. Moreover, discourses or individual practices can also be understood as forms of proxy representation. If a practice sees itself as a regular collective action through which future generations are to be heard and integrated into society, this can also be a form of proxy representation. An example of this is the practice of science, ranging from the individual climate scientist to the institutional level (for example, the IPCC). Science – particularly the climate science relevant to this book – is quite evidently a crucial proxy, without which the concerns of future generations would certainly not have received as much attention as they have in recent years. In scientific practice, the heterogeneity within a proxy becomes simultaneously evident. Discussions around the significance of Indigenous knowledge for climate policy provides an example of this (Abe et al. 2024). Both make the concerns of future generations audible in the present, but in separate ways and with different objectives. The recognised rules regarding how such conflicts should be addressed will vary, depending on the institution or practice (Latulippe & Klenk 2020; Wilkens & Datchoua-Tirvaudey 2022).

The law itself can also be a proxy. To take one example, if the constitution of a state refers to future generations as legal subjects to be considered and protected, then this is also a form of proxy representation for future generations. The embodiment of future generations' interests in multilateral treaty obligations or in principles of customary international law is also a form of proxy representation.

Concepts of representation are intertwined with the concept of interests. Future generations share with current generations the important attribute that their multiple interests cannot be reduced to a single dimension or currency (Driver 2014). In the past, it was often assumed that such interests were objectively 'out there', with the proxy representative having only to reveal them (Tanasescu 2014). This view is challenged by Mihnea Tanasescu, who maintains that proxy representation involves a strong 'creative and relational' dimension: the proxy brings into existence the interests concerned through an active process whereby the representor necessarily injects a normative element in terms of how they would like the world to be reformed (Tanasescu 2014). Similarly, Robyn Eckersley argues that proxy representation assumes the possibility that the proxy has knowledge of either future generations or ecological systems being represented (Eckersley 2004). We agree with Eckersley's position that knowledge in this context – spanning both scientific and Indigenous – must necessarily be interpreted through cultural and other social norms, but that this does not deny the existence of knowledge independent of the existence of the knowing agents or representatives (Eckersley 2004).

At the national level, a range of different mechanisms of proxy representation can be distinguished. The first category of proposals focuses primarily on the executive branch and aims, for example, to establish ombudsmen, guardians, or trustees (Weiss 1989; Birnbacher 1988; Thompson 2010). Ombudsmen emerge from a Scandinavian tradition that provides extensive powers to investigate complaints made by individual citizens relating to the actions of bureaucrats and public entities. Their findings are normally non-binding (Lawrence & Linehan 2021: 5); they also have important standard-setting and educational functions (McCormack & Hansen-Lohrey 2021). In the West, ombudspersons have become institutionalised in the formal political system. They can, for example, examine laws in terms of their consequences for future generations and make recommendations where laws do not adequately consider the interests of future generations. This is about representation of future generations as an advocate. The task for such officials is sometimes also to develop concrete policy concepts that benefit future generations, to which legislative proposals from other areas must be oriented. Various future forums also fall into this category.[7]

Proposals for a second category are directed at the reform of parliamentary representation. Dobson (1996), for example, suggests electing experts to parliament as representatives of future generations. Eleki (2005) develops a similar proposal, earmarking 5 per cent of parliamentary seats for representatives of future generations. Other authors favour establishing a third chamber of Parliament to deal with future issues (Roderick 2010). Jonathan Boston points to a wide range of so-called commitment devices that can help factor in long-term interests in parliamentary-style democracies: from reforming auditing processes through to appointing a scientific advisor to the Parliament to highlight long-term climate impacts (Boston et al. 2019). In New Zealand, for example, the strategy has been to appoint a Parliamentary Commissioner for the Environment (Boston 2021a).

[7] For a survey of various types of national institutions for future generations, see Lawrence & Linehan (2021).

Corresponding to the liberal theories described earlier and their focus on legal instruments, a third group of proposals involves reforms to the legal system to facilitate representation of future generations (both direct and indirect) or embedding the rights of future generations in constitutional provisions (Boston 2021b). In terms of the judiciary, an important possibility is to give standing (the right to sue) to NGOs to bring claims on behalf of future generations, or to allow such organisations or scientists to lodge *amicus curiae* briefs that highlight the distinctive interests of future generations (Lawrence & Köhler 2017).[8]

A fourth group of proxy presentations that goes beyond the formal political system includes, for example, strengthening social movements (Thompson 2005) and paying greater attention to cultural actors (such as religious communities) as proxies for the concerns of creation or future fellow human beings. Religious communities have increasingly become a topic in many contemporary political theories (Gerten & Bergmann 2012; Reder & Müller 2012). Even in a post-secular society, these groups can contribute importantly to representation of the future – precisely because of their creation-theological perspective towards the future. This applies equally to the diverse civil society activities: the 'Fridays for Future' school strikes are a case in point.

A further possibility involves citizens' assemblies which bring together a wide diversity of citizens – including young people below the voting age – to debate issues and then formulate recommendations which are then fed into the formal political process. Such mechanisms have been used in many jurisdictions, including Scotland (Linehan 2021).

Looking at the literature on proxy representation, it is striking that a single type of proxy representation is not usually proposed as a vehicle for giving sustainable attention to nature or future generations in political processes; more often, different forms are combined. For example, Simon Caney (2016) proposes a combined strategy involving a government manifesto for the future, a parliamentary committee, a future vision day, and an independent future council.

From this initial survey of forms of proxy representation, it becomes clear that there are already many approaches at the national level involving further development of democratic representation to include future generations or nature. Several of the models for representation of future generations at the national level have provided inspiration for moves at the international level to represent future generations. (Part III of this book explores several modes of representation at the international level in detail.) At this point, it is important to set out in general terms the various modalities for representation of future generations in relation to the global legal order and related institutions.

[8] *Amicus curiae* briefs allow a person or organisation that is not a direct party to a particular case to assist the court by providing expert information.

2.4 Existing Forms of Proxy Representation in International Law

The general rule is that, before international courts and tribunals, only states or individuals can rely on violations of their own rights. Put differently, only individuals or states suffering damage to their own interests have standing to bring claims before such tribunals. Prima facie, this creates an insurmountable problem for future generations bringing claims before such tribunals, or being represented by a proxy in some shape or form, because only potential (rather than actual) damage can be the basis of a claim.

In this section, however, we demonstrate that there are already several examples in the international legal order of claims being brought before an international tribunal in relation to damage or harm that was not suffered by the person or entity bringing the claim – but on a proxy basis.[9] These examples – set out as short case studies – show that the notion of claims being brought by states or entities on behalf of future generations is not as radical as it might seem. Rather, it involves only incremental reform to international law and institutions.

In relation to each of these short case studies, we examine: (i) who can bring a claim; (ii) on behalf of whom; (iii) whose rights are violated; and (iv) what assumptions are made in terms of the rights/interests of the person or entity violated.

2.4.1 League of Nations Mandate System

Under the League of Nations mandate system, and as confirmed by the ICJ in the 1971 case *Legal Consequences for States of the Continued Presence of South Africa in Namibia* (*Namibia case*), all members of the League had an obligation to act under the mandate system in the interests of the inhabitants of the country/entity covered by the mandate. In the *Namibia* case, the ICJ accepted the principle that, even following the dissolution of the League of Nations, South Africa had an obligation according to which the well-being and development of the peoples living in such territories formed 'a sacred trust of civilisation' (*Covenant of the League of Nations* 1919: art. 22). The duties here flowed from a treaty between the League and South Africa, which took on the obligations of a trustee in relation to the people of Southwest Africa. This system involved the mandate power being under an obligation to 'promote to the utmost the material and moral well-being and the social progress of the inhabitants of the Territory subject to the present Mandate' (The League of Nations 1920: art. 2) which, in turn, involved the mandatory making assumptions about the interests of the people it purported

[9] This section relies on an unpublished paper by Matthias Hartwig and Peter Lawrence; it is incorporated here with Hartwig's permission.

to represent. In turn, the ICJ in its advisory opinion of 1971 in the *Namibia* case made assumptions about the interests of the people covered by the mandate; for example, concluding that the apartheid system was not in the interests of the people of Southwest Africa (now Namibia) and that it was in violation of the UN Charter. In this example, then, the inhabitants of a particular mandate could not directly bring their interests before the ICJ. Nevertheless, this system involved the notion that the mandate state should act on behalf of the persons covered by the mandate, with a set of assumptions being made about their interests.

Addressing our criteria, we can say that, under this system: (i) any individual state member of the League can bring a claim against the mandatory for violation of the mandate (treaty between the League and the mandatory); (ii) such a claim could be brought on behalf of the inhabitants of the mandate; (iii) such a claim could relate to violations of the 'best interests' of the inhabitants of the mandate (for example, through the system of apartheid); and (iv) it was assumed that the inhabitants of the mandate possessed basic human rights (not couched in the language of human rights), including the right to be free of apartheid, and that the mandatory should exercise its governance over the mandate respecting these rights.

2.4.2 **Erga Omnes** *Claims under the International Law Commission Articles on State Responsibility*

In the *Case Concerning the Barcelona Traction, Light and Power Company Limited* (*Barcelona Traction* case 1970), the ICJ drew a distinction between obligations owed to a particular state and those owed to the international community as a whole 'in view of the importance of the rights involved, States can be held to have a legal interest in their protection; they are obligations erga omnes' (*Barcelona Traction* case 1970: 33), referring to the outlawing of acts of aggression, and of genocide, and principles and rules concerning the basic rights of the human person, including protection from slavery and racial discrimination. The International Law Commission (ILC) in its articles on state responsibility codified this concept in article 48, which provides that:

> 1. Any State other than an injured State is entitled to invoke the responsibility of another State … if:
>
> (a) the obligation breached is owed to a group of States including that State, and is established for the protection of a collective interest of the group; or (b) the obligation breached is owed to the international community as a whole. (ILC 2001: art. 48)

The ILC in its commentary emphasised that a state acting under article 48 would be acting not based on its individual capacity by reason of its suffering injury, but rather 'in its capacity as a member of the group of states to which the obligation is owed or indeed as a member of the international community as a whole' (ILC 2001: 126). The preconditions for this to occur are, first, that the obligation is owed to a group to which the state invoking responsibility belongs and, second, that the obligation has been established 'for the protection of the collective interest' (ILC 2001: 137). The obligation can be derived from treaties or customary international legal obligations. Examples of such collective interests include in relation to the environment or security of a region; the ILC makes clear that the interest extends beyond that of individual member states to a 'wider common interest' (ILC 2001: 126). An example is the *Treaty of Versailles* (1919), which established an international regime for the Kiel Canal to keep the canal open to foreign vessels. This broader common interest was upheld in the case of *S.S. Wimbledon, Britain et al. v. Germany* (*Wimbledon* case 1923) by the Permanent Court of International Justice (PCIJ). Japan joined this litigation, although not directly affected by the disruption of the passage of the *Wimbledon* (flying a French flag) through the canal.

The list of obligations which may fall into the category of obligations owed *erga omnes* is not static and may develop over time. As mentioned earlier, the ICJ in the *Barcelona Traction* case considered that outlawing aggression and genocide would fall within this category, as would the 'basic rights of the human person, including protection from slavery and racial discrimination' (*Barcelona Traction* case 1970: 33). In the *East Timor Case (Portugal v. Australia)* (*East Timor* case 1995), the ICJ added the right of self-determination to the list of obligations owed *erga omnes*.

It is crucial to note, however, that establishing an obligation owed *erga omnes* as a matter of state responsibility is distinct from establishing jurisdiction of an international tribunal to hear such a claim. Thus, the ICJ in the *Barcelona Traction* case stated that 'the instruments which embody human rights do not confer on States the capacity to protect the victims of infringements of such rights irrespective of their nationality' (*Barcelona Traction* case 1970: 48). The upshot is that, where an international obligation falls into the category of *erga omnes*, a state does not have to demonstrate that it has suffered damage as a precondition to bringing a claim, but the state still needs to demonstrate that the tribunal concerned has jurisdiction to hear the case.

Applying our matrix, first, under article 48, we ask, 'Who can bring a claim?' A state other than the injured state can bring a claim, provided there is a breach of an obligation owed to a group of states including that state, or the obligation breached is an obligation owed to the international community. Second, we ask, 'On whose behalf is such a claim brought?' The claim may be brought on behalf of the beneficiary (for example, in relation to human rights obligations) but also on behalf of the international community, which is considered to have an interest in upholding the obligation involved. Third, we ask, 'Whose rights are violated?' Under article 48, the rights of the third state are notionally violated, regardless of whether they in fact suffer injury. Fourth, we ask, 'What assumptions are made in relation to the rights or interests violated?' The assumption made is that it is in the interests of both individuals benefiting from the obligations in question and the entire international community to ensure that the norms, including basic human rights norms, are upheld.

2.4.3 Claims brought under the European Convention on Human Rights

Under the *European Convention on Human Rights* (ECHR) (1950), only a person, state or NGO whose interests are violated can make a claim before the European Court of Human Rights (ECtHR 2023). However, under article 33 of the Convention, a state can bring a claim when another state (that is a party to the Convention) violates the human rights of a person. This mechanism is quite distinct from diplomatic protection in that there does not need to be a link of nationality between the person whose rights are violated and the other state bringing the claim. The mechanism can be used in relation to violations against individuals and systemic issues. In relation to individual alleged violations, the exhaustion of local remedies is required, but this is not required in relation to claims of systemic violations. An interesting example is the case brought by *Denmark, France, Norway, Sweden and the Netherlands v. Turkey* (ECtHR 1983), when Turkey dissolved its Parliament, which included also a claim of systemic violation. The case was settled. This interstate procedure has been used with increasing frequency in recent years (Risini & Eicke 2024).[10]

Applying our matrix, under article 33 of the *European Convention on Human Rights*: (i) a state can bring a claim on behalf of an individual whose rights have been violated under the ECHR; (ii) provided there is evidence that the individual's rights are violated or there is systematic violation of rights; and (iii) the assumption in relation to such claims is that it is in the interest of all states within this regional human rights mechanism to have strong compliance with the obligations contained in the ECHR. The striking proxy representational feature in this example is that such claims can be brought, regardless of whether the applicant country is affected and regardless of whether the victim is one of its nationals or a national of another member state.

[10] As of 19 August 2024, there was a total of 37 pending or completed interstate applications using article 33. See 'Interstate Applications', European Court of Human Rights. Available at www.echr.coe.int/inter-state-applications.

2.4.4 American Convention on Human Rights

The Inter-American Commission on Human Rights provides that NGOs and other associations can bring cases before the Commission in relation to the violation of the interests of third persons in relation to the *American Convention on Human Rights* (ACHR) (1969). However, neither NGOs nor individuals can go before the Inter-American Court on Human Rights (IACtHR), only states can do this. Article 23 of the Rules of Procedure of the Inter-American Commission on Human Rights reads:

> Any person or group of persons or non-governmental entity legally recognized in one or more of the Member States of the OAS may submit petitions to the Commission, on their behalf or on behalf of third persons, concerning alleged violations of a human right recognized in, as the case may be, the American Declaration of the Rights and Duties of Man, the American Convention on Human Rights (Inter-American Commission on Human Rights 2013: art. 23).

The NGO or association does not need to demonstrate that it has suffered damage itself. It is sufficient that the NGO claims the violation of the rights of persons under the protection of the ACHR. Interestingly, most cases before the Inter-American Commission on Human Rights have been initiated by NGOs.

Thus, in summary, under the Inter-American system of human rights, an NGO can bring a claim on behalf of third persons whose rights under the ACHR are violated on the assumption that it is in the community interest to have strong compliance with the obligations set out in the ACHR.

2.4.5 Aarhus Convention

The *Convention on Access to Information, Public Participation in Decision-making and Access to Justice in Environmental Matters* (Aarhus Convention) (1998) encompasses three main principles:

1. access to information on environmental matters;
2. participation of persons and groups in the decision-making process on the construction of specific technical installations such as refineries, coke ovens, or nuclear power plants; and
3. access to justice.

The last provision is the most relevant in the context of our topic. Access to justice is granted for the violation of the right to access to information and for the violation of any substantial or procedural violation of any decision related to participation in the decision-making process. It is left to the national legislature to identify the group of persons and organisations which might have a right or interest in such a proceeding (Aarhus Convention 1998: art. 9 § 2). However, 'for the purposes of this definition, non-governmental organizations promoting environmental protection and meeting any requirements under national law shall be deemed to have an interest' (Aarhus Convention 1998: art. 2 § 5).

These provisions mean that NGOs working in the field of environmental protection will be entitled to bring a claim, even if these organisations or their members are not directly affected by the act or omission which is impugned. Many national legal systems which grant standing before national courts (mostly administrative courts in environmental matters) only where there is a subjective right or interest at stake, have had to modify their rules to meet the international legal requirements of the Aarhus Convention. As a result, the protection of the environment before a court becomes possible independent of individual interests. From a strictly procedural point of view, an environmental NGO (ENGO), such as Greenpeace, would be acting on its own behalf in articulating the interests of nature. From a broader perspective, however, the ENGO is acting on behalf of nature and thereby in the interests of future generations. In this sense, the ENGO is representing nature and future generations.

In summary, under the Aarhus Convention, ENGOs can bring a claim on behalf of third persons whose rights under the Convention are violated, on the assumption that strong compliance with the Convention's obligations is in the community's interest.

2.4.6 Case Studies: Conclusions

What can be gleaned from these case studies? A common thread is that a person whose rights are violated is not able, owing to their vulnerability, to defend their own rights. This vulnerability provides the justification for allowing another entity (whether it be a state in relation to which they are not a citizen, or an NGO) to step in to make a claim on their behalf. Thus, under the mandate system of the League of Nations, there was limited freedom of political assembly and a lack of access to courts, both factual and de jure. In relation to the interstate complaints mechanism of the *European Convention on Human Rights*, the rationale here is that individuals whose rights are violated may not necessarily be able to bring claims to ensure compliance with the Convention, particularly in relation to systemic violations. A third state may be better placed to do this.

Another common thread in these examples is that the state or NGO which is making a claim on behalf of the vulnerable person or persons is not doing so as an agent of this person or persons; rather, it is making reasonable assumptions as to the essential basic interests or rights of this person or persons.

These short case studies demonstrate that the international legal order already contains mechanisms which involve the proxy representation of persons who are vulnerable and not necessarily in a position to make claims on their own behalf. This is made possible by reasonable assumptions being made about the core interests of such persons. Thus, for example, an assumption is made that inhabitants of mandate territories under the League system have an interest in not living under a system of apartheid. Similarly, it is assumed that citizens living in countries covered by the *European Convention on Human Rights* have an interest in the Convention being fully implemented.

The upshot of these case studies is that the notion of international tribunals representing future generations in relation to climate change litigation involves only a modest reform, rather than a radical departure from existing international legal rules and mechanisms. In Section 2.5, we explain the various forms proxy representation of future generations in the international legal order could take.

2.5 Proxy Representation of Future Generations in the International Legal Order and Its Functions

Indirect representation of future generations in the international legal order can take place, if a particular rule of international law reflects the interests of future generations. Such rules can be found in treaties or rules of customary international law; they can be substantive or procedural. In terms of substance, on the face of it, the international environmental law principle of sustainable development and the related concept of intergenerational equity (both enshrined in the *Paris Agreement* and other treaties) should – at least in theory – ensure that future generations' interests are incorporated into climate law and policy-making. The *United Nations Framework Convention on Climate Change* (UNFCCC) (1992) requires parties to implement it guided by the following principle: 'the Parties should protect the climate system for the benefit of present and future generations of humankind, on the basis of equity' (UNGA 1992: art. 3(1)). The Preamble to the *Paris Agreement* refers to the need, 'when taking action to address climate change', to promote various principles, including 'intergenerational equity' (*Paris Agreement* 2015: preambular para 11). The status of this principle in customary international law remains disputed and its content rather vague, in that it does not specify what weight should be given to future generations vis-à-vis the current generation (Lawrence 2014; Scholtz 2021). Nevertheless, its inclusion in the UNFCCC (1992) and the *Paris Agreement* (2015) makes it clear that intergenerational equity should be considered in interpreting and implementing these global treaty instruments.

The concept of sustainable development is strongly linked to intergenerational equity in that one of its most influential formulations defines sustainable development as 'development that meets the needs of the present without compromising the ability of future generations to meet their own needs' (World Commission on Environment and Development 1987: 43). Nevertheless, developing countries have been concerned that sustainable development may imply limitations on their right to develop (Bodansky et al. 2017: 54). Reflecting this concern, Article 3(4) of the UNFCCC (1992) provides that 'the Parties have a right to, and should, promote sustainable development' (see also Bodansky et al. 2017: 129). In international law, the concept of sustainable development has been described as an 'interstitial norm' – meaning a norm that, without being legally binding or clearly defined, can nevertheless play a role in shaping the interpretation and application of customary or treaty norms (Lowe 1999; Viñuales 2021).

Indirect representation of future generations may occur in the global legal order, if a particular treaty regime adopts sufficiently stringent rules to ensure that the interests of future generations are protected in relation to the subject matter covered by the treaty. This has occurred in relation to the *Montréal Protocol on Substances That Deplete the Ozone Layer* (1987), which has included rules of sufficient stringency to ensure protection of the ozone layer to the benefit of future generations.[11]

The proposition that global politics should also take future generations into account and that new political programmes are needed for this purpose is becoming more prevalent (Lawrence 2020). While the Sustainable Development Goals (SDGs) adopted by the United Nations in 2015 (UN 2015) do not explicitly refer to the interests of future generations, many of the goals imply a requirement to consider the interests of future generations (Soltau 2021).

Unfortunately, to date, the mitigation measures under the climate regime fall well short of what is required. As mentioned earlier, emission reduction pledges made under the *Paris Agreement* will – when combined – see global warming continue to rise well above the 1.5°C ceiling identified by scientists (UNEP 2022).

A range of other possibilities for representation of future generations in the global legal order have procedural dimensions linked to courts. In March 2023, the UN General Assembly passed a resolution asking the ICJ to pronounce on whether failure by states to take strong mitigation measures in relation to climate change violates their obligations under international law, including in relation to future generations (see Chapter 6). Further options include a Pacific island state bringing a claim in the ICJ against a large emitter state on behalf of both its current and future generations, and indirect representation such as *amicus curiae* briefs by NGOs or scientists highlighting the impacts on future generations in relation to an ICJ case (Lawrence & Köhler 2017). A further possibility is for a tribunal (such as the ICJ itself) to act as a proxy or guardian of future generations. This was proposed

[11] Thanks to parties' commitment to the *Montréal Protocol* (1987), the ozone layer is predicted to recover by the middle of this century (see UNEP n.d.).

by Christopher Weeremantry (*Nuclear Tests Case (New Zealand v. France)* 1974: 341) but has not been taken up by the Court to date (see Chapter 6).

Further options include seeking clarification from international human rights bodies or tribunals along the lines that human rights obligations extend into the future to ensure the protection of future generations. In the climate change context, this involves certain preventative obligations to mitigate or put in place adaptation measures. There has been some progress in recent years in jurisprudence in this area in relation to the application of the *European Convention on Human Rights* (Karlsson-Niska 2020). While the global human rights regime remains relatively underdeveloped, recent cases have begun to push further development of this regime in this area, with young people bringing cases in which they purport to speak on behalf of both their own interests and future generations (see Chapter 7).

At the international level, proxy representation can perform a range of political and legal functions. First, proxy representation may perform a *proxy representative function*, which occurs when the proxy purports to speak or act on behalf of future generations ('direct representation'). As discussed earlier, this contrasts with the situation where the proxy does not purport to speak on behalf of future generations but highlights their interests, for example, a scientist highlighting the impacts of climate change and biodiversity on future generations. We will refer to this as 'indirect representation'.

A second function of proxy representation in the international legal order involves the idea of a *proxy compliance function*, where the proxy functions to ensure compliance with existing international legal rules which operate to the benefit of future generations. This will involve links to the substantive and procedural rules of the institution in question, which must empower the particular proxy institution, court, or tribunal to perform such a function. To be effective in performing this function, there will need to be sufficient carrots and sticks to ensure compliance – involving capacity building to assist countries struggling with implementation, as well as sanctions where countries have the means but not the political will to comply. (While this aspect of the global climate regime is very important, space precludes its discussion in this book.)

Third, there is a function of proxy representation that we call a *proxy reform function*. The essence of this function is that the proxy is proactive in advocating reform to existing international legal institutions and rules to ensure better protection of the interests of future generations. This could occur, for example, if a newly created UN Special Envoy for Future Generations advocated a strengthening of the global climate regime.

Fourth, there is a *proxy norm entrepreneurial function* which occurs where the proxy plays a leadership role in persuading others to adopt a particular norm which benefits future generations; for example, a UN Special Envoy could advocate for the norm of *intergenerational equity* entailing that an assessment of the impacts of current policies on future generations be incorporated across all UN programmes. The concept of 'norm entrepreneurs' is linked to constructivist concepts of international relations (Finnemore & Sikkink 1998; Wendt 2001). Intuitively, it would seem likely that there is a strong relationship between the legitimacy of the norm being advocated and the legitimacy of the leadership of the proxy representative. Put differently, if the norm being advocated is not seen as in the interests of all countries, then a proxy representative advocating for this norm will have an uphill battle. Conversely, if the norm is perceived as being in the interest of all states, this may facilitate the proxy norm entrepreneurial function.

In accordance with the aim of this book, these conceptual distinctions appear useful in terms of understanding in a more nuanced way the modes in which representation of future generations works in relation to the global legal order, as well as its role in creative reform strategies. A proxy representative of future generations, for example, may perform some or all these functions to varying degrees (considered further in Chapter 8). A central argument of this book is that the most effective proxy representative will maximise the performance of all these functions. In line with pragmatist logic, the evaluative development of (political) practices is always about achieving the best possible consequences for all parties involved. By breaking down proxy representation into these elements, we can make a more nuanced analysis of what, exactly, a proxy representative is and should be doing. As we shall see, this breakdown also allows for a more nuanced analysis of the democratic legitimacy of proxy representatives considered in the case studies presented in Part III.

2.6 Synthesis

A starting point of this chapter was that traditional concepts of representation based on agency do not work in relation to future generations. We nevertheless saw that proxy representation of future generations does fit within Rehfeld's concept of audience-based representation and Saward's concept of surrogacy-based representation. We proposed a definition of representation in the legal context, central to which was the concept of representation being authorised directly by law. We moved on to define proxy representation, distinguished between direct and indirect variants, and sketched various modes of proxy representation at the national level which have provided inspiration for proposals at the international level. We then described a range of existing forms of proxy representation in the international legal order (both direct and indirect), spanning the League of Nations mandate system through to more contemporary human rights mechanisms, to demonstrate that proxy representation of future generations represents a modest, rather than radical, reform of international law. We saw that the extent to which indirect representation of future generations is incorporated in the international legal order in terms of environment-related principles in the climate regime is limited. We presented a matrix setting out the range of functions that proxy representation might perform, and argued that, by distinguishing these functions, a more nuanced understanding of the functions of existing modes of proxy representation, as well as reform proposals, might be had.

References

Abe, H., Wenning, M. & Fritsch, M. (2024). *Intercultural Philosophy and Environmental Justice between Generations Indigenous, African, Asian, and Western Perspectives*, Cambridge: Cambridge University Press.

American Convention on Human Rights (ACHR) (1969) (adopted 22 November 1969; entered into force 18 July 1978), 1144 UNTS 123.

Adler, R. (2024). The Green Climate Fund: A Case Study in the Legitimacy of Global Climate Finance Governance. Unpublished PhD Thesis, University of Tasmania.

Birnbacher, D. (1988). *Verantwortung für zukünftige Generationen*, Stuttgart: Reclam.

Bodansky, D., Brunnée, J. & Rajamani, L. (2017). *International Climate Change Law*, Oxford: Oxford University Press.

Boston, J. (2021a). Parliamentary Commissioner for the Environment, New Zealand. In Segger, M.-C., Szabo, M. & Harrington, A.-R., eds., *Intergenerational Justice in Sustainable Development Treaty Implementation: Advancing Future Generations Rights Through National Institutions*. Cambridge: Cambridge University Press, 434–60.

Boston, J. (2021b). Protecting Long-term Interests: The Role of Institutions as Commitment Devices. In Linehan, J. & Lawrence, P., eds., *Giving Future Generations of Voice: Normative Frameworks, Institutions and Practice*. Cheltenham: Edward Elgar, 86–107.

Boston, J. & Lempp, F. (2011). Climate Change: Explaining and Solving the Mismatch between Scientific Urgency and Political Inertia. *Accounting, Auditing & Accountability Journal*, 24 (October), 1000–21.

Boston, J., Bagnall, D. & Barry, A. (2019). Foresight, Insight and Oversight: Enhancing Long-term Governance through Better Parliamentary Scrutiny. *Institute for Governance and Policy Studies*, Report for the New Zealand Parliament, June 2019. Available at: www.victoria.ac.nz/__data/assets/pdf_file/0011/1753571/Foresight-insight-and-oversight.pdf.

Caney, S. (2015). Responding to Global Injustice: On the Right of Resistance. *Social Philosophy and Policy*, 32(1), 51–73.

Caney, S. (2016). Political Institutions for the Future: A Fivefold Package. In González-Ricoy, I. & Gosseries, A., eds., *Institutions for Future Generations*. Oxford: Oxford University Press, 135–55.

Case Concerning the Barcelona Traction, Light and Power Company Limited. (*Barcelona Traction* case) (1970) 46 ILR 178.

Convention on Access to Information, Public Participation in Decision-Making and Access to Justice in Environmental Matters (Aarhus Convention) (1998) (adopted 25 June 1998; entered into force 30 October 2001), 2161 UNTS 447.

Convention on Biological Diversity (1992) (adopted 5 June 1992; entered into force 29 December 1993) 1760 UNTS 79.

Covenant of the League of Nations (1919) (adopted 28 June 1919; entered into force 10 January 1920) (108 LNTS 188, UKTS 4, 225 CTS 195), OXIO 358.

Dobson, A. (1996). Representative Democracy and the Environment. In Lafferty, W. M. & Meadowcroft, J., eds., *Democracy and the Environment*. Cheltenham: Edward Elgar, 124–39.

Driver, J. (2014). The History of Utilitarianism. In Zalta, E. N. & Nodelman, U., eds., *The Stanford Encyclopedia of Philosophy*. Winter 2014 ed. Metaphysics Research Lab, Stanford University. Available at: https://plato.stanford.edu/archives/win2014/entries/utilitarianism-history.

East Timor Case (Portugal v. Australia) Judgement (1995) 105 ILR 226.

Eckersley, R. (2004). *The Green State: Rethinking Democracy and Sovereignty*, Cambridge, MA: The Massachusetts Institute of Technology Press.

Ekeli, K. S. (2005). Giving a Voice to Posterity: Deliberative Democracy and Representation of Future People. *Journal of Agricultural and Environmental Ethics*, 18(5), 429–50. DOI: 10.1007/s10806-005-7048-z.

European Convention on Human Rights (formal title: *Convention for the Protection of Human Rights and Fundamental Freedoms*) (ECHR) (1950) (adopted 4 November 1950; entered into force 3 September 1953), 213 UNTS 221.

European Court of Human Rights (ECtHR). (1983). (9940/82, 9942/82, 9944/82, 9941/82, 9943/82) Commission (Plenary) – Decision – *France, Norway, Denmark, Sweden, Netherlands v. Turkey*.

European Court of Human Rights (ECtHR). (2023). *Factsheet – Climate change*. Available at: www.echr.coe.int/documents/d/echr/FS_Climate_change_ENG.

Finnemore, M. & Sikkink, K. (1998). International Norm Dynamics and Political Change. *International Organization*, 52(4), 887–917.

French Civil Code 1804 (Art 389). Available at: https://files.libertyfund.org/files/2353/CivilCode_1566_Bk.pdf.

Gerten, D. & Bergmann, S., eds. (2012). *Religion in Environmental and Climate Change. Suffering, Values, Lifestyles*, New York: Bloomsbury Academic.

González-Ricoy, I. & Gosseries, A. (2016). Designing Institutions for Future Generations. In González-Ricoy, I. & Gosseries, A., eds., *Institutions for Future Generations*. Oxford: Oxford University Press, 3–23.

Inter-American Commission on Human Rights (IACHR). (2013). *Rules of Procedure of the Inter-American Commission on Human Rights*.

International Law Commission (ILC). (2001). *Draft articles on Responsibility of States for Internationally Wrongful Acts, with Commentaries*.

Intergovernmental Panel on Climate Change (IPCC). (2023). Summary for Policymakers. In Lee, H. & Romero, J., eds., *Climate Change 2023: Synthesis Report. A Report of the Intergovernmental Panel on Climate Change. Contribution of Working Groups I, II and III to the Sixth Assessment Report of the Intergovernmental Panel on Climate Change*. Geneva: IPCC.

Karlsson-Niska, T. (2020). Climate Change Litigation and the European Court of Human Rights – A Strategic Next Step? *Journal of World Energy Law & Business*, 13(4), 331–42. DOI: https://doi.org/10.1093/jwelb/jwaa028.

Karnein, A. (2016). Can We Represent Future Generations? In González-Ricoy, I. & Gosseries, A., eds., *Institutions for Future Generations*. Oxford: Oxford University Press, 83–97.

Larenz, K. & Wolf, M. (2004). *Allgemeiner Teil des Bürgerlichen Rechts*, 9th ed., München: C. H. Beck.

Latulippe, N. & Klenk, N. (2020). Making Room and Moving Over: Knowledge Co-production, Indigenous Knowledge Sovereignty and the Politics of Global Environmental Change Decision-making. *Current Opinion in Environmental Sustainability*, 42, 7–14.

Lawrence, P. (2014). *Justice for Future Generations, Climate Change and International Law*, Cheltenham: Edward Elgar.

Lawrence, P. (2020). Global Guardians for Future Generations: Remedying a Blind Spot of Democracy? In Tamoudi, N., Faets, S. & Reder, M., eds., *Politik der Zukunft. Zukünftige Generationen als Leerstelle der Demokratie*. Bielefeld: Transcript, 191–214.

Lawrence, P. (2021). International Institutions for Future Generations and Democratic Legitimacy. In Cordonier Segger, M.-C., Szabo, M. & Harrington, A.-R., eds., *Intergenerational Justice in Sustainable Development Treaty Implementation: Advancing Future Generations Rights Through National Institutions*. Cambridge: Cambridge University Press, 597–614.

Lawrence, P. (2022). Justifying Representation of Future Generations and Nature: Contradictory or Mutually Supporting Values? *Transnational Environmental Law*, 11, 553–79.

Lawrence, P. & Köhler, L. (2017). Representation of Future Generations through International Climate Litigation: A Normative Framework. *German Yearbook of International Law*, 60, 639–66.

Lawrence, P. & Linehan, J. (2021). Introduction. In Linehan, J. & Lawrence, P., eds., *Giving Future Generations of Voice: Normative Frameworks, Institutions and Practice*. Cheltenham: Edward Elgar, 1–21.

Lawrence, P. & Wong, D. (2017). Soft Law in the Paris Climate Agreement: Strength or Weakness? *Review of European, Comparative & International Environment Law*, 26(3), 276–86.

Legal Consequences for States of the Continued Presence of South Africa in Namibia (*Namibia* case), ICJ Reports (1971) 16.

Linehan, J. (2021). Reforming Political Institutions for the Future: New Reform Proposals for Legislatures and Citizens' Assemblies. In Linehan, J. & Lawrence, P., eds., *Giving Future Generations a Voice: Normative Frameworks, Institutions and Practice*. Cheltenham: Edward Elgar, 169–89.

Lowe, V. (1999). Sustainable Development and Unsustainable Arguments. In Boyle, A. & Freestone, D., eds., *International Law and Sustainable Development: Past Achievements and Future Challenges*. Oxford: Oxford University Press, 19–37.

Luban, D. (2015). Human Rights Pragmatism and Human Dignity. In Cruft, R., Liao, S. M. & Renzo, M., eds., *Philosophical Foundations of Human Rights*. Oxford: Oxford University Press, 236–78.

MacKenzie, M. K. (2016). Institutional Design and Sources of Short-termism. In González-Ricoy, I. & Gosseries, A., eds., *Institutions for Future Generations*. Oxford: Oxford University Press, 24–48.

McCormack, P. C. & Hansen-Lohrey, C. (2021). Accountability, Government Decisions and Future Generations: Lessons from the Australian Ombudsman. In Linehan, J. & Lawrence, P., eds., *Giving Future Generations a Voice: Normative Frameworks, Institutions and Practice*. Cheltenham: Edward Elgar, 128–48.

Montréal Protocol on Substances that Deplete the Ozone Layer (Montréal Protocol) (1987) (adopted 16 September 1987; entered into force 1 January 1989), 1522 UNTS 3.

Nuclear Tests Case (New Zealand v. France) ICJ Reports (1974) 253.

Paris Agreement (2015) (adopted 12 December 2015; entered into force 4 November 2016), 3156 UNTC 79.

Reder, M. & Müller, J. (2012). Cultures and Religions. In Edenhofer, O., Wallacher, J., Lotze-Campen, H., Reder, M., Knopf, B. & Müller, J., eds., *Climate Change, Justice and Sustainability*. Dordrecht: Springer, 111–18.

Rehfeld, A. (2006). Towards a General Theory of Political Representation. *Journal of Politics*, 68, 1–21.

Risini, I. & Eicke, T. (2024). Inter-State Applications under the European Convention on Human Rights – Situating the Instrument in the Current Human Rights Landscape. *International Human Rights Law Review*, 13(1), 41–73.

Roderick, P. (2010). *Taking the Longer View: UK Governance Options for a Finite Planet*. A Report for the Foundation for Democracy and Sustainable Development and WWF-UK, London. Available at: www.fdsd.org/wordpress/wp-content/uploads/Takingthe-longer-view-December-2010.pdf.

Rogelj, J., Shindell, D., Jiang, K., et al. (2018). Mitigation Pathways Compatible with 1.5°C in the Context of Sustainable Development. In Masson-Delmotte, V. et al., eds., *Global Warming of 1.5 °C. An IPCC Special Report on the Impacts of Global Warming of 1.5°C above Pre-industrial Levels and Related Global Greenhouse Gas Emission Pathways, in the Context of Strengthening the Global Response to the Threat of Climate Change, Sustainable Development, and Efforts to Eradicate Poverty*. Cambridge/New York: Cambridge University Press, 93–174. DOI: 10.1017/9781009157940.004.

Saward, M. (2008). Representation and Democracy: Revisions and Possibilities. *Sociology Compass*, 2(3), 1000–13.

Saward, M. (2009). Authorisation and Authenticity: Representation and the Unelected. *The Journal of Political Philosophy*, 17(1), 1–22.

Scholtz, W. (2021). Equity. In Rajamani, L. & Peel, J., eds., *The Oxford Handbook of International Environmental Law*, 2nd ed., Oxford: Oxford University Press, 335–50.

Soltau, F. (2021). The 2030 Agenda for Sustainable Development: What Are Its Implications for Future Generations? In Linehan, J. & Lawrence, P., eds., *Giving Future Generations a Voice: Normative Frameworks, Institutions and Practice*. Cheltenham: Edward Elgar, 108–26.

S. S. Wimbledon, Britain et al. v. Germany (*Wimbledon* case) (1923) PCIJ Series A01.

Tanasescu, M. (2014). Rethinking Representation: The Challenge of Nonhumans. *Australian Journal of Political Science*, 49(1), 40–53.

The League of Nations. (1920). *Mandate for German Samoa*. Available at: https://nzhistory.govt.nz/media/photo/league-nations-mandate-german-samoa.

Thompson, D. F. (2005). Democracy in Time: Popular Sovereignty and Temporal Representation. *Constellations*, 12, 245–61.

Thompson, D. F. (2010). Representing Future Generations: Political Presentism and Democratic Trusteeship. *Critical Review of International and Political Philosophy*, 13(1), 17–37.

Tremmel, J. (2018). Zukunftsräte zur Vertretung der Interessenkommender Generationen. Ein praxisorientierter Vorschlag für Deutschland. In Mannewitz, T., ed., *Die Demokratie und ihre Defekte*. Heidelberg: Springer, 107–42.

United Nations. (2015). Transforming Our World: The 2030 Agenda for Sustainable Development. Resolution adopted by the General Assembly, UN Doc. A/RES/70/1.

United Nations Environment Programme (UNEP). (2022). *Emissions Gap Report 2022*. Available at: www.unep.org/resources/emissions-gap-report-2022.

United Nations Environment Programme (UNEP). (n.d.). *About Montréal Protocol*. Available at: www.unep.org/ozonaction/who-we-are/about-montreal-protocol.

United Nations Framework Convention on Climate Change (UNFCCC) (1992) (adopted 9 May 1992; entered into force 21 March 1994), 1771 UNTS 107.

Van Asselt, H. (2016). The Role of Non-state Actors in Reviewing Ambition, Implementation, and Compliance Under the Paris Agreement. *Climate Law*, 6(1), 91–108.

Viñuales, J. E. (2021). Sustainable Development. In Rajamani, L. & Peel, J., eds., *The Oxford Handbook of International Environmental Law*, 2nd ed., Oxford: Oxford University Press, 285–301.

Weiss, E. B. (1989). *In Fairness to Future Generations. International Law, Common Patrimony, and Intergenerational Equity*. Tokyo: Dobbs Ferry, United Nations University, Transnational Publishers.

Wendt, A. (2001). Driving with a Rearview Mirror: On the Rational Science of Institutional Design. *International Organization*, 55(4), 1019–49.

Wilkens, J. & Datchoua-Tirvaudey, A. R. C. (2022). Researching Climate Justice: A Decolonial Approach to Global Climate Governance. *International Affairs*, 98(1), 125–43.

World Commission on Environment and Development (WCED) (1987). *Our Common Future*, Oxford: Oxford University Press.

3

The Democratic Ideal and Its Normative Value for Future Generations

3.1 Democracy and Future Generations: An Ambivalent Relationship

Democracy is often seen as the best possible form of political rule and, in this sense, an 'ideal'. Democracy as a political system of governance often corresponds with the territorial form of the nation-state. Its main idea is to develop fair and transparent procedures of political decision-making for those people who are affected by its decisions within this national territory. In the past, it was clear who belonged to the democratic *demos*, mostly understood as the citizens of a state. However, current political, economic, and cultural phenomena challenge democracy – both as a theoretical concept and as a form of political organisation. This challenge has come particularly from long-term phenomena such as climate change, with its human and ecological impacts. Democracies struggle to ensure that such long-term consequences are considered in political decision-making (Boston 2016). Some people therefore speak of a crisis of democracy. One reason for this is that people who are affected by these consequences do not have the opportunity to be represented. On the one hand, this relates to the limitation of the *demos* of democracy to the citizens of a nation-state; on the other, it relates to the fact that future generations cannot raise their voices or vote in political processes.

As we have already argued, representation generally – and proxy representation, in particular – plays a significant role within democratic institutional designs. In this book, we address the question of whether, and to what extent, proxy forms of representation offer an important and useful way to close this democratic blind spot. Our thesis is that various forms of proxy representation already exist, both on the national level and in the global legal order, and that further developing proxy-style mechanisms therefore represents an incremental, rather than a radical, reform.

In this chapter, we explore a philosophical perspective which provides a basis for criticising and reforming existing forms of international legal forms of proxy representation that are addressed in Part III. We argue that reflecting on the democratic interpretations of proxy representation will help us to further develop international legal reforms. We begin by arguing that the democratic ideal applies at the international level for the same reasons it applies at the national level, in that it increases the likelihood that decision-makers will be held to account and reduces the risk of tyranny through the abuse of power, as well as increasing the likelihood of just outcomes. We demonstrate that the international community has endorsed the value of democracy as an ideal through a range of UN instruments, while the right to democracy as part of international law remains contested (Section 3.2).

The philosophical argument is structured in two steps. First, we reconstruct central theoretical models of democracy and inquire how an expansion of representation mechanisms for future generations could be conceptualised within these justificatory narratives (Section 3.3). Second, we analyse the values that underlie democratic practices and can be helpful for advancing proxy representation at the international level, by providing criteria for such reforms (Section 3.4). This involves analysing the discourses of intergenerational justice (Section 3.4.1), solidarity (Section 3.4.2), and vulnerability (Section 3.4.3). We then turn to examine how these discourses can be translated into political forms of proxy representation by drawing on the all-affected principle (AAP), which requires that those affected by a decision have a role in making that decision, and which is argued to be an element of most, if not all, theories of democracy (Section 3.5.1). We hypothesise that the AAP provides a basis for extending the *demos* to include future generations, which thus justifies proxy forms of representation to enable their representation (Section 3.5.2). We go on to argue that human rights constitute a practice of global values which provides a powerful normative orientation for climate law and policy-making – a vital part of the context of this book (Section 3.6). We close the chapter with some concluding remarks (Section 3.7).

3.2 Democracy as an Ideal at the International Level

As a preliminary argument, it is important to explicitly justify why we turn to democratic theory as the starting point for thinking about forms of proxy representation in the global legal order.[1] We argue that, even at the global level, the idea of democracy, including its implicit values, is a central and well-founded frame of reference for the analysis and reform of international law and related institutions.

[1] This section is based on Lawrence (2020: 88–99).

Theories of democracy have been developed with the national, and not the international, level of decision-making in mind. Indeed, some theorists have argued that democracy cannot apply at the international level. According to Robert A. Dahl (1999; see also Christiano 2011: 69, 81), for instance, this is because international institutions are created by states, many of which are not democratic. A second strand of this argument involves pointing out that there is no international organisation through which individual citizens around the world can find representation. Both arguments, however, are unconvincing. As David Held (1995) points out, the notion that democracy is inexorably linked and limited to sovereign states flies in the face of dramatic changes over recent decades, with states (particularly in Europe) now interlocked through complex international structures spanning defence, environment, and human rights. Held (1995) maintains that the AAP – which involves those affected by a decision having a say in the decision – and the concept of cosmopolitan democracy provide a basis for creating new deliberative decision-making centres beyond national territories to supplement existing political units based on sovereignty.

Deeper consideration of the purpose of democracy points in the same direction. The purpose of the democratic ideal is to ensure that public decision-making reflects the will of the people to the greatest possible extent, and that decision-makers are held to account, thereby reducing as much as possible the risk of tyranny through abuse of power. A further argument is that democratic decisions are more likely to result in just outcomes.[2] These considerations apply equally to the international and national levels. While it is true that many states are undemocratic, democracy as an ideal is not an all-or-nothing concept: the democratic ideal can and should serve as a valuable blueprint for reform at the international, as well as the national, level (Lawrence 2020: 92).[3]

Indeed, the democratic ideal has been at least formally accepted by the international community in several UN instruments. Thus, while the term 'democracy' is not included in the *Charter of the United Nations* (1945), the organisation indirectly bases its legitimacy on the concept of democracy, reflected in its opening words: 'We the Peoples of the United Nations'. The Universal Declaration of Human Rights (UDHR), adopted by the General Assembly in 1948, is more specific, stating that 'the will of the people shall be the basis of the authority of government' (UNGA 1948) and guaranteeing to everyone rights essential for effective political participation. While the UDHR was adopted at a time when UN membership

[2] Sen uses evidence of the role of democracy in reducing hunger and war, so not direct measures of justice but nevertheless, useful indicators. He states: 'Attention must be paid to the extensive evidence that democracy and political and civil rights tend to enhance freedoms of other kinds (such as human security) through giving a voice, at least in many circumstances, to the deprived and the vulnerable' (Sen 2009: 348).

[3] For a model of democratic legitimacy applicable to international institutions, see Dingwerth (2007). For application of this model to institutions to represent future generations, see Lawrence (2021a: 597–614).

was much smaller, with many then colonies yet to assert independence, this was followed up in the 1960s (after extensive decolonisation and with a much larger UN membership) with the *International Covenant on Civil and Political Rights* (ICCPR), adopted by the UN General Assembly in 1966. This Covenant enshrined many of the political rights and civil liberties that underpin democracies, including obligations on states to respect the right of individuals to participate in public affairs (OHCHR 2023a). The *United Nations Millennium Declaration*, adopted by the UN General Assembly in 2000 proclaims that, 'Democratic and participatory governance based on the will of the people best ensures' a range of human rights, including rights to live in 'dignity', to be 'free from hunger, and from the fear of violence, oppression or injustice' (UNGA 2000: para 6).[4]

The UN Human Rights Council has made the link between democracy, human rights, and legitimacy even more explicit. In March 2015, the UN Human Rights Council adopted a resolution '[r]eaffirming that democracy is based on the freely expressed will of people to determine their own political, economic, social and cultural systems and their full participation in all aspects of their lives' and 'stressing that human rights, democracy and the rule of law are interdependent and mutually reinforcing' (HRC 2015: preambular paras 7, 14). In 2015, governments committed to the 2030 Agenda for Sustainable Development, including a world in which 'democracy, good governance and the rule of law as well as an enabling environment at national and international levels, are essential for sustainable development' (United Nations 2023b: para 9; see also United Nations 2023c). The agenda process clearly demonstrates that the idea of democracy is a critical component of the debate on global governance in the face of climate impacts, even though many states are not democracies.

While there is convincing evidence that the international system reflects the value of democracy, whether one can go further than this and claim a right to democratic governance as part of the fabric of international law remains controversial amongst international legal scholars (Klabbers et al. 2021; Fox & Roth 2020). Since 1945, the democratic entitlement norm has always been in tension with the norm of non-intervention in the affairs of other states and the right of states to choose their own system of government as part of the concept of the sovereign equality of states (Ginsburg 2021: 105). Following the fall of the Berlin Wall in 1989, the mood began to change. As Thomas Franck famously claimed in 1992, there was an emerging right to democratic governance in international law (Franck 1992). Subsequent scholars claimed there was an inherent 'human right to resist tyranny' backed up by the right of humanitarian intervention (Tesón 1992: 68). Others resisted such claims, motivated by a concern

[4] The UN instruments referred to in this paragraph are quoted in Lawrence (2021a: 600).

that this discourse could justify a type of neocolonialism in which powerful (Western) states used it to justify military intervention and impose democracy on weaker states (Rasulov 2021: 35).

Nevertheless, Brad R. Roth takes the view that many highly regarded scholars have concluded that the principle that the will of the people (involving fairly run elections) should be the basis of government authority is well grounded in customary international law binding on all states (Roth 2021: 51). Moreover, the liberal-democratic governance norm has not only been embraced (in part, through the UN instruments mentioned earlier), but has also found expression in the right to democracy being enshrined in regional treaties in Europe, Central and South America, and Africa, while the effective enforcement of democratic rights under these regional treaties has been mixed (Ginsburg 2021: 125, 129).

However, there has recently been an increase in the number of countries around the world moving away from democracy and towards forms of autocratic rule, while authoritarian states have tended to reinterpret human rights and democracy discourse rather than rejecting them outright (Ginsburg 2021: 29). In summary, then, while the precise scope and status of rules of international law relating to democracy remain contested, the international legal system demonstrates solid support for the norm of democracy as a value of the international community, sufficient for grounding our normative argument justifying proxy representation of future generations. In other words, the *ideal* of democracy has found strong endorsement as a universally held value at the global level. We acknowledge that the extent to which adherence to this value at the societal level occurs is variable and contested.[5] We now turn to reflect on the possibilities and structural limitations of democratic theory in dealing with future generations.

3.3 Future Generations as a Blind Spot in Different Theories of Democracy

Different traditions of theorising about the political sphere have opened many ways of dealing with the ecological crisis. Theoretical models of democracy provide different responses to the question of how such long-term ecological consequences should be incorporated in political decisions. To discuss which model is best suited to deal with long-term consequences such as climate impacts, some important theoretical perspectives of democracy first need to be distinguished. In the following, we turn our attention to the most important theoretical models of

[5] A 2024 Pew Research Centre global survey found reduced but still solid majorities across the 24 countries surveyed supporting representative democracy as a good form of government, while there was strong criticism of how it was implemented (Wike et al. 2024).

democracy of the last three decades: realist, liberal, deliberative, communitarian, and poststructuralist theories of democracy.

3.3.1 Realist Theories of Democracy

Historically, some 'realist' theories of democracy are based on the work of Joseph Schumpeter (see, for example, Schumpeter 1950). These approaches often interpret democracy as a purely formal method of selecting preferred opinions and implementing decisions. Elections are at the heart of this model. Democracy in this approach means nothing more than free and fair elections. This mechanism is intended to ensure that everyone can potentially participate in decisions. This results in a thin and formal understanding of democracy. In some approaches, elites also play a special role in this process, especially in interpreting social reality and implementing political decisions.

In this approach, additional normative elements, such as an inherent orientation towards justice, are neglected. Indeed, such formal-realistic models of democracy usually refrain from normative statements, since they do not want to give preference to any value system: free elections ensure that the most plausible value system will prevail, which is then implemented politically. No predefined values precede the formal mechanisms of democracy.

Omitting normative elements is also one key reason why formal approaches, by definition, encounter fundamental problems in dealing with the consequences of political action for people who are not involved in these formal procedures: that is, elections. In view of the current ecological crisis, such a purely formal and normatively thin understanding of democracy is problematic. A democracy whose self-understanding is primarily (or even solely) based on elections will find it difficult to approach current problems, such as global conflicts or long-term ecological consequences, because it has no theoretical or practical foundation for dealing with something 'new' beyond the interests of living citizens who possess the right to vote.

Of course, representatives in democratic elections often promise to rule for the benefit of future generations. If they stuck to their promises, the electoral system would work. However, the entire process is skewed by vested interests favouring short-termism and other structural problems, such as short election cycles (Boston 2016: 13, 65–66, 68). Formal interpretations of democracy have no basis for responding to a situation where elected representatives make promises to protect the interests of future generations or nature, then breach such promises. Realists refrain from making normative value assumptions and yet precisely produce those problems to which they should provide an answer as a form of political rule. They try to deal with ecological challenges only through the instrument of elections and, thus, aggravate the problem because long-term consequences will never receive sufficient attention through elections alone. Such a model is incapable of providing a normative grounding for new forms of representation as a response to the current ecological crises.

3.3.2 Liberal Theories of Democracy

Turning to liberal theories of democracy, we can observe that these approaches also tend to involve a formal model of democracy, but with a particular focus on freedom and rights. In terms of its theoretical basis, methodological individualism plays a key role within the liberal theory. Democracy is based on the freedom of the individual, which is interpreted as the supreme good (and one that must be protected). This focus on the individual distinguishes liberalism from realist approaches. In liberal theory, freedom and equality are the inescapable cornerstones of democracy. Democracy as a form of political order is based on the normative goal of ensuring equal freedom for all citizens. Thus, it is not only about the formal procedure of voting but also the freedom and equality that provide the normative framework which precedes them.

Politically, on this normative basis, liberal theories of democracy imply a strong focus on rights as a foundation for dealing with social challenges. Behind this idea is the demand for freedom and equality, combined with a methodical individualism. In their origin, liberal rights always focus on ways to enable and secure the individual's ways of acting. In the tradition of John Rawls, who promoted liberalism theoretically from the 1970s, the principle of justice plays a key role in liberalism, alongside freedom and equality. Most often, the ethical question of justice is about the distribution of goods or personal rights and includes future persons.[6]

In this context, models of intergenerational justice play a particularly significant role in this tradition. The theoretical justification of intergenerational justice always rests on an argument or assumption about how much individuals owe each other. In consequence, these duties are translated into rights of future generations.[7] However, ecological consequences also play a role in this tradition connected to the emphasis on rights. For example, the question of whether future generations can be interpreted as rights-holders or whether legal frameworks should be designed in such a way that long-term consequences can be considered, bearing in mind human beings' reliance on well-functioning ecological – including

[6] See the discussion of Rawl's just savings principle in relation to intergenerational justice in Heyd (2009).

[7] There has been intensive discussion about whether, and to what extent, people living in the future today can be interpreted as bearers of rights. Traditionally, persons born in the future have no rights until they are born (because a person cannot possess rights until they exist). There is nevertheless an ethical duty to consider their interests as they will, upon being born, possess rights (Vanderheiden 2008: 137).

climate – systems. Even if liberal theories often tend to focus on the present, there are important points of contact for the consideration of the interests of future generations in current democratic decisions.

3.3.3 Deliberative Theories of Democracy

Deliberative theories in the tradition of Jürgen Habermas play a prominent role in the current discourses on democracy. These theories have much in common with liberal approaches but shift the focus from strict methodological individualism to joint procedures of negotiation and discourse. The starting point for understanding deliberative democracy is the idea of conversation. For Habermas, democracy is a hypothetical conversation and democracies are all the better and more ethically legitimate: the more opinions they hear in these conversations, the more transparent their procedures for processing these conversations into political decisions and the more participation oriented their institutions. Political decisions are ethically justified when they potentially involve all concerned in the sense of 'communicative reason'. 'Communicative reason' constitutes shared, transparent, and noncoercive discourse between participants and serves as the legitimating framework. Democracy aims at the political establishment of as many participatory procedures as possible to enable a broad involvement of citizens (understood as participants in discourse). The formal model of democracy is thus supplemented or extended by a deliberative model.

In its origins, this model of democracy focused on the living citizens who (can) participate in the procedures. In view of ecological crises, Habermas and representatives of this paradigm have already thought about extensions of the argumentation. In this theoretical model, future generations or other non-human living beings, for example, could be understood as discussion partners with whom a hypothetical agreement on important political decisions is to be reached, if it is ethically legitimate. A further extension of the theory involves the consideration of forms of proxy representation beyond the formal political system; for example, through social movements or certain discourses that might encapsulate the interests of future generations. Through these modifications, the deliberative model is rethought and reconfigured in the face of the ecological crisis (Dryzek & Pickering 2019).

3.3.4 Communitarian Theories of Democracy

Other theories of democracy argue that the political basis of democracy rests on the community rather than the individual (Sandel 1998; Taylor 1989; Walzer 1983, 1994). Different approaches to the community play a role – including republican, communitarian, and pragmatic perspectives. Many of these theories (for example, in the communitarian tradition) see themselves more as an alternative normative theory in contrast to a liberal theory of justice as developed by Rawls. Although these are not theories of democracy in a narrow sense, they, too, imply certain ideas of the political and democracy that are relevant to the considerations in this book. In all varieties of these theoretical paradigms, democracy is (closely) linked to the community and its normative self-understanding which is, in turn, implemented through democracy. Democratic processes are therefore understood less as a negotiation between citizens as individuals than as political processes that are an expression of the normative self-understanding of a community. In this tradition, the individual is always theoretically and practically subordinate to the community.

Ecological consequences are incorporated in this model insofar as they are integrated into the normative self-understanding of the community. This is less about forms of representation in the political system than the normative foundations of the community which, in turn, entail new narratives about who belongs to the community. These approaches can spur fresh narratives which incorporate future generations or understandings of the environment as part of the political community. Thus, De-Shalit (1995: 15–16) extends the concept of community into the future to create the idea of a 'transgenerational community' which can provide a strong basis for ethical obligations towards future generations grounded in rational self-interest, given that one's identity is necessarily linked to one's past and continues into the future. A limitation of this approach, however, is that it only offers a rationale for obligations towards descendants of one's own country and provides no basis for cutting climate emissions to benefit people living in poverty in other countries (Barry 1999: 99). This limitation can be overcome by linking communitarian theory to cosmopolitan theories of justice, which rest on the assumption that obligations are owed to other persons, regardless of where and when they happen to live (Lawrence 2014: 55–57). While doubts have been raised as to whether there is a genuine justice community involving shared values and institutions at the international level, Vanderheiden (2008) has argued persuasively that there are *elements* of such a global community in place in the global climate regime. Moreover, in the climate change context, there is causal interdependence between people: nobody can opt out of cooperative schemes to mitigate emissions, if these schemes are to be effective (Vanderheiden 2008: 98).

3.3.5 Post-structuralist Theories of Democracy

The last group of models consists of post-structuralist theories of democracy. Authors such as Judith Butler and Jacques Derrida belong to this school of theories, as do the so-called radical theories of democracy following Ernesto Laclau and Chantal Mouffe (1985). These theories are based on a broad understanding of the political. When they think about the political field and democracy, these theorists focus less on elections, rights, and institutions. For them, all forms of social movements and political engagement within and beyond this formal political field play a key role. Further, they pay attention to the asymmetries of power and mechanisms of exclusion that, in their view, characterise every political field, including democracies.

In addition, these approaches focus less on democratic consensus and more on political conflict as the central part of democracy. From this perspective, liberal or deliberative theories are in danger of underexposing the need for the ongoing social struggle for political equality in favour of (economic) distributional issues. Post-structuralists reflect, for example, more on the material and discursive preconditions of justice which are always related to unequal power structures, thereby highlighting the concrete social situation of vulnerable lives to attain a more equal society. The normative focus is usually on precarious forms of life and vulnerability (Derrida 1992; Butler 2004).

It is remarkable that these post-structural theories of democracy have, until now, given little thought to ecological challenges or future generations. On the one hand, this might be because they fundamentally pose the (philosophical) question of the foundations of political governance and that concrete questions of implementation play a subordinate role. On the other hand, these approaches appear well suited to address two aspects of these questions. First, the new materialist turn (which expands understandings of agency to include the 'more-than-human') helps to underpin an ecological understanding of democracy. Judith Butler (2020) follows this argumentation, interpreting Karl Marx as a relational thinker who emphasises the interconnectedness of humans and nature. Second, future generations would be potential forms of precarious life, neglected to date but deserving of attention. Such a focus could flow from a power analysis of current economic structures in terms of their implications for future generations. Again, Butler's concepts of relationality and vulnerability might be helpful in integrating future generations in the critique of political mechanisms (Reder & Faets 2024).

3.3.6 Pragmatist Theories of Democracy

Pragmatist philosophers, such as John Dewey, argue that democracy should always begin with an empirical observation of current problems. This method is founded on Dewey's epistemological concept (see Chapter 1, Section 1.2), which views political knowledge as originating from the processing of experiences. Therefore, inquiry as an element of politics involves a multi-stage process. In his *The Theory of Inquiry*, Dewey identifies the steps that typically constitute this process: identifying a situation that is experienced as a problem; creating a hypothesis about the various aspects of the problem; developing practical solutions; and, finally, undertaking an evaluation aimed at proving the validity of the solution.

To realise such an experimental modus of democracy in political reality, pragmatist theories argue that democracies should recognise various social practices and their potential to deal with political problems practically. From an ethical point of view, the genesis and validity of democratic norms are always connected, which means that the validity of these norms can only be proved by reconstructing social practices and related norms embedded in these practices. Dewey's ('only') guiding principle, which arises from the primacy ascribed to experience, is the recognition of the variety of experiences. Dewey calls this duplication of experiences 'growth', which means that those social, political, and economic practices should be promoted that enable the growth of individual and collective experiences in democracies.

Against this background, pragmatists argue that democracies should not focus on developing ideal institutions or democratic procedures, but on dealing experimentally with people's experiences. Thus, democracies would recognise experiences as the fundamental starting point of democratic practice. As Dewey (1937: 457) explains, 'democracy is much broader than a special political form, a method of conducting government, of making laws and carrying on governmental administration by means of popular suffrage and elected officers'. Rather, it represents

> a way of life, social and individual. The key-note of democracy as a way of life may be expressed; it seems to me, as the necessity for the participation of every mature human being in formation of the values that regulate the living of men together: which is necessary from the standpoint of both the general social welfare and the full development of human beings as individuals (Dewey 1937: 457).

The ideal of democracy arises from practices and not from theory. Therefore, democratic policy should be aware and reconstruct (individual and collective) actions that are most likely to enable the development and promotion of human experiences. Hence, the quality of democracy appears in whether, and to what extent, social behavioural patterns and political procedures contribute to the development of citizens and society as a whole – which also extends to citizens who will be born in the future. Again, the central attribute of democracy is its experimental character. Politics starts from concrete experiences and from the problems that arise from these experiences. Politics should analyse these problems thoroughly, formulate hypotheses to solve them, and evaluate the extent to which these hypotheses prove themselves in practice. This experimental structure is infinite in principle, which is why democracy is only conceivable as an open-ended process (Bohman 1999): 'Democracy is not just one form of social life among other workable forms of social life; it is the precondition for the full application of intelligence to the solution of social problems' (Putnam 1995: 217).

Such an understanding of democracy also leads to reforms of institutional structures of participation and representation in democracies, especially if they are to widen the *demos* to include the excluded and marginalised. For example, to consider the negative impacts of climate change on future generations, democracies need to develop mechanisms of representation through which the possible experiences (and interests) of future generations can be represented today. The debates about proxy representation within existing institutions, new election schemes, or radical counter-hegemonies demonstrate the need for democratic reform.

3.3.7 Comparison of Models of Democracy

The various paradigms of democratic theory illustrate that democracy, understood as the self-determination of the *demos*, can be conceptualised in many ways. Depending on its theoretical assumptions, democratic practice focuses on different mechanisms and political procedures as central features of democracy, advocating for their promotion and safeguarding.

In line with the pragmatic orientation of this book, we make two points about the diversity of democratic theories. First, pragmatism itself favours a particular understanding of democracy: one that does not envision an ideal or fixed institutional structure, but instead requires democratic practice to be continuously developed, evaluated, and improved, especially in times of crisis. This understanding provides a compelling basis for enhancing the consideration and representation of future generations, as there is currently no blueprint or fixed ideal for this evolution.

Second, this pragmatic model integrates many elements from other paradigms within a comprehensive framework. Rights and institutions (realist and liberal models) are acknowledged as integral to democracy, serving as part of the experimental improvement of democratic practice. Communicative deliberation, essential for reconciling diverse perspectives, is also crucial to pragmatism's development of democracy (deliberative model). Additionally, this deliberation is never context-free but always embedded within a particular set of cultural practices and semantics, which can be utilised for this experimental democracy (communitarian model). Finally, the pragmatic approach, like post-structuralist theories, focuses on experiences of suffering and exclusion from democratic processes.

Thus, the pragmatist understanding of democracy does not contradict the other paradigms; rather, it seeks to bring their most compelling elements into an inclusive framework. In this sense, the pragmatist approach has an inclusive potential compared to other models, as it connects various democratic aspects. However, it also notes that other models tend to absolutise certain democratic aspects, thus missing the democratic essence in pragmatist terms: the open, evaluative, and experimental adaptation of democracy's idea to the challenges of each era.

The inclusive nature will also become evident in the values embedded within democratic practices. While some democratic models focus primarily on one value or make it their normative centre (for example, liberal approaches focus on justice; radical democracies on vulnerability; and communitarian approaches on solidarity), the pragmatic approach does not play these values off against one another. Instead, pragmatic approaches illustrate how the interplay between these values can form an inclusive normative basis for addressing political crises, such as the question of how to consider future generations.

At the pragmatic intersection of different democratic theories, another central characteristic of democracy emerges that is crucial both theoretically and practically for the inclusion of future generations. In all models, there is an implicit negotiation of who belongs to the *demos* of democracy and, thus, who should be involved in democratic procedures (such as representation). From a narrowly cultural perspective, one might argue that a particular linguistic or cultural community defines the boundaries of the *demos*. However, while this view may have significance in the practice of nation-state democracy, it appears contingent and, on a theoretical level, weak in terms of legitimacy.

In contrast, a key theoretical characteristic of democracy is the principle of affectedness by decisions. The assumption behind this principle is that democratic decisions always have a particular scope. If people constitute the sovereign – the *demos* of democracy – then all decisions must be justified and legitimised with respect to this *demos* (the people). Conversely, this means that all those affected by democratic decisions should participate in them.

The inclusion of all affected parties, whether as rights-bearing subjects (liberal), discourse partners (deliberative), or participants in a political practice (pragmatist), thus becomes a central quality of democracy. This AAP is a fundamental principle of democratic self-determination. Some questions will arise throughout the book concerning the AAP: Is it necessary, from a democratic theory perspective, to include future generations in present political decisions as affected parties? As we shall see, this generates a strong legitimating argument for developing proxy representation for future generations (see Section 3.5.2).

One final concept must be addressed explicitly within this comparative analysis of democratic theories: the concept of interest. In some democratic theories, as we have already noted, the concept of interest plays a significant role, especially in formal and liberal conceptions. Generally speaking, interest refers to the concerns, calculated benefits, or advantages of a person or, in some theoretical frameworks, also of a group of people. Thus, interest is a perspectival concept, traditionally not focused on the common good but on individual calculations and objectives. In democratic theory, the reference to interests serves as a heuristic concept to relate and balance these various perspectives within the political context.

This book's exploration of interest is rooted in both theory and practice, where it has become an influential conceptual framework. However, interest here is not used in a narrowly individualistic sense. Instead, interest always focuses on individual perspectives within relational networks of social and political connections, from which they cannot be isolated. Interest, therefore, does not mean setting individual concerns as absolutes. Moreover, interest should not be equated with rational calculation in the sense of the Homo Economicus model. While the emphasis on interest does follow its own 'logic', this does not mean that political balancing of interests should be understood as purely optimising rational preferences.

Instead, it seems meaningful to interpret interest in a broader sense. The considerations in this book draw on different formations of the concept of interest. When speaking of the interests of future generations, it is meant first to consider and integrate their perspective into the political process, especially because they are often inadequately represented. Second, the concept underscores the fact that there are other interests besides those of future generations, which may conflict with them; for instance, the interests of currently living impoverished populations in the Global South. Thus, we tie the discussion of proxy representation for future generations back to normative reflections on democracy. The values implicit in democratic practices provide a framework for making such judgements compellingly.

There is also a third way of using the term interest. It is in the interest of everyone – that is, the entire *demos* – to represent future generations appropriately. For example, a human rights perspective holds that the world community has an interest in upholding and protecting the rights of all people, including those yet to be born. When interests are discussed in the following chapters, all these meanings will be considered and interconnected.

3.4 Normative Foundations for the Representation of Future Generations

The reconstruction of these six models of democracy – which play a significant role not only in theory but also on the level of the practical self-understanding of democracies – shows first that all approaches must make (partly fundamental) theoretical changes to be able to respond to long-term ecological crises. It is already apparent that the various models of democracy sketched earlier differ in how well they are capable of being applied to ecological challenges involving long-term consequences such as climate change.

If representation is viewed as a cornerstone of democracy, then the question becomes whether and how representation can be theoretically rethought and re-operationalised in the face of ecological challenges. What could such a development of proxy representation look like, at both national and international levels?

And how could it be ethically justified or oriented? In this regard, philosophy provides some insights. Building on the pragmatic methodology underpinning this book, the next step in our argument involves identifying potential ethical criteria for this transformation of representation. Pragmatists are not concerned with establishing an ideal principle; rather, they reconstruct social and political practices and inquire about the values implied within them that are suitable for the further development of these practices. To further develop proxy representation in this direction, especially at the international legal level, it is important to reconstruct and discuss the values implied in the democratic practices, which can serve as an important impulse for this advancement. The advantage of this approach is that it does not impose principles from external sources onto reality; instead, normative proposals for improvement are developed from within the political practice itself.

Of course, the point of view from which the forms of representation are reconstructed and assessed plays a significant role. To avoid a narrowing of this process, the pragmatist approach implies deliberative elements. To critically assess one's own conditionality, the pragmatist aims to integrate as many different stakeholders as possible to include as many different perspectives of critique as possible. The goal is to assess the forms of representation from as many perspectives as possible and their potential implications for respecting the values outlined regarding future generations.

Such an approach also takes seriously the diversity and heterogeneity of various proxies, which can often come into conflict with each other. Not all forms of proxy representation of future generations have the same impacts. Ombudspersons, constitutions, the IPCC, and international courts and tribunals may have divergent impacts and imply divergent conclusions in terms of exactly how future generations could best be represented and what the best political solutions might be. From a pragmatist perspective, this diversity and its resulting conflicts are not seen as problems but as a productive force for democratic change. Democracy, irrespective of its self-conception, thrives on diversity. This certainly applies to proxy representation as well. Nonetheless, it is essential to inquire about the inherent values that are particularly crucial for discussion and clarification.

Turning our attention now to democratic practices, both within their national contexts and the international system, three values currently play a particularly key role: justice, solidarity, and vulnerability. These values are present in all the conceptions of democracy outlined earlier, albeit in diverse ways. The following will outline these three values and demonstrate their potential contributions to the ethical and political inclusion of future generations in present political practices. Put in pragmatist terms, the focus is on reflecting upon various paths of ethical and political improvement with the aim of better representing future generations in current international law and policy-making.

We justify the selection of these three values in two ways. First, they play a significant role in democratic practices that address the question of future generations. Of course, other values could also have been chosen because they also form the normative fundament of democracy. For example, dignity, freedom, and justice play a key role in democratic practices and in theoretical discourses about democracy. We will demonstrate in the course of our argument that there are numerous connections and overlaps between these and the three selected values. In some cases, parts of the normative reconstruction of individual values can quite obviously be translated into other value discourses. Nonetheless, the selection of the three values seems particularly productive because they open different dimensions of reflection (for example, justice and freedom often lie close to each other in the liberal tradition). Moreover, the three normative perspectives can also provide productive impulses for the further development of future ideas about representation. Therefore, we focus on justice, solidarity, and vulnerability, while simultaneously connecting these to other normative discourses.

3.4.1 Intergenerational Justice

The first and currently most powerful discourse, which draws primarily from the liberal and deliberative tradition of normative democratic theory, is intergenerational justice. This follows on from the key theories of justice in the twentieth century and involves extending them from a temporal perspective to incorporate future generations.

The current ethical discourse on *intergenerational justice* is characterised by a variety of partly controversial positions regarding the interpretation of normative demands of future generations; put differently, what ethical duties we owe towards future generations. The different conceptions can mostly be classified along the classical categories of ethical theorising and their critics, which originate from a range of traditions including: the discourse-theoretical (Ekardt 2015; Ott 2007); contractarian (Gardiner et al. 2009; Heyd 2009; Rawls 1971); egalitarian (Gosseries 2001; Scanlon 2005); responsibility (Jonas 1979); teleological (Thompson 2017); and utilitarian (Birnbacher 1988; Parfit 1984), amongst others.

A starting point of many of these theories is a specific concept of 'future generations'. Before the normative claim of intergenerational justice can be substantiated, the question of the (temporal) framework of action and its actors must be clarified. It can be observed that many models of the current discourse transfer the action-theoretical context to a transtemporal framework. This means that generations are defined as actors who are sometimes at odds with each other. Thus, the origin of all questions of intergenerational justice lies in how to resolve conflicts between two or more distinct actors. The generations therefore become (individual) agents of action. Principles of fairness, justice, or distribution are then formulated in relation to these different actors (for different definitions of future generations, see Tremmel's theory of intergenerational justice; Tremmel 2009: 19–20).

However, whether and how future generations can be philosophically grasped and related to those who are alive now diverges strongly: while discourse theory as well as contractarianism develop their concept of a 'generation' in the tradition of a transgenerational interaction of rational communication partners, egalitarianism as well as sufficiency theory, following principles of harm, refer to different models of overlapping generational cohorts. Deontological approaches interpret duty and its fulfilment according to ethical standards as fundamental to judging whether an action is morally justified. When considering intergenerational justice, this principle is applied to determine duties owed by contemporaries to human beings born in the future.

Regardless of the differences between approaches to intergenerational justice, the issue of threshold plays a key role in all paradigms. For intergenerational justice, the question is not only to whom we owe something but also how much and of what. One answer is provided by the threshold or subsistence conception (Meyer 2003; Gosseries & Meyer 2009), which defines a minimum of goods (in a broad concept of goods that also includes opportunities or rights) which must be protected to be able to live in a human way. This minimum is tied to the condition of being human. Normally, this means the provision of basic goods (such as food, water, and clothing). Social goods (such as access to the labour market, education, or political participation) can also play a key role, depending on the theory. This is clearly shown by the capability approach (Dijk 2021). In addition, basic preconditions for human beings staying above the threshold – such as a functioning (or at least non-threatening) environment, including the climate system – are assumed to complement the threshold. According to this thesis, we act in an *inter*-generationally just manner if we act to ensure that this threshold remains in place in the future.

This understanding of justice is related to equality in two ways. First, it is about substantial equality regarding the provision of basic needs. The threshold concept implies the normative assumption that all people are entitled to a life in dignity, which means that they should be provided with at least the same basic form of life fulfilment. Second, it is also about equality under the law. Because this life above a threshold value is granted to all people equally as a legal entitlement, it is often formulated in the logic of human rights. Intergenerational justice as the fulfilment of a threshold value (whether formulated as needs or capabilities) is therefore linked to the understanding of equality.

One threshold theory of intergenerational justice is the theory of human rights. Climate change violates both the rights of persons alive and those in the future (Bell

2011: 9). Reder and Köhler argue that the normative core of human rights rests on the principles of freedom, equality, solidarity, and participation which constitute a normative guideline for climate policy-making. They further argue that 'a decent life for all humans is the centre of the normative foundation of human rights' (Reder & Köhler 2016: 132). Human rights thus form a well-defined threshold that must also be respected for future generations (Caney 2010a).

Behind this extension of human rights to future generations lies a particular understanding of law. Rights are understood, in the sense of Habermas, as a dynamic system of claims. As the legal system evolves, people respond to new conflicts and problems. The enactment of new laws, up to and including constitutional changes, is based on this dynamic understanding of law. If future generations can claim human rights, this implies that they are potentially also legal subjects. This is controversial because the status of a legal subject traditionally presupposes existence. From a legal-philosophical perspective, however, the view has gained acceptance that future humans are potentially legal subjects, and that they acquire this status upon birth. After all, the legal system is based on the same idea: children do not need to apply for the status of a legal subject; rather, it is automatically granted to them at birth. This expansion of the understanding of law can also be applied generally to future generations.

In this book, we define intergenerational justice as requiring the observance of the human rights of future generations necessary for them to lead a decent life. This provides a justification for our responsibility towards future generations. In terms of the international legal framework of human rights, we interpret 'necessary to lead a decent life' as entailing a threshold which means, at the very least, a requirement on all states to meet the minimum essential level required of *all* human rights set out in the human rights covenants.[8] Threshold theories do not preclude us from doing more for future generations than the threshold dictates, but this is then not a question of justice but of altruism. Threshold theories do not focus on individual fates but set conditions of a liveable existence *qua* being human.

[8] While economic, social, and cultural rights *are* to be progressively achieved under Article 2 of the *International Covenant on Economic Social and Cultural Rights* (ICESCR) (1966), the UN Human Rights Committee has clarified that

> at the very least, minimum essential levels of each of the rights is incumbent upon every State party. Thus, for example, a state party in which any significant number of individuals is deprived of essential foodstuffs, for essential primary care, of basic shelter and housing, or of the most basic forms of education is, prima facie, failing to discharge its obligations under the Covenant (UN Committee on Economic Social and Cultural Rights (CESCR) 1990: para 10).

The Committee goes on to state that the Covenant establishes such a 'minimum core obligation', while an assessment as to whether a state has discharged this minimum core obligation must take account of 'resource constraints applying within the country concerned' (CESCR 1990: para 10). The Committee has stated that 'a failure to prevent foreseeable human rights harm caused by climate change … could constitute a breach of the obligations [of the ICESCR]' (CESCR 2018: para 6).

From a normative perspective, such threshold approaches do not intend to pitch individual human rights against others or to speak of 'core' human rights. Human rights can only be adequately understood in their multidimensionality. This means, for example, that individual freedoms or rights for the satisfaction of basic needs have the same status as social or cultural rights. It is only in the combination of these dimensions that human rights take on their normative significance. For instance, when the Inuit in Canada lose their physical, mental, and cultural foundation due to climate change and the melting of ice, this threat can only be captured in its multidimensionality. Human rights, in their various facets, are, however, an instrument capable of doing just that. The UN Human Rights Committee has made it clear that, at the very least, common minimum essential levels must be met by every state party to the *International Covenant on Economic Social and Cultural Rights* (ICESCR) in relation to each of the rights set out in the Covenant (UN Committee on Economic, Social and Cultural Rights (CESCR) 1990: para 10).

3.4.2 Solidarity

In addition to the debate on intergenerational justice, the question of solidarity has played a key role for some years. This has implications both for the normative foundations of democracy in general and for its consideration of future generations. In the late 1990s, Kurt Bayertz elaborated an important theory of social and political solidarity (Bayertz 1999; Scholz 2008). In the tradition of Durkheim, Bayertz's concept of social solidarity is based on the observation that the rational voluntarism of liberal political theories is misleading. The image of the isolated, rationally willing citizen that underlies many democratic societies is inaccurate. Rather, human beings are always already involved and integrated in a complex and dynamic network of social relations and interactions, from which normative claims arise beyond rational-wilful consent. Solidarity means recognising that people live in relations from which normative claims arise. These moral demands refer to the fact that all parts of the relational network should be considered, that no one should fall out of the network, and that special attention should be paid to those whose lives are precarious. It flows from this view that solidarity entails not just help or assistance for the vulnerable, but also a fundamental change of economic structures to protect the vulnerable.

Relationality as the basis for climate ethics therefore emphasises that all people worldwide relate to each other in a dynamic network of relations. Political decisions or economic actions in one part of the world have massive effects on ecological conditions elsewhere and thus on the lives of people in other parts of the world. Solidarity understood as relationality thus means that normative claims go beyond the boundaries of one's own community, culture, or nation. Solidarity always means global or transcultural solidarity, even if such global solidarity only exists in plurality (Gould 2007; Reder & Heindl 2020). In terms of a pragmatist theory of solidarity, the demand for global solidarity implies, for example, that people at different nodes of the relational network feel solidarity with other people (or living beings) and thus bring their concerns into the (political) field of vision. Values (such as solidarity) arise from the interconnectedness of people.

Second, the theorem of relationality implies a fundamental critique of a purely anthropocentric approach for environmental ethics and does so within the framework of a new pattern of thinking: relationality as the social-theoretical basis of solidarity always means to be in connection with all other living beings, including ecosystems. What constitutes human experience or shapes human action is not only other people but also ecological conditions or other living beings, such as non-human animals. Of course, the objection has been made that reciprocal relationships cannot be conceptualised between all living beings, and certainly not between humans and non-human nature. However, this reciprocity only exists between many people who are in solidarity with each other hypothetically and not factually. Moreover, studies giving meaning to the idea of human beings having solidarity with non-human animals have emerged in recent years (Cojocaru 2021). In a similar direction, this study emphasises an obligation to solidarity with other animals arising from the interconnectedness between humans and nature.

Third, solidarity means that environmental ethics should not fall into a presentist thinking of the political, which is inherent in some liberal political theories (Tahmoudi et al. 2020). Solidarity as recognition of relationality also means thinking about the lives of future generations. Thus, environmental ethics must be much more strongly considered as a temporal-diachronic frame of reflection when thinking about solidarity.

Conceiving of solidarity in a relational manner takes inspiration from Indigenous ontologies. According to Indigenous belief systems in Canada, Aotearoa-New Zealand, and Australia, for example, individuals have a responsibility to maintain a balance between the elements of nature in which they are a part: this duty exists in a context in which one's identity is interconnected with the identities of one's ancestors and future generations conceived within a circular, rather than a linear, concept of time (Abe et al. 2024; McGregor 2018; Winter 2021).

Bayertz (1999) and Scholz (2008) focus not only on social solidarity but also on political solidarity. This, too, contains important impulses for the debate on climate ethics. Historically, political solidarity has had two facets. On the one hand is the transfer of social relationality into the political institutions of the democratic constitutional state. From a historical point of view, the institutional protection against social risks – in short, the welfare state – can be viewed as an important expression of political solidarity. These institutions ensure that no one falls outside the relational net. For environmental ethics, this dimension of political solidarity means an increased focus on institutions and the law to safeguard these institutional arrangements, which provides a link to more liberal thinking about intergenerational justice (Reder et al. 2018).

On the other hand, political solidarity has a second dimension that is grounded in, amongst other things, the labour movement and its militant demands. In this second respect, political solidarity pays particular attention to the crises of the time and seeks transformative solutions beyond existing legal and political institutions. It asks how political commitment can be reawakened and a militant commitment to a different world strengthened. Political solidarity entails a fundamental critique of existing political and economic conditions. It is not so much a matter of expanding existing meanings, but of developing fundamentally new frames of thought, starting from the political. The aim is to work transformatively towards a different society in the future (Reder & Stüber 2020). Again, the normative background of this critique is the theorem of relationality: political structures and processes are criticised when individual parts, people, living beings, and nature are ignored or even deliberately overlooked. It aims for structures based on solidarity which overcome these blind spots.

In this context, it is particularly important for researchers to understand which (new) forms of solidarity practice are developing in the wake of transnational social upheavals, how these can be theoretically interpreted, and what conclusions can be drawn from this for the understanding of society or the political. Empirically, many cultural and political practices are emerging that emphasise solidarity with future generations. From 'Fridays for Future' school strikes to religious communities and academic think-tanks, many practices advocate solidarity with future generations. These practices reflect a concern for intergenerational justice. Only if people feel connected in their concrete practices with people living in the future can moral and legal claims be justified within the framework of a theory of justice.

A further link between solidarity and intergenerational justice is that, for intergenerational solidarity to be meaningful, current generations must accept an ethical obligation to ensure that future generations meet a minimal, subsistence level above a certain threshold. This has striking parallels with the concept of social solidarity sketched earlier. Just as social solidarity can be interpreted as ensuring nobody falls below a minimum social welfare net, intergenerational solidarity can similarly be interpreted as ensuring that future generations do not fall below a threshold of minimal subsistence. In the climate change context, we have seen that such a threshold can be defined as meeting the requirements of human rights.

The language of solidarity is strongly reflected in the UN Secretary-General's 2013 report, *Intergenerational Solidarity and the Needs of Future Generations*

(UNSG 2013) and 2021 report, *Our Common Agenda*, which argues for a new social contract to provide the basis for a rejuvenated multilateralism to solve pressing global problems (UNSG 2021: 22). The social contract is to extend to future generations (UNSG 2021: 38–39) which, on the face of it, is problematic, given the lack of reciprocity between contemporaries and future generations (Lawrence 2022: 48–50). Nevertheless, solidarity allows an extension to future generations based on shared interests. The Secretary-General's 2021 report defines solidarity as 'a fundamental value by virtue which global challenges must be managed in a way that distributes costs and benefits fairly, in accordance with basic principles of equity and social justice and ensures that those who suffer [the most] or benefit the least receive help from those who [suffer the least or] benefit the most (UNSG 2021: 14)'.[9]

The Secretary-General's 2021 report was the springboard for the development by the UN High-Level Committee on Programmes (HLCP) – which brings together a number of UN agencies – of a set of common principles on future generations. These common principles aim to ensure agreement on a set of common values across the United Nations system for use in a range of contexts, including strategic planning, policy advice, and programming (United Nations 2023a: 2). 'Global solidarity' and 'global responsibility' are identified as key values to foster to ensure that the UN system responds to the global ecological crisis (United Nations 2023a: 4).

It has been pointed out that this definition is rather narrow in its focus on wealth distribution (Koroma 2012: 114), and a slightly broader definition finds support in UN instruments which adds two further elements: (i) 'shared responsibility for managing worldwide economic and social development, as well as threats to international peace and security'; and (ii) 'respect for nature' entailing prudence in the management of all living species as resources 'in accordance with sustainable development' to ensure that the 'immeasurable riches provided to us by nature [are] preserved and passed on to our descendants' (UNGA 2000: para 6). The *Millennium Declaration* adopted by the UN General Assembly in 2000 proclaims that all three elements (wealth distribution, peace/security, and sustainability) are 'fundamental values essential to international relations in the 21st century'.

An advantage of this framing based on solidarity is that it may avoid the possible divisiveness of rights-based language, which some countries perceive as manifesting a Western bias. A further advantage is that, by emphasising common threats, the language of solidarity underscores the need to cooperate, and the idea

[9] This definition draws on UNGA res. 57/213, which in turn was reflected in the Millennium Declaration of the United Nations General Assembly, UNGA res. 55/2 of 8 September 2000, para 6.

that 'we are all in this together'. Solidarity is often linked to the notion that the 'all' encompasses the global community, rather than the nation-state. The recent resurgence of nationalism places this framing under strain.

One disadvantage of this framing is that the content of obligations which flow from solidarity remains vague. Arguably, then, a solidarity framing needs to be supplemented by obligations of intergenerational justice – particularly the principle of 'intergenerational equity' understood as a minimum, an obligation on contemporaries to ensure that future generations enjoy human rights necessary to lead a decent life (see Section 3.4.1), and an obligation to preserve the ecological integrity of the planet (Drysek & Pickering 2019: 89). Fleshing out such a concept in a treaty has not been done to date, but would arguably be a logical extension of the solidarity framing we argue for here (see Chapter 8).

Indeed, the principle of intergenerational equity has been argued to point in the direction of a trust-type relationship between human beings and resources, which is a type of proxy representation. The fact that human beings have inherited natural resources, and that no generation has a superior claim to these resources than any other, has been argued to give rise to the concept of the trust, whereby the current generation has a duty to conserve and maintain planetary resources for future beneficiaries (Shelton 2010: 143).

The element of solidarity involving shared responsibility for resources, mentioned earlier, finds expression in the special international legal regimes created for the deep seabed and the moon, both of which involve the idea of the 'common heritage of humankind': that is, a communal safeguarding of areas of resources which cannot be claimed by individual sovereign states, with this communal management being exercised as a trust for the benefit of future generations (Shelton 2010: 143). The International Seabed Authority (ISA), established by the *UN Convention on the Law of the Sea* in 1982 (UNCLOS 1982: art. 136) with the aim of regulating and controlling deep seabed mineral mining in areas outside national jurisdiction on behalf of humankind, acts 'as a kind of trustee on behalf of mankind as a whole' (Jaeckel et al. 2017: 150). As South Africa pointed out in the UN General Assembly in 2009, the 'common heritage of humankind' principle is not only about benefit sharing but also 'about solidarity; solidarity and the preservation and conservation of the good we all share and therefore should protect' (Jaeckel et al. 2017: 150). This regime is infused with both *intra-* and *inter*-generational equity-type elements, including the preservation of marine-protected areas for the benefit of future generations (Jaeckel et al. 2017: 155). However, creating trust-type mechanisms for the benefit of future generations and implementing them is not the same thing. The ISA regime has come under criticism for a lack of transparency in the operations of its Finance Committee and commercialisation, putting the regime at risk (Nyka 2021: 18).

3.4.3 Vulnerability

Finally, in addition to solidarity with future generations, the question of vulnerability as a normative-political framework for reflection on intergenerational issues currently plays an increasingly significant role in theory and practice. Vulnerability has recently emerged as a counter-concept to traditional normative-political framings. In the debates on climate change, discussions on vulnerability have long played a key role; for example, in relation to the IPCC (Edenhofer et al. 2012). Many non-governmental organisations (NGOs) have also increasingly adopted a focus on vulnerability during the last decade. This focus on vulnerability accentuates issues that are often neglected by traditional theories and political practices.

The evolving debate shows that there are quite different forms of vulnerability, such as natural, social, economic, and cultural. Climate change impacts involve exposing particular groups to different forms of vulnerability. For example, heat waves, extreme weather events, and an increase in vector-borne diseases make increasing numbers of people vulnerable in terms of health impacts (IPCC 2023). Those most vulnerable include the elderly, the young, disabled persons, women, and people living in poverty. Climate change magnifies existing vulnerabilities and is now seen as a key factor in social development (UNDP 2020, 2022). Vulnerability can be understood as a basic dimension of all living things, for which it is necessary to develop a new critical sensitivity beyond established social security narratives and institutions, as Butler (2016) argues.

However, it is also evident that not all people are equally vulnerable (Goodin 1986). Rather, individuals and communities are vulnerable in different ways due to social, societal, or personal dispositions. The risks of being injured – as shown, for example, by studies in the context of capability research – are very unequally distributed, beginning with children, women, refugees and displaced persons, people from the countries of the Global South and, especially, future generations. At the same time, determining who is considered vulnerable and should therefore be given greater protection is always an expression of political power that must be problematised. Who is (most) vulnerable and who defines this is highly controversial in the current discourse. *Ex negativo*, the question is asked about those who are not perceived, who are discriminated against, or who are completely excluded from the social, political, or economic processes.

Vulnerability is also a counterfoil to justice, which is often strongly aligned with the economic model of distributive justice.[10] From this perspective, solidarity

[10] Of course, vulnerability might also be conceptualised within a distributive justice approach. Some approaches within the climate debate proceed in this way. We have decided to differentiate between justice and vulnerability for two reasons. First, within the philosophical literature, most authors interpret vulnerability as a critique and alternative to justice. For example, philosophers pointed out that Rawls' conception of justice implies the conception of rational, autonomous, and independent human beings (and

means primarily giving a voice to those who are currently not visible in such distributive calculations. In contrast, the discourse on vulnerability is understood as a critique of democratic orders that fail to adequately consider the vulnerability of future people. If democracies are normatively oriented towards the vulnerable, they must also pay special attention to them through their forms of representation as one basic form of democratic procedure.

There is also a strong link between vulnerability and intergenerational justice. If intergenerational justice in the climate context is equated with ensuring that future generations can enjoy the human rights necessary for a decent life, this finds further justification in the link to vulnerability. This is because meeting human rights requirements is a vehicle for ensuring that future generations are not vulnerable. Adopting legal rules and policies that ensure that future generations have sufficient food, subsistence, and shelter is clearly vital in terms of helping them to have the necessary resilience to withstand climate impacts. As discussed further in this book (Section 8.5), this framing has implications for the mandate of appropriate institutions to represent future generations, in that the requirement to address human rights that are vital to vulnerabilities should be central to such mandates. Given human beings' reliance on functioning ecosystems, protection of these ecosystems also needs to be incorporated in the relevant mandates of proxy institutions.

The central question in this next step of our reflection is how current concepts of proxy representation can be further developed to respond appropriately to the current ecological crises, particularly the climate crisis. What impulses can emerge from democratic-theoretical and ethical considerations in this regard? The concluding reflections of this chapter address these questions.

3.5 Theoretical Strategies for Reforming Representation

3.5.1 Normative Impulses for the Discourse on Proxy Representation

The discourses on justice, solidarity, and vulnerability provide a normative basis for the transformation of representation both at the national and international levels. Whether and how this normative demand can be translated into political forms of proxy representation is a central concern of what follows in this section. In this context, our thesis is that the three discourses of justice, solidarity, and vulnerability are interconnected, even if they come into tension with each other – which they certainly do. From a pragmatist perspective, however, this tension does not pose a fundamental problem because pragmatists expect such contradictions. These

citizens) and, thus, focuses too little on the concrete forms of vulnerability (Reder & Faets 2024). These debates reflect the demarcations between the two values. Second, for methodological reasons, it seems reasonable to differentiate between the two values to emphasise their potential for addressing the question of representation of future generations, even if they are linked.

tensions should be used productively to improve the respective political practice – in this case, the forms of representation – as a whole.

All three normative discourses form fundamental dimensions of the democratic *ethos*. Democracy depends on the solidarity of people, in the sense of a recognition of social connectedness, to be able to negotiate claims to justice in the first place. The focus on those who are excluded (or not included) clearly plays a significant role in all theories of democracy, particularly in relation to theories which conceive of democracy as being more than the formal act of elections. These criteria can easily be linked to other normative theories: thus, for example, to the extent that theories of intergenerational justice entail the fair distribution of goods between generations, these theories also imply a conception of vulnerability.

Future generations are particularly vulnerable because they are not involved in current decisions but will suffer from their consequences. Ensuring a minimum subsistence level of protection of the rights of future generations can help ensure that they are protected in relation to the vulnerabilities future individuals and groups face, considering the threat of climate change. Moreover, this action of recognising the vulnerable through proxy representation amounts to an important expression of solidarity: it ensures that intergenerational solidarity has meaningful content in the climate change context and is not merely an abstract slogan. Proxy representation can then be seen as a political mechanism aimed at giving a voice to the particularly vulnerable; its legal forms can also play a key role when the law shifts to the logic of protecting the particularly vulnerable.

The development of new forms of proxy representation of future generations grounded on these three normative discourses can help push us in the direction of long-term climate law- and policy-making, and, at the very least, make visible the long-term consequences of current short-term political decisions. By personalising these consequences and understanding future generations as part of a constantly forming and expanding *demos*, these consequences can be integrated into the logic, mechanisms, and procedures of political procedures. In this way, problems such as climate change can be dealt with politically, and vulnerable future people can be normatively considered.

From a meta-perspective, all three ethical discourses draw attention to two aspects that are important for a transformation of representation. First, democracies and their theoretical underpinnings currently tend to place too much emphasis on methodological individualism or the concept of community and thus pay too little attention to social relationality. Second, they still focus too much on the present. Democracy is primarily concerned with the present. Yet, human life is always temporal, connected to the past and the future. Democracy should therefore no longer be understood exclusively in the present, but diachronically, that is, across time. A concrete consequence of this could be to understand proxy representation of future generations not just as a corrective to existing theories of democracy, but also as a fundamental element of the theoretical foundations of democracy itself.

In addition, in a globalised world, the social and the political sphere can only be thought of in terms of a relationality that extends beyond traditional national borders. This means that normative claims do not stop at these borders but must extend to all people worldwide. If political action by states always has global effects, these must be considered normatively, and political mechanisms must be adapted accordingly. This applies equally to the diachronic character of social relationality. People are necessarily temporal beings, and their existence always necessarily spans many generations. This manifests itself in the discussion of intergenerational justice. Generations are not discrete actors opposed to one another but, rather, fluidly interwoven in interlocking relationships. For states and the global (legal) order to normatively reflect this reality, appropriate mechanisms must be developed to adequately account for this social diachronic relationality. This approach of relationality is a good normative basis for the development of new forms of representation.

Furthermore, the approach of relationality, through its focus on the reciprocal relationships between humans and the environment or nature, offers the basis of a rigorous critique of a strictly anthropocentric approach. These interrelationships give rise to normative claims not only for humans but also for non-human nature which need to be recognised. The development of new forms of proxy representation is therefore an imperative in relation to future generations of human beings, but also in relation to non-human nature. While we do not further develop the idea of representation of nature in this book, it is important to emphasise that this extension is logically required.

Let us conclude this first argument: to be able to integrate the concerns of future generations appropriately into political mechanisms, politics – both on the national and international levels – should pay greater attention to the diachronic relationality of the social than it has in the past. In this context, it becomes clear that democracy is not a timeless ideal, but a political practice that must be constantly readjusted in terms of its normative pillars in view of new challenges – such as climate change.

Proxy representation can then become an institutionalised critique accompanying all political processes on the operational level. Proxy representatives of future generations have the potential to examine and critique whether current political decisions have considered the interests of future generations adequately and implemented a convincing understanding of intergenerational justice. Such forms of self-criticism embodied in political procedures – aimed at questioning political decisions measured against the normative foundations of democracy – have always been a key characteristic of democracies. Proxy representation of future generations is one such institutionalised form of critique.

3.5.2 *Future Generations as Part of the National and International* Demos

In liberal, deliberative, republican, and communitarian traditions, the aim is to reflect critically on the determination of those who are to be represented. In the language of democratic theory: because representation is always founded on a concept defining who belongs to the *demos*, we must rethink the concept of *demos*. We must ask afresh: who should be involved in democratic decision-making and why?

Such a critical debate on the *demos* can also be found in post-structuralist approaches. These approaches share with liberal, deliberative, and communitarian traditions the intention that we should pay more attention to those who are excluded from current political decisions. From post-structuralist perspectives, however, it is not so much about broadening the *demos* (legal subjects, discourse partners, and so on). Some radical democratic theorists, for example, even argue that the *demos* could never be understood as an interaction between rational agents or an ethnic, cultural, and historical community; rather, the *demos* is the voice of the excluded (Rancière 2010). Political discussions therefore always revolve around the question of who receives too little (or no) attention and should therefore receive more attention as part of the *demos*. Democracy is thus ultimately a struggle about the question of who is excluded. This is also true from a temporal perspective, as future generations tend to be excluded in current political decisions.

This consideration is also critical at the international level. It is crucial to reflect upon and engage in political discussion about who should be included in political and legal mechanisms. If there are compelling arguments for an expansion of the *demos* of the democratic idea into the future, these arguments also apply at the international level. Here, too, it involves expanding the global community as a reference point for global political decisions into the future (Lawrence 2021b: 22–41).

Although the different traditions of theorising politics and democracy differ in terms of justification, they seem to agree that representation needs to be reformed with a view to better incorporating global and long-term consequences of political action and, thus, providing a rationale for proxy representation of the excluded. If democracies focus on those who do not have the power to be adequately represented in the political sphere, they will create new forms of representation for those who do not belong to the *demos* in the traditional understanding. This means that democracy must cope with its own paradoxical character; namely, it must give an account of those who are not part of democratic procedures.

From this perspective, it becomes clear that democracy – and representation as a fundamental political mechanism – are not (fixed) ideals. Rather, representation is a political mechanism that must always be developed while considering new challenges: the long-term consequences of political decisions are one such challenge today. Thus, political forms of representation should be reconfigured to meet this challenge with the underlying rationale of democracy in mind. In terms of representation, two possibilities arise. First, representatives could be bound to constitutional norms within the legal framework of the democratic nation-state. For example, future generations' interests can be anchored in the constitution, requiring all representatives – at least in theory – to consider their interests and integrate them in political decisions (Dobson 1999). As mentioned earlier, at the international level there is no constitution, while the UN Charter fulfils some roles like a constitution (Cot 2011: para 63). Incorporating future generations' interests in an international agreement is a further possibility (see Chapter 8). A second category of possibilities is more focused on the political level. The aim on this level would be to develop new political forms of proxy representation of future generations which purport to represent the distinctive interests of this group to better integrate their interests into national and international political processes. But what exactly does proxy representation mean? What are its different forms? And how can they be ethically and legally justified?

Thus, the central question is how the democratic idea of representation can be further developed in the face of ecological crises, not only at the national but also at the international level. Our thesis is that democratic representation – regardless of the theoretical tradition through which it understands itself – is best suited to respond to ecological crises in the sense of providing a powerful rationale for participation by all – including future generations, despite the various limitations previously outlined. For this purpose, it is important not to limit democracy to the nation-state. Democracy can provide a powerful ideal which justifies further development of new forms of proxy representation at both the national and international levels, while the particularities of the international system need to be considered in designing such mechanisms at this level. Thus, our concern is to ask how democratic representation at the national level can not only be further developed, and (where feasible) transferred to the global level. We focus our considerations on different forms of proxy representation.

A powerful rationale for the further development of democratic forms of proxy representation is found in the AAP (Bohman 2007; Fung 2013; Näsström 2011). This principle means that all people affected by a political decision should be 'involved' in them. In the current world, in which democracies – and, indeed, states generally – make many decisions that have a massive impact on people in other regions or in the future, the question is whether this principle remains valid and, if so, what this means for democracy and proxy representation of future generations. But what the AAP in general, and 'involvement' in particular, means is controversial. The term 'involved' could suggest direct participation, whereas some may argue that representation is sufficient. Moreover, in the recent period, 'speaking for others' has been suspected of entailing yet another form of 'hegemonic paternalism', suggesting that representation of those affected should be as direct as possible; in other words, that those affected should speak for themselves (Bernstorff 2021: 150). However, as has been pointed out, even if the most affected have the possibility to speak in international institutions, they are being heard 'because they also claim to speak on behalf of other similarly affected persons' (Bernstorff 2021: 150). The extent to which international NGOs provide a legitimate voice to those affected has recently been challenged on the grounds that they may lack internal accountability, democratic processes, and be dominated by the Global North. In response, at least 19 international institutions have constructed mechanisms to ensure those affected (or mostly affected) gain a voice (Bernstorff 2021: 148). An example of this is the Committee relating to the 2006 UN *Convention on the Rights of Persons with Disabilities* (CRPD 2006), where the procedural rules limit representation on the Committee to organisations with at least half of the members being persons with disabilities and being led by persons with disabilities (Bernstorff 2021: 48–49).

In addition, the question of representation is controversial, because it could mean the concrete representation of all people affected (for example, via elections) and the representation of future interests (Goodin 2007). Certainly, democracies would reach their limits if they were to involve *all those concerned* in representation in a formal or agency-based sense. Democracy would then always mean 'world democracy', in which (almost) all people worldwide could vote and thus authorise the representatives (Valentini 2014).

The AAP does not necessarily imply such a concept of representation and a world state. It does, however, require the interests of people living now (and in the future) be factored into decision-making action in relation to climate change, including the development of new forms of representation to ensure that this occurs. This means that, even if democracies cannot currently allow all people to vote equally, they should – using the AAP as an *ideal* or blueprint for reform – at least develop new forms of participation and representation, so that excluded groups are at least hypothetically considered or indirectly involved. Democracies must discuss what the *demos* means in our current circumstances – that involves making political decisions which entail wide-ranging global and long-term consequences for people who are not part of the 'traditional *demos*'. At the international level, this means using the AAP as a blueprint for reform, which provides a powerful justification for exploring new forms of proxy representation in the international system.

A further justification for the expansion of the *demos* flows from the pragmatist method. If political action implies political consequences that contradict their own normative foundations (according to the central values of democracy), then institutions come into self-contradiction. So, for example, if a political community is committed to human rights and their protection as part of its normative self-understanding but at the same time does not respect the human rights of future generations with its climate policy decisions, this is a contradiction that must be resolved. Governance structures must expand the *demos* to avoid contradicting their own normative foundations. Again, how far this expansion goes is the subject of democratic negotiation. And, for this negotiation, vulnerability can again provide a framework: because it is primarily about the consideration and representation of those who are particularly vulnerable.

Let us demonstrate what the AAP means, for example, for the democratic understanding of deliberation. In many traditional theories, the circle of those included in deliberation refers to the *demos* limited to the nation-state. But how does this work in relation to the many decisions of democratic deliberation processes that affect people beyond this *demos*? Deliberative theories integrate this question with an extension of the understanding of deliberation. Future generations are then interpreted as equal 'partners' in hypothetical discourses. According to the ethical discourse principle, their opinions and interests must also be considered appropriately in the political process – especially in the form of representation (necessarily by proxy). Another form of discourse-ethical argumentation also speaks of the representation of discourses; for example, of long-term ecological discourses which embody the interests of future generations (Dryzek & Niemeyer 2012). This proposal circumvents the problem of conceptualising future generations as speaking beings in a reciprocal relationship to currently living ones. However, identifying who is entitled to decide which discourses count under this model remains challenging, if it is a group of experts who appoints them. In both directions, the reform of representation is about broadening the perspective of the discourse: whether it is about broadening the group that is (allowed to be) part of the discussion or the discourses about that group.

Republican or communitarian models of politics have responded to long-term problems by extending the political community in many ways that reflect the AAP by expanding the possibility for those affected by a decision to have a voice. These theories reflect on traditional concepts of the boundaries of the (democratic) community. In these models, future generations are interpreted less as rationally speaking citizens of a discourse community or rights holders than as part of the democratic community itself. To integrate future generations into political considerations and decisions, the concept of republican community that underlies these theories is extended in time. This extension is then accompanied by a legitimation of their concerns within republican procedures, usually also through proxy representation. The debate over whether younger children are already part of the political community and should therefore be more involved in political procedures is an example of such a broadening of the democratic community (Gutwald & Reder 2023; Schweiger 2022). In this theoretical tradition, the concept of representation is developed by reflecting on and broadening the understanding of the political community. The political community traditionally referred to the linguistically capable, reasonable citizens. This, for example, excluded both children and future generations because they were assumed to be irrational or not capable of speech at all.

Republican or communitarian traditions respond by developing a new narrative, rather than concrete (for example, rights-oriented) proposals for the further development of representation. Instead, these models argue that we need to redefine what constitutes the political community. As we argue in this book, community thus redefined includes not only currently living people but also children or people who are not yet alive.

At the same time, the idea here is also to expand the political community to the global level. In a highly interconnected world, political, economic, and ecological crises (such as climate change) are inextricably global problems that require global legal responses. If responding to these crises not only requires formal procedures but also a minimum of political community, then this community must increasingly be expanded beyond the national-societal framework. The debates in the social, cultural, and normative framework of the UN climate regime's conference of parties (COPs) in the last decades demonstrate this: without a minimum of community in the sense of a willingness to solve the problem together, nothing moves forward politically. That is why these models argue for the construction of a global political community, for example, in the sense of thin morality, as Michael Walzer argues. If sovereignty-related concerns and self-interest – particularly on behalf of the wealthy countries – undermine this actual community, reflected in the rather weak global climate regime, does this undermine this argument? We would say that it does not because the fact that a minimum level of global community cooperation is a precondition for successfully addressing climate change is sufficient (Vanderheiden 2008: 105).

3.6 Legal Constraints and Human Rights as (Normative) Global Legal Practice

One structural problem is that, in both the actor-centred authorisation model of representation and Rehfeld's audience-based concept, representation is not normatively or legally bound in a strict sense. Of course, in democratic states, the actions of elected representatives must be in accordance with the applicable legal foundation (for example, the constitution) or there must be an audience that accepts that someone is speaking on behalf of somebody else. However, the actions of the representatives are not bound in a strict sense in either model. They are free to stand up for what they consider to be right, according to their party/political affiliation and also their personal judgement – if they are accepted as a representative by the relevant audience. Thus, representatives in many democracies (so far) are not legally bound to consider or even include the interests of future generations in their decisions if this is not mandated by the legal framework, for example, the constitution. How can this limitation be considered – and, if possible, overcome – from the standpoint of the various models of democracy? For this purpose, a first look at the liberal understanding of democracy is helpful.

At the national level, attempts to overcome this limitation are often made using legal instruments. Some democracies have already established legal mechanisms which bind representatives making decisions to consider future generations. Debates about anchoring environmental concerns, such as the interests (and rights) of future generations, in constitutions are one example. From the perspective of liberal or deliberative theories, such legal frameworks are a central instrument through which future generations – for example, in the perspective of Habermas – not only become objects, but also bearers of fundamental rights. This means that future generations will not only have to bear the consequences of political action but also that they can – at least, indirectly – become subjects of law if such rights are granted to them in the constitution.

In the liberal tradition, which is oriented towards law as a political instrument, thought has been given to future generations as bearers of rights. However, this broadening of the understanding of law was (and still is) not self-evident. Originally, critics pointed out that only those persons who are also factually alive can be legal entities. The counter-argument, which increasingly finds acceptance in current legal and political discussions, is based on the observation that at every moment more persons are born who, upon being born, automatically acquire legal status.[11] Thus, there is neither a distinct boundary between present and future legal subjects, nor do we ever deny people this status when they are born. Future human beings can thus be considered to constitute legal subjects – though still in a provisional sense, because they are not yet born. This fact does not diminish the normative and legal claim of their rights, which gives rise to intergenerational obligations on the shoulders of contemporaries (Vanderheiden 2008; Meyer 2003). Bell (2011) argues, for example, that it is the potential for harm in the future which gives rise to all human rights obligations and corresponding rights. Thus, the fact that an obligation arises in relation to persons who are not yet born at the time a particular

[11] We put aside the question of whether rights *in utero* also arise and take no position on this issue. See Donger (2022: 274).

action is taken is irrelevant to whether an obligation – with corresponding rights – arises in the first place. Moreover, a constitution – or other legal mechanism – can require decision-makers to consider the interests of future generations, without necessarily ascribing them rights.

It has been argued that support for the rights of future generations could imply opposition to abortion (Donger 2022: 274). However, the right to life of future generations is not a 'right to be born' but, rather, 'a right to life-sustaining conditions for those who are already living', with climate litigation by youth plaintiffs placing the emphasis on the latter (Donger 2022: 274).

At the international level, there is no global constitution. The UN Charter performs some elements of such a role (Cot 2011: para 63) but does not contain strong provisions for restraining states' action in terms of impacts on future generations. A non-binding *Declaration on Future Generations*[12] was adopted at the UN *Summit of the Future* held in 2024, but largely contains vague obligations repeating provisions found in other UN instruments, reflecting states' zealous protection of their sovereignty.

Another important international practice in this perspective is that of human rights (see also the reflections on the relation between intergenerational justice and human rights in Chapter 3). Human rights provide a basis for a universal (global) morality and are also the legal fundament for the orientation of politics. From this perspective, human rights – extended to include the human rights of future generations – can provide both a constraint on decision-makers (to ensure protection of the human rights of future generations) and a rationale for proxy representation. From a pragmatist point of view, human rights practices have validity based on their incorporation in various global practices. The UDHR – agreed by consensus by the global community – seeks to provide answers to the multifaceted, specific experiences of injustice (Walzer 2005; Habermas 2010). From that perspective, human rights embody a cosmopolitan approach: 'The same rights that apply within the state also apply at the global level' (Caney 2010b: 23). As emphasised in the considerations on intergenerational justice, a multidimensional understanding must be applied – which contradicts an understanding of core human rights.

However, human rights are always in need of further development because of emerging social problems and sources of injustice. This is also true in view of new

[12] The idea of a global charter for future generations was proposed by Edith Brown Weiss (1989) in her pathfinding book, *In Fairness to Future Generations: International Law: Common Patrimony, and Intergenerational Equity*. As this book went to press, the United Nations Summit of the Future on 22 September 2024 adopted *The Pact for the Future*, para 32 of which noted the proposal for an Envoy for Future Generations but did not agree to create one. For all outcomes of this summit – including the *Pact for the Future* and *Declaration on Future Generations* – see United Nations (2024). In October 2024 a senior UN official announced at a major international conference that the Secretary-General was intending to proceed to create such an envoy (Day 2024) (see Chapter 8 of this book).

global challenges, including the multiple connections between climate change and poverty. Therefore, it is convincing to analyse the effects of climate impacts from a human rights perspective, as Caney clearly point out: 'My argument is simply that a human rights perspective has important insights and any account of the impacts of climate change which ignores its implications for people's enjoyment of human rights is fundamentally incomplete and inadequate' (Caney 2010a: 89). From this perspective, human rights provide an ethical threshold, which could be a convincing basis for climate and development politics.

Human rights serve as a threshold for a dignified life, applicable to both present and future generations and, in this sense, can function as a narrative to justify proxy representation from a moral and legal perspective. After all, proxy representation represents an institutional form of safeguarding the human rights of future generations. This institutional-participatory element is an integral part of human rights practice and therefore can be applied to proxy representation based on the internal logic of human rights. This demonstrates an initial connection between ethical and legal discourse in justifying and advancing the forms of representation for future generations within the internal legal system. Parts II and III of the book focus on these practices and mechanisms in the international legal system and related institutions.

3.7 Final Remarks

In this chapter, we demonstrate that philosophical reflections can help to legitimise and further develop proxy representation of future generations, both from the perspective of the ideal of democracy and of the ethical considerations embodied in the discourses of justice, solidarity, and vulnerability. These values can act as a springboard for thinking about new mechanisms for representation of future generations. Moreover, the values implicit in these discourses can be the basis for further developing current practices, institutions, and international legal rules.

Of course, representation always tends to refer to the *demos* as an ontologically attendant entity which is, in most cases, to be defined by territorial demarcations. Current theories sometimes still conceptualise the *demos*, for reasons of legitimacy, based on its representation – which necessarily entails that the *demos* must be somehow limited, according to normative assumptions about who belongs to it and who does not (Benhabib 2004; Habermas 1998). In other words, representation paradoxically implies the production of those who are not represented.

Thus, for all political and legal pathways to establish new mechanisms of representation, it is necessary to examine who is represented and by whom. For example, if the normative core of democracy is the protection of the vulnerable, then all democracies have always been challenged to critically question their own demarcation of the *demos* and to reflect on which vulnerable people beyond the *demos* are negatively influenced by its decisions. To bypass such limitations of the *demos*, it seems useful to conceive of proxy representation not solely as a narrowly defined political mechanism. Proxy representation can also happen, for example, through civil society protest and resistance groups that demand a practice of solidarity with future generations beyond such a narrow definition, while outside the scope of this book. The emerging importance of social movements has parallels with the growing influence of non-state actors in developing and implementing international law (Lawrence 2021c: 153–68). Representation as institutionalised critique, for example, is obviously dependent on forms of protest and public discussion.

Finally, although we highlight the potential democratic theory has for our purposes, we also observe the problem that some theories of democracy tend to answer the normative questions raised only in relation to the nation-state. As we have seen, this does not go far enough because global and long-term consequences of political action are always intertwined, and there are strong interconnections between national and international law. Therefore, all states are increasingly challenged to understand their actions as transnational and to conceptualise them accordingly. Normatively, those who are excluded often do not live within this nation-state framework. For example, those who will suffer most from climate impacts are the future generations in the Global South. This consideration shows the importance of a transnational or even cosmopolitan perspective. Thus, proxy representation should not be narrowed to the national level, but always conceptualised from a global perspective. This is a central aim of our book.

References

Abe, H., Wenning, M. & Fritsch, M. (2024). *Intercultural Philosophy and Environmental Justice between Generations Indigenous, African, Asian, and Western Perspectives*, Cambridge: Cambridge University Press.

Barry, B. (1999). Sustainability and Intergenerational Justice. In Dobson, A., ed., *Fairness and Futurity: Essays on Environmental Sustainability and Social Justice*. Oxford: Oxford University Press, 93–117.

Bayertz, K. (1999). Four Uses of Solidarity. In Bayertz, K., ed., *Solidarity*. Dordrecht: Kluwer, 3–28.

Bell, D. (2011). Does Anthropogenic Climate Change Violate Human Rights? *Critical Review of International Social and Political Philosophy*, 14(2), 99–124.

Benhabib, S. (2004). *The Rights of Others*, Cambridge: Cambridge University Press.

Bernstorff, J. von. (2021). New Responses to the Legitimacy Crisis of International Institutions: The Role of 'Civil Society' and the Rise of the Principle of Participation of 'The Most Affected' in International Institutional Law. *European Journal of International Law*, 32(1), 125–57.

Birnbacher, D. (1988). *Verantwortung für zukünftige Generationen*, Ditzingen: Reclam.

Bohman, J. (1999). Democracy as Inquiry, Inquiry as Democratic: Pragmatism, Social Science and the Democratic Division of Labour. *American Journal of Political Science*, 43, 590–607.

Bohman, J. (2007). *Democracy across Borders: From Dêmos to Dêmoi*, Cambridge, MA: The Massachusetts Institute of Technology Press.

Boston, J. (2016). *Governing for the Future: Designing Democratic Institutions for a Better Tomorrow*, Bingley: Emerald.

Brown Weiss, E. (1989). *In Fairness to Future Generations: International Law: Common Patrimony, and Intergenerational Equity*, Tokyo: The United Nations University; Dobbs Ferry, NY: Transnational Publishers.

Butler, J. (2016). Rethinking Vulnerability and Resistance. In Butler, J., Gambetti, Z. & Sabsay, L., eds., *Vulnerability in Resistance*. Durham & London: Duke University Press, 12–27.

Butler, J. (2020). The Inorganic Body in the Early Marx: A Limit-Concept of Anthropocentrism. *Radical Philosophy*, 206, 3–17.

Butler, J. (2004). *Precarious Life: The Powers of Mourning and Violence*, London: Verso.

Butler, J. & Athanasiou, A. (2013). *Dispossession: The Performative in the Political*, Cambridge: Polity.

Caney, S. (2010a). Climate Change, Human Rights and Moral Thresholds. In S. Gardiner, S. Caney, D. Jamieson & H. Shue, eds., *Climate Ethics Essential Readings*. Oxford: Oxford University Press, 163–77.

Caney, S. (2010b). Human Rights and Global Climate Change. In Pierik R., & Werner, W., eds., *Cosmopolitanism in Context: Perspectives from International Law and Political Theory*. Cambridge: Cambridge University Press, 19–44.

Charter of the United Nations, XV UNCIO 335, *amendments in* 557 UNTS 143, 638 UNTS 308 and 892 UNTS 119.

Christiano, T. (2011). Is Democratic Legitimacy Possible for International Institutions? In Archibugi, D., Koenig-Archibugi, M. & Marchetti, R., eds., *Global Democracy: Normative and Empirical Perspectives*. Cambridge: Cambridge University Press, 69–95.

Convention on the Rights of Persons with Disabilities (CPDR) (2006) (adopted 12 December 2006 in UNGA resolution A/RES/61/106; entered into force 3 May 2008), 2515 UNTS 3.

Cojocaru, M. D. (2021). *Passionate Animals: Emotions, Animal Ethics, and Moral Pragmatics*, Lanham, MA: Lexington Books.

Cot, J. P. (2011). United Nations Charter. In R. Wolfrum, ed., *Max Planck Encyclopaedia of International Law*, Oxford: Oxford University Press.

Dahl, R. (1999). Can International Organisations be Democratic? A Sceptic's View. In Shapiro, I. & Hacker-Cordon, C., eds., *Democracy's Edges*. Cambridge: Cambridge University Press, 19–36.

Day, R. (2024). *Coming Soon A UN Envoy for Future Generations*, United Nations University (October 9, 2024). Available at: https://unu.edu/cpr/blog-post/coming-soon-un-envoy-future-generations.

De-Shalit, A. (1995). *Why Posterity Matters: Environmental Policies and Future Generation*, London: Routledge.

Derrida, J. (1992). In Drucilla, C., Rosenfield, M. & Carlson, D., eds., *Deconstruction and the Possibility of Justice*. New York: Routledge.

Dewey, J. (1937). Democracy and Educational Administration. *School and Society*, 45, 457.

Dijk, N. van (2021). The Capability Approach as a Road Map for Re-thinking Intergenerational Justice. In Linehan, J. & Lawrence, P., eds., *Giving Future Generations a Voice: Normative Frameworks, Institutions and Practice*. Cheltenham/Camberley: Edward Elgar, 42–61.

Dingwerth, K. (2007). *The New Transnationalism: Transnational Governance and Its Democratic Legitimacy*, London: Palgrave Macmillan.

Dobson, A. (1999). *Fairness and Futurity. Essays on Environmental Sustainability*, Oxford: Oxford University Press.

Donger, E. (2022). Children and Youth in Strategic Climate Litigation: Advancing Rights through Legal Argument and Legal Mobilisation. *Transnational Environmental Law*, 11(2), 263–89.

Dryzek, J. & Niemeyer, S. (2012). *Foundations and Frontiers of Deliberative Governance*, Oxford: Oxford University Press.

Dryzek, J. & Pickering, J. (2019). *The Politics of the Anthropocene*, Oxford: Oxford University Press.

Edenhofer, O., Wallacher, J., Lotze-Campen, H., Reder, M., Knopf, B. & Müller, J. eds. (2012). *Climate Change, Justice and Sustainability: Linking Climate and Development*. Dordrecht, Heidelberg, New York, London: Springer.

Ekardt, F. (2015). *Theorie der Nachhaltigkeit: Rechtliche, ethische und politische Zugänge – am Beispiel von Klimawandel, Ressourcenknappheit und Welthandel*, 3rd ed., Baden-Baden: Nomos.

Fox, G. H., & Roth, B. R., eds. (2020). *Democracy and International Law*, Cambridge: Cambridge University Press.

Franck, T. (1992). The Emerging Right to Democratic Governance. *American Journal of International Law*, 86(1), 46–91.

Fung, A. (2013). The Principle of Affected Interests: An Interpretation and Defense. In Smith, R. M. & Nagel, J. H., eds., *Representation: Elections and Beyond*, Philadelphia, PA: University of Pennsylvania Press, 236–68.

Gardiner, S., Caney, S., Jamieson, D. & Shue, H. (2009). *Climate Ethics: Essential* Readings, Oxford: Oxford University Press.

Ginsburg, T. (2021). *Democracies and International Law*, Cambridge: Cambridge University Press.

Goodin, R. E. (1986). *Protecting the Vulnerable. A Reanalysis of Our Social Responsibilities*, Chicago, IL: University of Chicago Press.

Goodin, R. E. (2007). Enfranchising All Affected Interests, and Its Alternatives. *Philosophy and Public Affairs*, 35(1), 40–68.

Gosseries, A. (2001). What Do We Owe the Next Generation(s). *Loyola of Los Angeles Law Review*, 35(1), 293–354.

Gosseries, A. & Meyer, L. H. eds. (2009). *Intergenerational Justice*, Oxford: Oxford University Press.

Gould, C. C. (2007). Transnational Solidarities. *Journal of Social Philosophy*, 38(1), 148–64.

Gutwald, R. & Reder, M. (2023). How to Protect Children? A Pragmatic Approach: On State Intervention and Children's Welfare. *Journal of Ethics*, 27(1), 77–95.

Habermas, J. (1998). *Die Postnationale Konstellation: Politische Essays*, Berlin: Suhrkamp.

Habermas, J. (2010). The Concept of Human Dignity and the Realistic Utopia of Human Rights. *Metaphilosophy*, 41(4), 464–80.

Held, D. (1995). *Democracy and the Global Order. From the Modern State to Cosmopolitan Governance*, Cambridge: Polity Press.

Heyd, D. (2009). A Value or an Obligation? Rawls on Justice to Future Generations. In Gosseries, A. & Meyer, L. H., eds., *Intergenerational Justice*, Oxford: Oxford University Press, 167–88.

Intergovernmental Panel on Climate Change (IPCC). (2023). *Climate Change 2023: Synthesis Report. A Report of the Intergovernmental Panel on Climate Change. Contribution of Working Groups I, II and III to the Sixth Assessment Report of the Intergovernmental Panel on Climate*, Geneva: IPCC.

International Covenant on Civil and Political Rights (ICCPR) (adopted 16 December 1966; entered into force 23 March 1976), 999 UNTS 171.

International Covenant on Economic Social and Cultural Rights (ICESCR) (adopted 16 December 1966; entered into force 3 January 1976) 993 UNTS 3.

Jaeckel, A. et al. (2017). Conserving the Common Heritage of Humankind – Options for the Deep Seabed Mining Regime. *Marine Policy*, 78, 150–57.

Jonas, H. (1979). *Das Prinzip Verantwortung: Versuch einer Ethik für die technologische Zivilisation*, Berlin: Suhrkamp.

Klabbers, J. et al. (2021). International Law and Democracy Revisited. *European Journal of International Law*, 32(1), 9–15.

Koroma, A. G. (2012). Solidarity: Evidence of an Emerging International Legal Principle. In Hestermeyer, H. P. et al., eds., *Coexistence, Cooperation and Solidarity: Liber Amicorum Rüdiger Wolfrum*, Leiden: Brill, 103–29.

Laclau, E. & Mouffe, C. (1985). *Hegemony and Socialist Strategy: Towards a Radical Democratic Politics*, London: Verso.

Lawrence, P. (2014). *Justice for Future Generations, Climate Change and International Law*, Cheltenham: Edward Elgar.

Lawrence, P. (2020). Representation of Future Generations. In Kalfagianni, A., Fuchs, D. & Haydn, A., eds., *Routledge Handbook of Global Sustainability Governance*, London: Routledge, 88–99.

Lawrence, P. (2021a). International Institutions for Future Generations and Democratic Legitimacy. In Cordonier Segger, M. C., Szabó, M. & Harrington, A. R., eds., *Intergenerational Justice in Sustainable Development Treaty Implementation: Advancing Future Generations Rights through National Institutions*, Cambridge: Cambridge University Press, 597–614.

Lawrence, P. (2021b). Justifying Institutions for Future Generations Based on the Mitigation of Bias and Intergenerational Justice. In Linehan, J. & Lawrence, P., eds., *Giving Future Generations a Voice: Normative Frameworks, Institutions and Practice*, Cheltenham: Edward Elgar, 22–41.

Lawrence, P. (2021c). International Relations. In Rajamania, L. & Peel, J., eds., *The Oxford Handbook of International Environmental Law*, 2nd ed., Oxford: Oxford University Press, 153–68.

Lawrence, P. (2022). Justifying Representation of Future Generations and Nature: Contradictory or Mutually Supporting Values? *Transnational Environmental Law*, 11(3), 1–27.

McGregor, D. (2018). Indigenous Environmental Justice, Knowledge, and Law. *Kalfou*, 5(2), 279–96.

Meyer, L. H. (2003). Past and Future. The Case for a Threshold Conception of Harm. In Meyer, L. H., Paulson, S. L. & Pogge, T. W., eds., *Rights, Culture and the Law: Themes from the Legal and Political Philosophy of Joseph Raz*, Oxford: Oxford University Press, 143–59.

Meyer, L. H., Paulson, S. L. & Pogge, T. W. (2003). *Rights, Culture and the Law: Themes from the Legal and Political Philosophy of Joseph Raz*, Oxford, UK: Oxford University Press.

Näsström, S. (2011). The Challenge of the All-Affected Principle. *Political Studies*, 59(1), 116–34.

Nyka, M. (2021). International Seabed Authority and Environmental Deep-Sea Stewardship – Principles Governing the Protection and Use of Seabed Resources. *Maritime Law*, XXIX, 9–19.

Ott, K. (2007). Ethical Orientation for Climate Change Policies. In Rodi, M., ed., *Implementing the Kyoto Protocol. Chances and Challenges for Transition Countries*, Berlin, Germany: Lexxion, 13–20.

Parfit, D. (1984). *Reasons and Persons*, Oxford: Oxford University Press.

Putnam, H. (1995). *Pragmatism. An Open Question*, Oxford: Blackwell.

Rancière, J. (2010). *Dissensus on Politics and Aesthetics*, London: Continuum.

Rasulov, A. (2021). 'From the Wells of Disappointment': The Curious Case of the International Law of Democracy and the Politics of International Legal Scholarship. *European Journal of International Law*, 32(1), 17–47.

Rawls, J. (1971). *A Theory of Justice: Original Edition*, Boston, MA: Harvard University Press.

Reder, M. & Köhler, L. (2016). Human Rights and Climate Policy. In Bos, G. & Duwell, M., eds., *Human Rights and Sustainability, Moral Responsibility to the Future*, London/New York: Routledge, 123–36.

Reder, M. & Heindl, A. (2020). Politische Solidarität in transnationaler Perspektive. *WSI-Mitteilungen*, 73(5), 349–55. https://doi.org/10.5771/0342-300X-2020-5-349.

Reder, M. & Stüber, K. S. (2020). Solidarität in der Krise: Für ein Verständnis politischer Solidarität in Corona-Zeiten im Anschluss an H. Arendt. *Zeitschrift für Praktische Philosophie*, 7(2), 443–66. https://doi.org/10.22613/zfpp/7.2.18.

Reder, M. & Faets, F. (2024). Judith Butler and Future Generations: Transtemporal Relationality, Generational Trouble and Future-Oriented Ruthless Critique. *Philosophy & Social Criticism* (online first). https://doi.org/10.1177/01914537241232965.

Reder, M., Gösele, A., Köhler, L. & Wallacher, J. (2018). *Umweltethik: Eine Einführung in globaler Perspektive*, Stuttgart: Kohlhammer.

Roth, B. R. (2021). The Trajectory of the Democratic Entitlement Thesis in International Legal Scholarship: A Reply to Akbar Rasulov. *European Journal of International Law*, 32(1), 49–55.

Sandel, M. (1998). *Liberalism and the Limits of Justice*, 2nd ed., Cambridge: Cambridge University Press.

Scanlon, T. (2005). When Does Equality Matter? In Nida-Rümelin, J. & Thierse, W., eds., *Political Equality: Politische Gleichheit*, Essen: Klartext Verlagsgesellschaft, 109–25.

Scholz, S. (2008). *Political Solidarity*, Philadelphia, PA: University of Pennsylvania Press.

Schumpeter, J. A. (1950). *Capitalism, Socialism and Democracy*, New York: Harper.

Schweiger, G. (2022). *#Kinderarmut: Ein philosophischer Essay*, Marburg: Büchner Verlag.

Sen, A. (2009). *The Idea of Justice*, London, UK: Allen Lane.

Shelton, D. (2010). Intergenerational Equity. In Wolfrum, R. & Kojima, C., eds., *Solidarity: A Structural Principle of International Law*, Heidelberg: Springer, 123–61.

Tahmoudi, N., Faets, S. & Reder, M. (2020). *Politik der Zukunft: Zukünftige Generationen als Leerstelle der Demokratie*, Bielefeld: Transcript Verlag.

Taylor, C. (1989). *Sources of the Self: The Making of the Modern Identity*, Cambridge: Cambridge University Press.

Tesón, F. R. (1992). The Kantian Theory of International Law. *Columbia Law Review*, 92, 53–102.

Thompson, J. (2017). The Ethics of Intergenerational Relationships. *Canadian Journal of Philosophy*, 47, 313–26.

Tremmel, J. C. (2009). *A Theory of Intergenerational Justice*, Oxford: Earthscan.

United Nations. (2023a). *United Nations System Common Principles on Future Generations*, Report of the Chief Executives Board for Coordination (UN Doc. CEB/2023/1/Add.1) (4 May 2023).

United Nations. (2023b). *United Nations Sustainable Development Goals*. Available at: www.un.org/sustainabledevelopment/sustainable-development-goals/.

United Nations. (2023c). *Global Issues: Democracy*. Available at: www.un.org/en/global-issues/democracy.

United Nations. (2024). *Summit of the Future, Our Common Agenda*. Available at: www.un.org/en/summit-of-the-future/pact-for-the-future.

UN Committee on Economic, Social and Cultural Rights (CESCR). (1990). *General Comment No. 3: The Nature of States Parties' Obligations (Art. 2, Para. 1 of the Covenant)* adopted at the fifth session of the Committee on Economic Social and Cultural Rights on 14 December 1990, UN Doc. E/1991/23.

UN Committee on Economic, Social and Cultural Rights (CESCR). (2018). *Climate Change and the International Covenant on Economic Social and Cultural Rights*. Statement of the Committee on Economic, Social and Cultural Rights (8 October 2018).

United Nations Convention on the Law of the Sea (UNCLOS) (adopted 10 December 1982; entered into force 16 November 1994), 1833 UNTS 397.

UN Developmental Programme (UNDP). (2020). *The Next Frontier: Human Development and the Anthropocene*. Available at: https://hdr.undp.org/content/human-development-report-2020.

UN Developmental Programme (UNDP). (2022). *2022 Special Report, New Threats to Human Security in the Anthropocene: Demanding Greater Solidarity*. Available at: www.hdr.undp.org/en/2022-human-security-report.

UN General Assembly (UNGA). (1948). *Universal Declaration of Human Rights*. Resolution 217A (III). UN Doc. A/810 at 71. Available at: www.ohchr.org/en/resources/educators/human-rights-education-training/universal-declaration-human-rights-1948.

UN General Assembly (UNGA). (2000). *55/2. United Nations Millennium Declaration*. Resolution adopted by the General Assembly. UN Doc. A/RES/55/2.

UN Human Rights Council (HRC). (2015). *Human Rights, Democracy and the Rule of Law: Resolution adopted by the Human Rights Council*. UN Doc. A/HRC/RES/28/14, Geneva. Available at: https://digitallibrary.un.org/record/795311.

UN Office of the High Commissioner (OHCHR). (2023a). *About Democracy and Human Rights: OHCHR and Democracy*. Available at: www.ohchr.org/en/democracy.

UN Office of the High Commissioner (OHCHR). (2023b). *OHCHR and Climate Change*. Available at: www.ohchr.org/en/climate-change.

United Nations Secretary-General (UNSG). (2013). *Intergenerational Solidarity and the Needs of Future Generations: Report of the Secretary-General*. UN Doc. A/68/322, New York. Available at: https://digitallibrary.un.org/record/756820.

United Nations Secretary-General (UNSG). (2021). *Secretary-General's Report, Our Common Agenda*.

Valentini, L. (2014). No Global Demos, No Global Democracy? A Systemization and Critique. *Perspectives on Politics*, 12(4), 789–807.

Vanderheiden, S. (2008). *Atmospheric Justice: A Political Theory of Climate Change*, Oxford: Oxford University Press.

Wallacher, J., Michael, R. & Martin, K. (2009). Klimawandel, weltweite Armut und Gerechtigkeit. Begründung und Gestaltung einer integrierten Klima- und Entwicklungspolitik. *Zeitschrift für Umweltpsychologie*, 13/1, 52–67.

Walzer, M. (1983). *Spheres of Justice*, Oxford: Blackwell.

Walzer, M. (1994). *Thick and Thin*, Notre-Dame, IN: University of Notre Dame Press.

Walzer, M. (2005). *Politics and Passion: Towards a More Egalitarian Liberalism*, New Haven, CT: Yale University Press.

Wike, R. et al. (2024). *Representative Democracy Remains a Popular Ideal, But People around the World are Critical of How It's Working*, Washington, DC: Pew Research Center. Available at: www.pewresearch.org/global/2024/02/28/representative-democracy-remains-a-popular-ideal-but-people-around-the-world-are-critical-of-how-its-working/.

Winter, C. (2021). *Subjects of Intergenerational Justice*, London/New York: Routledge.

Part II

International Law and Institutions

4

Criteria for Evaluating Mechanisms for Representation of Future Generations

4.1 Introduction

Imagine it is 2060. Wild weather has swept through The Netherlands. The famous system of Delta Works has kept North Sea surges at bay, but the Rhine River has flooded, transforming swathes of the country into an inland sea (KNMI 2015).[1] Justice N'Doure from Senegal has just received news that her place of work – the International Court of Justice (ICJ) located in the Peace Palace in The Hague – will be temporarily moved to higher ground in the east of the country. She has been informed that personal belongings from offices in the building may be collected from a checkpoint near the Peace Palace. N'Doure has recently travelled from heatwave conditions in Senegal, which have devastated her country's crops. She finds an emergency worker willing to take her by boat to the checkpoint. As they approach, she notices that the contents of the Peace Palace library have been swept out by the floodwaters, and books are floating away. She reaches over the gunwale of the boat and picks up a tome. By a strange twist of fate, it is the 2025 volume of the *Annual Reports of the International Court of Justice*, which contains judgements of the Court in its Advisory Opinion on climate change.[2] The volume is water-damaged but still readable. She begins to read.

Of course, no one knows what the world will look like in 2060 (or 2080 or 2100) but the scene sketched here is within the current (grim) predictions of scientists. The point of this story is to highlight a theme of this chapter: that climate change requires a reconsideration of traditional concepts of legitimacy in relation

[1] Royal Netherlands Meteorological Institute, Ministry of Infrastructure and Environment, *KNMI'14 Climate Scenarios for the Netherlands* (KNMI 2015), which predicts that climate change will result in significantly increased winter rainfall with increased flood risks for the Rhine, Meuse, and smaller rivers in The Netherlands.

[2] At the time of writing, public hearings on the Advisory Opinion requested by the United Nations General Assembly (UNGA) in March 2023 had just concluded and the Court had begun its deliberations (UNGA 2023; ICJ 2024).

to institutions. This new understanding of legitimacy will need to embrace a more expansive concept than has previously been utilised, given that projected climate impacts pose serious risks to the entire international society and its institutions. As we shall see, concepts that have worked up until now need to be modified to be made fit for purpose in this new reality.

Elsewhere in this book, we argue that the democratic ideal of inclusivity provides a powerful rationale for proxy-style representation of future generations. We note, however, that representative-style institutions or mechanisms are only one possibility: mainstreaming future generations' interests in policy- and law-making may be more effective. Thus, new institutions for future generations require justification. Such justification can be made against the baseline of having no such institutions (non-implementation baseline) or in comparison to other competing proposals (comparative baseline) (Caney 2016: 141). To illustrate, is creating a new UN Special Envoy for Future Generations a better option than not having such an institution? Alternatively, is such an institution comparatively more effective when assessed against other proposals (relative baseline) proposed at this particular time and place, involving, for example, mainstreaming future generations' interests in various existing programmes and policies (Caney 2016: 141)?

Effectiveness is only one of several criteria for justifying and evaluating such institutions. Simon Caney's influential framework for evaluating institutions for the future involves the following criteria: effectiveness, moral legitimacy, political sustainability, and political accessibility (Caney 2016: 140–42).[3] Legitimacy and effectiveness are closely related to the values of justice, solidarity, and vulnerability elaborated in Chapter 3. While justice, solidarity, and vulnerability represent, in a way, the foundations of the democratic idea, legitimacy and effectiveness represent formal criteria that are necessary for the material values to be implemented in the political processes. There is, therefore, a complementary relationship between them.

Assessing the effectiveness of institutions oriented towards the future presents challenges. One obvious challenge is that the effectiveness of a particular institution cannot be assessed until the future unfolds. Moreover, if we seek to assess long-term effectiveness, this creates a clear challenge. On the other hand, this problem can be overstated: it will be evident to varying degrees when assessing the effectiveness of any institution. One way of (at least partly) overcoming this challenge is to consider the performance of comparable institutions. For example, Jonathan Boston (2016) suggests that, when considering the possible effectiveness of an ombudsman for future generations, we could look at the empirical record of

[3] Boston (2016) proposes criteria of effectiveness, feasibility, and desirability.

comparable ombudsman for children or other vulnerable groups. Measuring effectiveness can involve using an internal yardstick (an institution's own objectives) or an external yardstick (whether an institution addresses a problem more broadly). In this chapter, we use a hybrid approach that combines both elements.

It is also important to note at the outset that we define 'effectiveness' broadly. It is not limited to monetary values, which can flow from an uncritical, neoliberal-type framing. Thus, a particular institution for future generations may be effective in a broader sense of promoting particular values that filter through to policy-making, which then promotes more favourable values from a justice and democracy point of view – even where an economic rationalist evaluation would find it difficult to quantify the exact impact of the particular institution in monetary terms.

We turn first to a general discussion of criteria for evaluating proxy-style institutions for future generations (Section 4.2), then proceed to elaborate criteria for assessing the democratic legitimacy of international institutions (Section 4.2.1) and international tribunals (Section 4.2.2), before turning to criteria for effectiveness (Section 4.2.3), accessibility, and political sustainability (Section 4.2.4). We conclude with some final observations (Section 4.3).

4.2 Criteria for Evaluating Institutions to Represent Future Generations

Both the legitimacy and effectiveness criteria elaborated in this chapter involve value judgements embedded in normative framings. These include an intergenerational justice value – reflected in the idea that future generations should enjoy the human rights necessary to lead a decent life, and their full range of capabilities, as well as a democratic value with the idea that future people should enjoy the capacity to govern themselves effectively (Hoffmann & Dijk 2023). This entails the idea that the interests of future generations should be protected by enabling their participation in contemporary deliberative practices through proxy representation. Consistent with the pragmatist methodology of this book, these criteria involve an incremental extension of the application of existing values to new contexts.

Effectiveness is, in turn, linked to accessibility and political sustainability. Accessibility refers to the political feasibility of a reform proposal, addressing the question of whether it is likely to be implemented in the real world. A proposed reform might be attractive from a normative point of view but score low on accessibility, meaning that it ultimately lacks effectiveness because it is unlikely to be implemented. Political sustainability refers to whether a reform proposal will be sustained into the future, which, again, is a precondition for its ultimate effectiveness.

4.2.1 Democratic Legitimacy of International Institutions

It is crucial to proceed with a clear understanding of the interrelated concepts of legitimacy and effectiveness. In this book, we apply the following criteria to assess the democratic legitimacy of international institutions.

(a) Procedural (input legitimacy), involving inclusive/fair representation, accountability, and transparency and deliberation (discursive quality);
(b) Source-based (input legitimacy), involving expertise, legal legitimacy, tradition, and discourse; and
(c) Substantive (output legitimacy), involving effectiveness and equity.

The criteria are derived from Sylvia Karlsson-Vinkhuyzen and Antto Vihma (2009: 405), Klaus Dingwerth (2007, 2014: 1124–47), and Daniel Bodansky (1999).[4] The criteria for legitimacy of Karlsson-Vinkhuyzen and Vihma and Bodansky are for legitimacy *tout court*. Recognising that democratic principles are not the only basis for legitimacy, Dingwerth (2007: 28, 34) argues convincingly that including deliberation strengthens legitimacy, as it involves greater participation of those affected and also entails a discursive quality of the rule-making process. Democratic legitimacy also meshes well with the rationale for proxy-style mechanisms of representation argued for in Chapter 3. The criteria set out earlier are tailored to the context of this book, which includes both the decisions of international tribunals – the ICJ (Chapter 6) and UN Rights of the Child Committee (Chapter 7) – and an international institution for future generations, a proposed UN Special Envoy for Future Generations (Chapter 8). Each criterion is explained later.

It is important to note that we use legitimacy to refer to normative, rather than sociological or subjective legitimacy. Normative legitimacy refers to whether a claim of authority is well founded in some objective sense. Sociological or subjective legitimacy refers to societal acceptance of authority as a sociological fact (Bodansky 1999: 601; Karlsson-Vinkhuyzen & Vihma 2009: 409).

Legitimacy and effectiveness are distinct but strongly interconnected concepts. Under these criteria, on the one hand, substantial effectiveness (output legitimacy) contributes to democratic legitimacy. On the other hand, meeting the requirements

[4] These authors apply legitimacy criteria to the spectrum of 'soft' through to 'hard' legal norms – a different context but, arguably, the categories are still valid in terms of the institutions discussed in this book. Karlsson-Vinkhuyzen and Vihma (2009) state their criteria of legitimacy (not democratic legitimacy) as source based, procedural, and substantive. We adopt a different order here, with procedural (input legitimacy) listed first, given our focus book on proxy representation as a distinctive procedure. Nevertheless, we consider all the criteria to be weighted equally. We have augmented these criteria with the criterion 'deliberation' derived from Dingwerth's theory (2007: 24–32) – see the following discussion – to formulate criteria for *democratic legitimacy*. We acknowledge that these authors do not necessarily share the same conception of legitimacy; Dingwerth adopts a procedural understanding of democratic legitimacy linked to his particular understanding of democracy (Dingwerth 2007: 15).

of the various elements of procedural (input legitimacy) in turn contributes to effectiveness. Section 4.2.2 sets out specific criteria for the democratic legitimacy of international tribunals (a subset of the broader category of international institutions), before turning to deal with the effectiveness of both international tribunals and institutions for future generations more generally (Section 4.2.3).

The criterion of input or procedural legitimacy involves 'inclusive representation' and captures the idea that, for a decision to be democratically legitimate, all those affected by the decision should have a say in the making of the decision: the 'all affected principle' (AAP) (Ball 2006: 137; Goodin 1996: 835; Goodin 2007: 40; Pitkin 1967: 209). Future generations cannot participate directly in decisions being made now in relation to climate change but can do so through a proxy. The proxy can make reasonable assumptions about the interests of future generations, referring to their vulnerability and including their need for the stable climate and functioning ecosystems upon which their welfare will depend (Vanderheiden 2008: 129). In addition, while beyond the scope of this book, the mandate of a proxy should also reflect moral duties to ecosystems and non-human species (Hoffmann & Dijk 2023: 79).

In the context of proxy representation of future generations, youth representation of future generations can enhance legitimacy. While the findings of empirical research on whether young people are more concerned about the future than older people are mixed (Gonzalez-Ricoy & Rey 2019: 7), the interests of young people overlap significantly more with the interests of persons not yet born than do the interests of older people. Moreover, climate change will threaten the interests of people who are now younger over a larger span of their lives than the interests of people who are now older. Reflecting this truth, young people have initiated school strikes around the world, as well as launching climate litigation, where they purport to speak not just on behalf of their own interests, but also on behalf of future generations (Donger 2022).

The sub-criteria of 'accountability and transparency' are problematic in the context we are discussing because it would seem impossible to hold a proxy for future generations accountable to persons not yet born. Nevertheless, accountability can (at least indirectly) be achieved by ensuring that the proxy operates consistently with a mandate that reflects the interests of future generations (Lawrence 2021: 607). Moreover, the proxy could be held to account by non-governmental organisations (NGOs) having a role in monitoring the proxy's performance. Transparency in the proxy's activities is an important precondition for this monitoring to take place (Hale 2008: 73).

The sub-criterion 'deliberation' reflects the view that the process of deliberation is an essential element of democratic legitimacy, according to theories of deliberative democracy (Dingwerth 2007: 23). As Dryzek and colleagues observe:

> Deliberative democracy reconceptualizes governance as effective, inclusive, and transformative communication encompassing citizens and policymakers. The basic idea, applicable globally no less than at other levels of governance, is that the legitimacy of any collective decision rests on the right, capacity, and opportunity of those subject to or affected by that decision (or their representatives) to participate in deliberation that is consequential for the content of the decision (Dryzek et al. 2019: 1).

Deliberation is often seen as a vehicle for conveying citizen's views to representative institutions, thereby ensuring their democratic nature (Saward 2008). According to this approach, 'deliberation' must have particular attributes to be a touchstone of democratic legitimacy: it must be free of coercion and involve participants who give reasons for their proposals and are willing to critically assess others' proposals oriented towards reaching a consensus based on reasoned argument (Dingwerth 2007: 24, 31).

In Chapter 3, we demonstrated that deliberative democracy is a central approach within the debate on democratic theory. By focusing on the institutionalisation of the process of opinion and will formation through various forms of (proxy) representation, this approach is promising in terms of its theoretical and practical implications for the institutional recognition of future generations. Deliberative democracy provides a strong justification for a proxy to represent the interests of future generations in the deliberative process.[5] Indeed, Dryzek and Niemeyer (2008: 481) have argued in favour of a particular version of deliberation that involves articulating discourses rather than positions. If we consider proxies for future generations articulating the interests of persons not yet born, rather than representing them as such, this opens the possibility of a new mechanisms, such as a UN Special Envoy for Future Generations, meeting this criterion (see Chapter 8).

In Japan, social experiments in deliberative democracy have assigned particular groups to represent future generations (as of 2060) and others to represent existing generations (Hara et al. 2019: 1609; see also Uwasu et al., 2020). The groups were tasked with seeking consensus on policy priorities between these two groups. A fascinating result of these early studies is that negotiations between the groups resulted in a consensus in favour of a substantial number of policy priorities which favoured the interests of future generations (Hara et al. 2019: 1612). These studies suggest that human beings – when made fully aware of long-term impacts of policies – may be willing to support policies which benefit the interests of future generations. Moreover, representatives of future generations can negotiate on their behalf and creatively explore the possibility of finding policy settings which address both long- and short-term interests. Through this process, the aim would

[5] However, this raises the concern that it could involve an unelected elite deciding which discourses should be given weight in the policy process; see Niemeyer & Jennstål (2017: 247–65).

be to change the mainstream policy discourse to better reflect the interests of both current and future generations (Hara et al. 2019: 1615–16). In addition, proxy-style representatives of future generations could foster further similar types of social experiments and use the findings as a catalyst to move from such research experiments into real-life policy-making.

The criterion of 'source-based legitimacy' (input legitimacy) refers to information or knowledge that is seen as authoritative: expertise, legal legitimacy, tradition (including institutionalised processes which can be difficult to change), and discourses (Karlsson-Vinkhuyzen & Vihma 2009: 410–11).[6] In terms of proxy-style representatives of future generations, 'expertise' could refer, for example, to the knowledge that a UN Special Envoy for Future Generations has (or could draw upon) in relation to the types of policies which are most likely to be effective in relation to protecting the interests of future generations. A well-resourced UN Special Envoy (with expert staff) would increase its legitimacy (expertise). Such a mechanism could also draw on scientific expertise in relation to the impact of climate change on future generations by relying on the authoritative reports of the Intergovernmental Panel on Climate Change (IPCC) and consulting with this body.

'Legal legitimacy' involves authority based on being in accordance with law, which at the international level involves institutions acting in a manner consistent with the treaty which has established them – which, in turn, derives its legitimacy from states' consent to it (Bodansky 1999: 604–5).

'Tradition' as a source of legitimacy can include, for example, the legitimacy of the *United Nations Framework Convention on Climate Change* (UNFCCC) and *Paris Agreement* (2015) regime as the legitimate form of intergovernmental governance to address climate change (Karlsson-Vinkhuyzen & Vihma 2009: 410).[7] The case studies in this book involve innovative forms of proxy representation of future generations, involving new institutions (for example, the UN Special Envoy for Future Generations) and existing institutions taking on new roles (for example, the ICJ and the UN Committee on the Rights of the Child). The legitimacy of these forms may be enhanced by the existing legitimacy of the institutions in question; even the legitimacy of the new UN Special Envoy may be affected by the perceived legitimacy of similar UN special envoys.

The sub-criterion of 'discourse' can involve legitimacy being linked to particular discourses that are perceived as authoritative by relevant stakeholders.

[6] Some authors distinguish source-based legitimacy from input legitimacy. For example, Bodansky (1999: 612) distinguishes source/origin based (e.g., God, tradition, or consent), procedural (fair procedures), and substantive (desired outcomes) forms of legitimacy.

[7] Peer-reviewed scientific knowledge is also an important source of legitimacy for the UNFCCC/*Paris Agreement* regime (Karlsson-Vinkhuyzen & Vihma 2009: 410). State consent also provides a basis for the legitimacy of the UN climate regime (Bodansky 1999: 604).

In this book, we draw on elements of discourses that already enjoy considerable support to justify proxy-style mechanisms for the representation of future generations, such as discourses relating to solidarity and sustainable development, which includes the principle of intergenerational equity. These discourses can help justify and bolster the legitimacy of new, proxy-style institutions for future generations (see Section 8.2). But some versions of sustainable development that prioritise development over sustainability can work in the contrary direction (see Section 8.5).

Concepts of sustainability and intergenerational equity have a particular legal form and thus constitute legal discourses that have been taken up both in global climate negotiations in the UN system and in climate litigation around the world. Indeed, policy-makers have started to come under pressure from legal action taken against governments using international tribunals – climate litigation – which gives rise to questions about the democratic legitimacy of such tribunals.

The criterion 'substantive (output legitimacy)' covers effectiveness (see further 4.2.3). In this book, we treat effectiveness as a distinct criterion but note that enhancing effectiveness can contribute to the overall legitimacy of a mechanism or institution through its effect on output legitimacy.

Equity as a sub-criterion reflects the idea that substantive legitimacy involves both contributing to solving a particular problem and improving justice. Given the context of extreme global inequality, it is crucial that mechanisms do not just change behaviour or solve a particular problem, but also enhance justice. The connection with effectiveness is that norms or mechanisms perceived to be both legitimate and fair are more likely to be complied with (Karlsson-Vinkhuyzen & Vihma 2009: 413).

A weakness in the criteria for democratic legitimacy set out earlier is that they rest on deliberative practice only up to the present time, without in any way involving the practice or voices of future generations. This problem can be addressed by expanding our understanding of legitimacy. When political decisions are made that affect future generations, from a democratic theoretical perspective (which aims at the integration of all those affected by a decision), these decisions can only be considered legitimate if they appropriately consider the impacts on future generations' needs or interests.[8] Legitimacy only makes sense, then, if it is understood as also including what we refer to as 'future legitimacy'. This can also be justified from a normative standpoint: because, if decisions do not recognise and consider the needs and living conditions of future generations, they also disregard their vulnerability and cannot be considered legitimate from the standpoint of intergenerational justice.

[8] With thanks to Florian Sperk for providing the basis for the ideas elaborated in this paragraph.

The concept of 'future legitimacy' is underpinned by the concept that all generations are of equal value, thus requiring an assessment of legitimacy in terms of both current and future generations. Assessing a new UN Special Envoy for Future Generations against this benchmark would thus require an evaluation from the perspective of future generations. This, in turn, requires imagining that one is living decades in the future, in a world that is increasingly negatively impacted by climate change, and looking back to determine whether such a UN Special Envoy created now was sufficient to address the underlying threat posed by climate change to the international community and all its institutions, with all the consequences for intergenerational justice entailed in this threat.

An objection to this concept of 'future legitimacy' could be raised on the grounds that it would inherently prioritise the interests of future generations over current generations. To address this problem, it could be argued that the overarching legitimacy of a particular international institution must be based on the area of overlap between its legitimacy as traditionally understood – what we will refer to as 'present legitimacy' – and its 'future legitimacy'. This would ensure that legitimacy was conceived in a manner which – in terms of its normative framing – did not prioritise either future or current generations' interests but sought to maximise both.

4.2.2 Democratic Legitimacy of International Tribunals

International tribunals can be considered a subset of the broader category of international institutions. At a general level, therefore, the democratic legitimacy of such tribunals is related to the extent to which they fulfil the criteria (elaborated earlier) which apply to all international institutions. We will see, however, that these criteria require some adaptation to the specific functions that international tribunals perform.

The function of such tribunals is not singular, but includes the resolution of disputes, clarification of international law rules, and the promotion of justice (to which we will return in a moment). The functions of the ICJ are set out in its Statute – a treaty – which refers to the function of the Court as being to 'decide in accordance with international law such disputes as are submitted to it' (*Statute of the International Court of Justice* 1945: art. 38). At a formal level, the authority of the ICJ – and therefore its legitimacy – is derived from state consent to this treaty (Merrills 2011: 116–19). At first blush, it would seem that the Court should only apply international law and not develop it, but, on closer examination, the ICJ has several implicit functions. These include – as the principal judicial organ of the United Nations – supporting the UN's overall goal of maintaining peace and security and settling international disputes 'in conformity with the principles of justice and international law' as expressed in the *Charter of the United Nations* (1945:

art. 1(1); Giladi & Shany 2023: 107).[9] A further implicit function is the role of the Court in developing, not just applying, international law (Giladi & Shany 2023: 107). Indeed, commentators point out that the ICJ plays a much more activist role than is apparent from looking its Statute (Bogdandy & Venzke 2013: 52–7). Thus, where international law rules are unclear, the ICJ plays an important law reform role through interpreting rules in a particular direction or even further developing rules in a way that allows international law to adapt to new circumstances, in a manner extending well beyond the role of the Court as described in its Statute (Tams & Tzanakopoulos 2010).

Our argument is that, where international tribunals perform this function, courts such as the ICJ should undertake this task by applying a normative framework, according to which the role of the court – whatever other functions it has – should be the promotion of justice, extended to include intergenerational justice.[10] Thus, the first prong of our argument is that the effectiveness of the ICJ rests on the extent to which the tribunal acts to promote justice, extended to include intergenerational justice. This rests on the argument that furthering justice is an implicit goal of the Court. As we have seen, furthering equity or justice is a criterion for assessing output legitimacy, which involves examining closely the function or goals of the particular institution. Importantly, this is also a criterion for effectiveness, given this has been defined as including equity (see text described earlier).

In making this argument, we note that this does not preclude international tribunals also playing a key role in promoting other values, such as the resolution of disputes and the facilitation of trade. Our argument is that international tribunals ought to promote justice and, thus, protection of the most vulnerable groups. This rests on the fact that the international community has accepted in the *Charter of the United Nations* (1945: art. 1(3)) and a raft of global human rights instruments, including the Universal Declaration of Human Rights (UNGA 1948), the idea that all people, regardless of when and where they are born, are entitled to human rights (Beyleveld, Düwell & Spahn 2015; Lawrence & Köhler 2018: 645–46). It flows from this that the international legal order should promote justice defined as ensuring the protection of human rights (Buchanan 2004; Ratner 2015).

If one accepts that the international legal order should promote justice defined as protection of human rights, it follows that the legal order should also promote intergenerational justice, based on the premise that the entitlement to human rights is both universal and extends into the future (Caney 2009).[11]

[9] Giladi and Shany (2023: 107) describe this as a 'regime support' function implicit in the ICJ's dispute settlement function.

[10] This argument is based on Lawrence & Köhler (2018).

[11] Note that the idea that human rights extend to the right to a clean, healthy, and sustainable environment received endorsement by the international community in July 2022 (UN General Assembly 2022). See also the discussion of intergenerational justice in Chapter 3, Section 3.4.1.

To make the further argument that international tribunals ought to be democratically legitimate, we contend that several specific criteria must be met. These correspond with the general procedural (input legitimacy) criteria outlined earlier, which involve inclusive/fair representation, accountability, and transparency and deliberation (discursive quality). These criteria are modified to consider the context of international tribunals and the need to be responsive to the interests of future generations.

Thus, as a subset of all international institutions, international tribunals ought to be democratically legitimate and act on behalf of the people, the *demos*. In addition, the *demos* must be extended to include both current and future generations. Acting on behalf of the *demos* requires both:

- impartiality and independence, in terms of ensuring procedural fairness in relation to court/tribunal processes; and
- responsiveness to the *demos*, involving transparency, deliberation, and participation, including the involvement of affected individuals in the particular processes (von Bogdandy & Venzke 2014: 151–2). (As we shall see in the case studies on international tribunals, this involves responsiveness to the interests of future generations through proxy-style procedural mechanisms.)

In addition, international tribunals must meet the requirements of output legitimacy (see further).

The content of these further requirements of democratic legitimacy in the context of international tribunals are drawn from principles developed in Western Europe under the *Treaty on European Union* (TEU) (EU 2008; Bogdandy & Venzke 2014: 136 et seq.). These rules emerged through extensive deliberative processes involving democratic states over 20 years. *Prima facie*, this would seem open to criticism as being a narrowly Eurocentric approach; the answer to criticism is that these rules happen to have emerged in Europe but could have emerged anywhere (Bogdandy & Venzke 2014: 136). Their validity stems from the strength of the deliberative process which gave rise to the principles and from the involvement of democratic states in this process (Bogdandy & Venzke 2014: 137). Furthermore, there is a strong link to the pragmatist methodology of this book, in that these elements of democratic legitimacy have been proven to work well in practice.

As mentioned earlier, international institutions need to meet criteria of current and future legitimacy. Assessing an international tribunal and its decisions against the benchmark of future legitimacy would require making an evaluation (for example, of an ICJ Advisory Opinion on climate change decided in 2025) from the perspective of future generations. This, in turn, requires imagining that one is living in a future world looking back to determine whether such a decision taken by the Court was sufficient to address the underlying threat of climate change (to the international community and all its institutions, including the Court), with the consequences for intergenerational justice entailed in this threat.

As pointed out earlier, the overall legitimacy of an institution would be found in the area of overlap between present and future legitimacy, thus ensuring the maximisation of future and current generations' interests.

Bringing these thoughts together, the legitimacy of an international tribunal (both present and future) is dependent on the extent to which it performs its functions (that is, linked to its effectiveness) and the extent to which it promotes justice (extended to include intergenerational justice) are integral to these functions. There is a tension here in that, if a tribunal such as the ICJ ignored its Statute and proceeded to invent international law rules in areas where the rules are clear, it would potentially undermine its legitimacy. As Julius Stone (1954: 368) pointed out, tribunals such as the ICJ are dependent on retaining legitimacy in the sense of state consent. An overly creative ICJ would very quickly undermine its legitimacy in this sense.

On the other hand, the concept of future legitimacy underscores the importance of legitimacy from the standpoint of future generations. This is vital in terms of adjusting the concept to the threat climate change poses to the very existence of all institutions, including the ICJ. This provides an additional lens for viewing legitimacy, which is more responsive to the context in which the law-making process takes place. Thus, an ICJ decision that was too timid in relation to the threat of climate change would undermine both its present and future legitimacy.

We can now map out criteria for assessing the democratic legitimacy of international tribunals and see how these relate to the overarching criteria applicable to all institutions set out earlier (Section 4.2.1). Thus, for the purposes of this book, the *democratic legitimacy* of an international tribunal is assessed on the extent to which it:

1. operates consistently with the treaty which establishes its mandate, to which states have consented – corresponding to the general criteria element of source based (input legitimacy) in the form of legal legitimacy;
2. operates based on procedures ensuring the inclusive and fair representation of both current and future generations with, in particular:
   - impartiality and independence in terms of ensuring procedural fairness in relation to court/tribunal processes; and
   - responsiveness to the *demos*, involving transparency, deliberation, and participation, including the involvement of affected individuals in the processes, with future generations involved through proxy-style procedural mechanisms.
   - appropriately considers the impacts on future generations, their needs, or interests, thus ensuring *future legitimacy*. This involves assessing legitimacy

in terms of both current and future generations, with an evaluation being made as to whether a decision made by an international tribunal today would be legitimate from the perspective of future generations. (This could include imagining a world decade from now that has been increasingly negatively impacted by climate change and looking back to assess whether a decision taken by a particular tribunal today was sufficient to meet the needs of intergenerational justice.) These elements correspond to the general criteria elements of procedural (input legitimacy) involving inclusive/fair representation, accountability and transparency, and deliberation (discursive quality).
3. demonstrates expertise both in the form of legal expertise but also drawing on scientific knowledge relating to climate change – corresponding to the general criteria element of source based (input legitimacy) in the form of expertise; and
4. demonstrates output legitimacy defined in terms of taking decisions that:
   - are effective both in terms of fulfilling the particular functions of the international tribunal as set out in its statute/mandate and contributing to strengthening international law rules relating to climate change and their implementation (see Section 4.2.3); and
   - enhance substantive justice, extended to include intergenerational justice – corresponding to the general criterion of substantive (output legitimacy), involving effectiveness and equity applicable to all international institutions.

The case studies in this book on the ICJ and UN Committee on the Rights of the Child (see Chapters 6 and 7) demonstrate how the normative framework argued for in Part I can play a positive role in promoting intergenerational justice without undermining the legitimacy of the particular tribunal. These case studies demonstrate that there are possibilities for maximising current and future legitimacy.

4.2.3 Effectiveness

Caney (2016: 137–40) points out that short-term policies are not harmful *per se*; on the other hand, short-termism can be extremely harmful in relation to problems like climate change, where it involves shifting the burden to the next generation. He observes that assessing the effectiveness of future-oriented institutions involves making a judgement about the extent to which such institutions overcome causes of wrongful short-termism; this is his key criterion for effectiveness (Caney 2016: 140). He also notes that the causes of harmful short-termism involve institutional and human psychological factors. On the institutional side in democracies, there is the harmful impact of short electoral cycles which induce politicians to focus on the short term, while ignorance of the future impact of policy-making is compounded by the dominance of lobbyists pushing short-term, sectoral interests. In addition, there are short-term media cycles, auditing processes, and performance indicators (Caney 2016: 137–46).

The climate crisis is an example of a creeping environmental problem where incremental impacts make it harder to galvanise support for decisive, responsive action. This is compounded by the lack of identifiable future victims – which are usually represented by abstract statistics. Psychological factors involving positive illusions, procrastination, and self-interest also play a role. Caney sensibly points out that institutional reform proposals need to seek to reduce the impact of underlying negative psychological factors, or at least prevent these factors from impacting the policy-making process. Where possible, he points to the possibility of harnessing these factors to promote long-term interests (Caney 2016: 145–6).

Increased input legitimacy can result in greater effectiveness, which can, in turn, contribute to legitimacy. Karlsson-Vinkhuyzen and Vihma (2009) define the concept of effectiveness as having two dimensions. First, effectiveness refers to the extent to which a norm, rule, or institution achieves a specified objective or goal in relation to a particular norm or institution. Second, 'problem-solving effectiveness' refers to how a particular norm can impact behaviour where this is required to solve a particular problem (Karlsson-Vinkhuyzen & Vihma 2009: 405).

We saw earlier that the output legitimacy criteria used here involve an effectiveness criterion defined in terms of how well the particular institution functions in meeting the goals set out in its mandate (as interpreted by the particular tribunal and its constituencies, in the case of international tribunals), as well as how well it contributes to the strengthening and implementation of international law rules relating to climate change. This has synergies with a goal or functions approach to assessing the effectiveness of international tribunals (Shany 2012, 2014). In the ICJ Advisory Opinion (Chapter 6) and UN Committee on the Rights of the Child (Chapter 7) case studies, this effectiveness assessment also factors in how well the tribunal addresses the questions put to it by the parties (in the first case) and by the UN General Assembly (in the second case).

The international law rules on climate change are mostly contained in the UN climate treaty regime and in customary international law. Turning to the former, we use the *Paris Agreement* (2015) as a yardstick or goal for measuring effectiveness in the climate change context. The objectives of the *Paris Agreement* are set out in Article 2(1) as follows:

> This Agreement, in enhancing the implementation of the Convention, including its objective, aims to strengthen the global response to the threat of climate change, in the context of sustainable development and efforts to eradicate poverty, including by:
>
> 1. holding the increase in the global average temperature to well below 2°C above pre-industrial levels and pursuing efforts to limit the temperature increase to 1.5°C

above pre-industrial levels, recognising that this would significantly reduce the risks and impacts of climate change;
2. increasing the ability to adapt to the adverse impacts of climate change and foster climate resilience and low greenhouse gas emissions development, in a manner that does not threaten food production; and
3. making finance flows consistent with a pathway towards low greenhouse gas emissions and climate-resilient development (*Paris Agreement* 2015).

In summary, the *Paris Agreement* objectives include the 1.5°C/2°C mitigation goal, adaptation, climate resilience, and sustainability, plus financial flows consistent with low emissions/climate-resilient development. The *Paris Agreement* objectives are to be read in conjunction with Article 3 of the UNFCCC (1992), which includes the principle of equity – including by implication intergenerational equity, albeit expressed vaguely.[12]

Importantly, for our purposes, effectiveness is understood as including not only just the formal international law rules but also the potential for these rules to flow on to influence behaviour, of both states but non-state actors. This approach is consistent with Steinar Andresen's concept of effectiveness, that is broken down into 'output', 'outcome', and 'impact' elements, which can sharpen analysis in this area (Andresen 2021: 990). The 'output' involves the formal rules of a regime. In contrast, the 'outcome' variable examines actual behaviour. 'Impact' refers to the problem-solving ability of a regime. Our case studies assess the outcome and impact of the mechanisms/institutions, while recognising the methodological challenges in drawing conclusions about causal links (Andresen 2021: 991).

Thus, in the case studies of proxy representation set out in Part III, we evaluate particular international mechanisms in terms of their *effectiveness*, defined in accordance with:

1) how well they promote justice (including intergenerational justice) and the values of inclusiveness, solidarity, and addressing vulnerability (a normative dimension);[13]
2) how well they contribute to strengthening international law rules relating to climate change and their implementation, thus contributing to the modification of the behaviour of states and non-state and substate actors in the direction of these rules; and

[12] Article 3(1) of the UNFCCC provides that: 'The Parties should protect the climate system for the benefit of present and future generations of humankind, on the basis of equity and in accordance with their common but differentiated responsibilities and respective capabilities. Accordingly, the developed country Parties should take the lead in combating climate change and the adverse effects thereof'.

[13] Underdahl (2004: 28) emphasises that, in assessing the effectiveness of a particular regime, 'effectiveness' should be kept separate from 'fairness'. However, as we have already mentioned, the UN climate regime includes fairness within its framework in its various references to equity. Moreover, in terms of our ICJ case study (Chapter 6), we have seen that furthering justice is an implicit function of the Court.

3) in relation to international tribunals: how well they perform the functions specified in their particular statute both generally and in relation to the specific mandate for the particular case in question; for example, the UN General Assembly mandate for the ICJ Advisory Opinion on Climate Change (see Chapter 6) or the scope of the complaint, in the case of the UN Committee on the Rights of the Child (see Chapter 7).

Element (b) is, in turn, defined in accordance with the *Paris Agreement* 1.5/2°C overarching mitigation target, adaptation for current and future generations, climate resilience, low greenhouse gas emission development, and financial flows consistent with low emissions/climate-resilient development. It also includes the extent to which the mechanism strengthens customary international law rules relating to state responsibility for climate-related harms, involving liability, restitution, and compensation.[14] While these rules are backward looking, they are nevertheless relevant in terms of future generations' interests. This is because strong rules in this area can provide benefits for current generations but also incentives for the mitigation of greenhouse gas emissions, with positive consequences for future generations, and can also help fund adaptation efforts, both now and in the future.

Furthermore, we argue (see Section 6.5) that the 'principle of harm prevention' involving state responsibility for anthropogenic climate change-related harms should be extended to include harm to future generations. There are tensions here because some states are likely to be opposed to such an extension because it would conflict with their view that they should not be held responsible for past greenhouse gas emissions (Section 6.5). This highlights the fact that two of our case studies (Chapter 6 on the ICJ and Chapter 7 on the UN Committee on the Rights of the Child) involve mandates that combine 'future-related' elements with other 'non-future related' elements; for example, relating to international legal obligations for ongoing climate change related harm, and/or responsibility in relation to harm which has already occurred. This entails the particular tribunal balancing the interests of current and future generations, which will not always push in the same direction; this complicates the evaluation of effectiveness. This complication is not an issue in relation to the case study on the proposed UN Special Envoy for Future Generations (Chapter 8) because this involves a 'future-oriented' mechanism with

[14] See Wewerinke-Singh (2019). The UNFCCC has established a 'loss and damage' mechanism, the *Warsaw International Mechanism for Loss and Damage associated with Climate Change Impacts* established at COP19 (November 2013) of the UNFCCC. Available at: https://unfccc.int/topics/adaptation-and-resilience/workstreams/loss-and-damage/warsaw-international-mechanism. Article 8 of the *Paris Agreement* (2015) highlights the importance of addressing loss and damage but with the crucial caveat that it does not provide a basis for any liability or compensation. See Boyd et al. (2021: 1366). A fund for responding to loss and damage was established in 2022 at COP27, with a governing instrument agreed in 2023 at COP28. However, many key operational issues remain unresolved at the time of writing; initial contributions were only a small fraction of what experts consider is required. See Pill & Hammersley (2024).

a mandate envisaged to have a particular focus on future generations' interests. The UN Special Envoy will most likely have a mandate to highlight such interests and feed this information to decision-makers who will have the task of balancing current and future generations' interests.

We acknowledge that the functions of the ICJ, as set out in its Statute, and the UN Committee on the Rights of the Child are not to protect the climate system. However, as we demonstrate in the case studies, each tribunal has been tasked with examining international law rules broadly (in the case of the ICJ) and more narrowly (in the case of the UN Committee on the Rights of the Child)[15] in terms of their interaction with climate change. Further, given our argument that international tribunals should interpret international law rules in a manner that furthers justice (including intergenerational justice), we assess the extent to which these international tribunals, consistent with their particular mandates, interpret international legal rules in a manner which contributes to making more effective the substance and implementation of international law rules relating to climate change in a manner which furthers justice.

At this point, it is important to note the strong connection between democratic legitimacy and effectiveness. International tribunals that are democratically legitimate are more likely to be effective. Legal systems rely on subjects of the law accepting a court's decisions to fulfil their functions (Bogdandy & Venzke 2014: 154). Democratic processes usually promote acceptance (Bogdandy & Venzke 2014: 155); for this reason, enhancing the democratic legitimacy of international tribunals tends to enhance their effectiveness.

This is consistent with scholars' observations that international institutions that are perceived to be legitimate are likely to be more effective (Franck 1990; Stokke & Vidas 1998). Thus, we consider effective decisions of an international tribunal to be decisions which fulfil the particular functions of the tribunal or court as set out in its statute/mandate, as interpreted by the international tribunal and key constituencies. Given the climate change context of this book, we include the additional criterion that effectiveness is measured in terms of the contribution made by the decision of the international tribunal to strengthening international law rules relating to climate change.

The effectiveness of the decisions of these international tribunals needs to be considered broadly, in that their decisions interact with national law in a variety of ways. Thus, an ICJ advisory opinion (which is non-binding) might, for example, delineate principles of international environmental law which are then taken up by a national court in a climate litigation case and/or made binding or operative

[15] The UN Committee on the Rights of the Child monitors implementation of the *Convention on the Rights of the Child* (CRC) by its state parties, as well as the Optional Protocols to the Convention on involvement of children in armed conflict, sale of children, child prostitution, and child pornography (OHCHR 1996–2024).

within a particular national legal order through incorporation in legislation. While under-researched to date, anecdotal evidence suggests that ICJ rulings do feed into professional discourses at both the national and global decision-making level (Giladi & Shany 2023: 117).

As we noted earlier, assessing the effectiveness of future-oriented institutions also encompasses the extent to which they address the causes of harmful short-termism. Thus, in evaluating whether institutional proposals to represent future generations contribute to achieving the *Paris Agreement* goals set out above, we take a broad approach to assessing how these particular goals will be furthered, including through addressing sources of far-ranging, harmful short-termism in relation to climate policy (including institutional and social psychology factors). One significant cause of harmful short-termism is lack of awareness of the long-term impacts of policies. Proxy-style institutions can play a helpful role in combating harmful short-termism by raising awareness of the long-term impacts of laws and policies. Global proxy-style institutions can also have a catalytic role in putting pressure on states to adopt appropriate institutions at the national level. These various dimensions are discussed in relation to each of the case studies.

As observed in Chapter 1, the ultimate effectiveness of proposed new institutions for future generations cannot be judged in advance. As Jonathan Boston cautions, designing institutions for future generations is 'as much an art than a science', given the complex causal factors involved in accounting for short-termism (Boston 2021: 96). Nevertheless, new proxy-type mechanisms for representing future generations have the potential to put pressure on existing institutions to better incorporate the interests of future generations in their decision-making processes. The increasingly catastrophic impacts of climate change – and mounting evidence that the status quo is clearly not working – suggest that experimental proxy-style institutional mechanisms to represent future generations should urgently be pursued, even where the likelihood of success is slim. Given the intergenerational dimension, it is vital to consider effectiveness in terms of both the probability and magnitude of success. Importantly, the strategy of exploring proxy-style mechanisms can be pursued in parallel with efforts to mainstream future generations' interests in policy- and law-making.

4.2.4 Accessibility and Political Sustainability

In this context, accessibility refers to whether and how likely it is that we can get from 'here' to 'there' (Caney 2016: 142).[16] In other words, is a proposal likely to

[16] Caney borrows the notion of 'accessibility' from Allen Buchanan but uses it in a slightly different way. See Buchanan (2004: 61).

be implemented in the real world? Political sustainability refers to whether a proposed new institution can be sustained into the future – obviously a precondition for its effectiveness (Caney 2016: 141). Here, factors include whether the institution is embedded in a constitution, for example, thus making it more difficult to dismantle. At the international level, this could include whether the institution is embedded in a global treaty – which can create some resistance to its being rapidly undone. The structure of finances is also crucial in this respect, in terms of whether an institution is vulnerable to budget cuts. This risk can be lessened, for example, if the budget necessary for a particular future-oriented institution is part of the core budget of an international organisation.

4.3 Final Observations

The argument we make in this chapter mirrors the argument made by John Dryzek in relation to the arrival of the Anthropocene, which has focused attention on human impacts on functioning global ecosystems, thus providing impetus for an urgent and compelling case for reform of global institutions. The Anthropocene entails the idea that human beings are a dominant source of change to the planet, including its climatic system (Keys et al. 2019). Linked to this is mounting empirical evidence that the Earth's climatic system is approaching tipping points with potentially catastrophic consequences (Michel, Swingedouw, & Ortegav 2022: 5176; see also Cho 2021). This has led Dryzek (2015) to call for a rethink of political institutions, which should be tailored for this new era on the basis of 'ecosystemic reflexivity' as a first overriding virtue.[17] 'Ecosystemic reflexivity' involves integrating improved ways of listening to ecological systems – entailing broader participation of both nature and future generations – into human institutions (Dryzek 2015: 12).

This idea of fundamentally rethinking institutions is reflected in the concept of future legitimacy introduced in this chapter, which involves expanding legitimacy to consider the existential threat climate change poses to international society, its legal system, and institutions.

Returning to the thought experiment which opened this chapter, when Justice N'Doure rereads the ICJ Report of the judgement in the climate change advisory opinion, she will inevitably read it through the contextual lens of 2060. By incorporating a thought experiment of this kind into our concept of legitimacy, we hope to demonstrate that it is possible to conceive of the idea of legitimacy in a way which more accurately reflects the climate change context. As we have already noted, there is a risk that this approach could favour intergenerational justice and the interests of future generations over the needs of contemporaries and

[17] Dryzek & Pickering (2018) use the term ecological reflexivity.

intragenerational justice. However, this risk can be minimised by using the legitimacy criterion to cover those areas of overlap between the two frames of legitimacy (present and future) to ensure that we maximise both intragenerational and intergenerational justice and maximise effectiveness, given the link between legitimacy and effectiveness. We saw that some empirical studies have demonstrated that assigning persons to act on behalf of future generations can potentially lead to creative policy- and law-making that involves policy solutions which meet the interests of both contemporaries and future generations. This provides grounds for hope that proxy-style institutions for future generations can have positive impacts in policy- and law-making.

The effectiveness framework we present here involves criteria linked to the objectives of the *Paris Agreement*, as well as the idea that future-oriented institutions need to address the causes of harmful short-termism. While there are some clear-cut ways in which proxy-style institutions can serve this role – for example, through highlighting the impacts of rules or policies on future generations – it is striking that, to date, there is scant literature on how these processes work in relation to the particularities of international law and related institutions. International law and institutions are the creature of states, but they also have their own particular dynamics. International law does not operate directly within states but tends to be mediated through national institutions and mechanisms.[18] This poses further levels of complexity in terms of analysing how a particular proxy-style institution representing future generations can address causes of harmful short-termism. This constraint in analysing the effectiveness of proxy-style institutions at the international level is considered in the case studies in Part III. It is certainly an area where more research is needed to ensure reform efforts have the best chance of success.

References

Andresen, S. (2021). Effectiveness. In Rajamani, L. & Peel, J., eds., *The Oxford Handbook of International Environmental Law*, 2nd ed., Oxford: Oxford University Press, 988–1002.

Ball, T. (2006). Democracy. In Dobson, A. & Eckersely, R., eds., *Political Theory and the Ecological Challenge*. Cambridge: Cambridge University Press, 131–47.

Beyleveld, D., Düwell, M. & Spahn A. (2015). Why and How Should We Represent Future Generations in Policymaking? *Jurisprudence*, 6(3), 549–66.

Bodansky, D. (1999). The Legitimacy of International Governance: A Coming Challenge for International Environmental Law? *American Journal of International Law*, 93(3), 596–624.

[18] The interface between international law and national law depends partly on whether a particular state is in the dualist tradition, which requires domestic legislation to translate international legal obligations into national law, or whether the state follows the monist tradition, where international legal obligations are automatically incorporated into domestic law. See Dupuy (2011).

Bodandy, A. von & Venzke, I. (2013). On the Functions of International Courts: An Appraisal in Light of their Burgeoning Public Authority. *Leiden Journal of International Law*, 26(1), 49–72.

Bogdandy, A. von & Venzke, I. (2014). *In Whose Name?* Oxford: Oxford University Press.

Boston, J. (2016). *Governing for the Future: Designing Democratic Institutions for a Better Tomorrow*, Bingley: Emerald.

Boston, J. (2021). Protecting Long-term Interests: The Role of Institutions as Commitment Devices. In Linehan, J. & Lawrence, P., eds., *Giving Future Generations a Voice: Normative Frameworks, Institutions and Practice*. Cheltenham: Edward Elgar, 86–107.

Boyd, E. et al. (2021) Loss and Damage from Climate Change: A New climate Justice Agenda. *One Earth*, 4(10), 1365–70.

Buchanan, A. (2004). *Justice, Legitimacy, and Self-Determination: Moral Foundations or International Law*, Oxford: Oxford University Press.

Caney, S. (2009). Climate Change, Human Rights and Moral Thresholds. In Humphreys, S. ed., *Human Rights and Climate Change*. Cambridge: Cambridge University Press; reprinted in Gardiner, S., et al., eds., *Climate Ethics, Essential Readings*, Oxford: Oxford University Press.

Caney, S. (2016). Political Institutions for the Future: A Fivefold Package. In González-Ricoy, I. & Gosseries, A., eds., *Institutions for Future Generations*. Oxford: Oxford University Press, 135–55.

Charter of the United Nations (adopted 29 June 1945; entered into force 24 October 1945), XV UNCIO 335, *amendments in* 557 UNTS 143, 638 UNTS 308, and 892 UNTS 119.

Cho, R. (2021). How Close Are We to Climate Tipping Points? Columbia Climate School, Climate, Earth, and Society. *State of the Planet* (11 November 2021). Available at: https://news.climate.columbia.edu/2021/11/11/how-close-are-we-to-climate-tipping-points/.

Convention on the Rights of the Child (CRC) (adopted 20 November 1989; entered into force 2 September 1990), 1577 UNTS 3.

Dingwerth, K. (2007). *The New Transnationalism: Transnational Governance and Its Democratic Legitimacy*, London: Palgrave Macmillan.

Dingwerth, K. (2014). Global Democracy and the Democratic Minimum: Why a Procedural Account Alone is Insufficient. *European Journal of International Relations*, 20(4), 1124–47.

Donger, E. (2022). Children and Youth in Strategic Climate Litigation: Advancing Rights through Legal Argument and Legal Mobilization. *Transnational Environmental Law*, 1(2), 263–89.

Dryzek, J. (2015). Institutions for the Anthropocene: Governance in a Changing Earth System. *British Journal of Political Science*, 46(4), 1–20.

Dryzek, J. & Niemeyer, S. (2008). Discursive Representation. *American Political Science Review*, 102(4), 481–93.

Dryzek, J. & Pickering, J. (2018). *Politics of the Anthropocene*, Oxford: Oxford University Press.

Dryzek, J. et al. (2019). *Deliberative Global Governance*. Cambridge Elements, Earth System Governance, Cambridge: Cambridge University Press.

Dupuy, P.-M. (2011). International Law and Domestic (Municipal) Law. In Peters, A. & Wolfrum, R., eds., *The Max Planck Encyclopaedia of International Law* (online ed.), Oxford: Oxford University Press.

European Union. (2008). *Treaty on European Union*, 13 December 2007, 2008/C 115/0.

Franck, T. M. (1990). *The Power of Legitimacy among Nations*, Oxford: Oxford University Press.

Giladi, R. & Shany, Y. (2023). Assessing the Effectiveness of the International Court of Justice. In Espósito, C. & Parlett, K. eds., *The Cambridge Companion to the International Court of Justice*. Cambridge: Cambridge University Press, 101–20.

Gonzalez-Ricoy, I. & Rey, F. (2019). Enfranchising the Future: Climate Justice and the Representation of Future Generations. *WIREs Climate Change*, 10, e598, 1–12. https://doi.org/10.1002/wcc.598.

Goodin, R. (1996). Enfranchising the Earth, and Its Alternatives. *Political Studies*, 44(5), 835–49.

Goodin, R. (2007). Enfranchising All Affected Interests, and Its Alternatives. *Philosophy and Public Affairs*, 35(1), 40–68.

Hale, T. N. (2008). Transparency, Accountability, and Global Governance. *Global Governance*, 14, 73–97.

Hara, K., Yoshioka, R., Kuroda, M., Kurimoto, K. & Saijo T. (2019). Reconciling Intergenerational Conflicts with Imaginary Future Generations: Evidence from a Participatory Deliberation Practice in a Municipality in Japan. *Sustainability Science*, 14(6), 1605–19. https://doi.org/10.1007/s11625-019-00684-x.

Hoffmann, J. & Dijk, N. van. (2023). How to Design better Institutions for the Future: An Evaluative Framework. In Dijk, N. van Playing the Long Game: Considering the Interests of Young People and Future Generations in Climate Law-making. Unpublished PhD Thesis, University of Tasmania, 67–85.

International Court of Justice. (2024). Obligations of States in Respect of Climate Change. Press Release 2024/81, 13 December 2024: Available at: www.icj-cij.org/case/187.

Karlsson-Vinkhuyzen, S. I. & Vihma, A. (2009). Comparing the Legitimacy and Effectiveness of Global Hard and Soft Law: An Analytical Framework. *Regulation & Governance*, 3(4), 400–20.

Keys, P. W., Galaz, V. & Dyer, M. et al. (2019). Anthropocene Risk. *Nature Sustainability*, 2, 667–73. https://doi.org/10.1038/s41893-019-0327-x.

KNMI [Royal Netherlands Meteorological Institute]. (2015). Ministry of Infrastructure and Environment. KNMI'14 Climate Scenarios for the Netherlands.

Lawrence, P. (2021). International Institutions for Future Generations and Democratic Legitimacy. In Cordonier Segger, M. C., Szabó, M. & Harrington, A. R., eds., *Intergenerational Justice in Sustainable Development Treaty Implementation: Advancing Future Generations Rights through National Institutions*. Cambridge: Cambridge University Press, 597–614.

Lawrence, P. & Köhler, L. (2018). Representation of Future Generations through International Climate Litigation: A Normative Framework. *German Yearbook of International Law*, 60, 639–66.

Merrills, J. (2011). *International Dispute Settlement*, Cambridge: Cambridge University Press.

Michel, S. L. L., Swingedouw, D. & Ortega, P. et al. (2022). Early Warning Signal for a Tipping Point Suggested by a Millennial Atlantic Multidecadal Variability Reconstruction. *Nature Communications*, 13. https://doi.org/10.1038/s41467-022-32704-3.

Niemeyer, S. & Jennstål, J. (2017). The Deliberative Democratic Inclusion of Future Generations. In González-Ricoy, I. & Gosseries, A., eds., *Institutions for Future Generations*. Oxford: Oxford University Press, 1–21.

Paris Agreement (adopted 12 December 2015; entered into force 4 November 2016), 3156 UNTS 79.

Pill, M. & Hammersley, G. (2024). A Climate Loss and Damage Fund that Works. *Lowy Institute Policy Briefs* (9 September 2024). Available at: www.lowyinstitute.org/publications/climate-loss-damage-fund-works.

Pitkin, H. (1967). *The Concept of Representation*, Los Angeles, CA: University of California Press.

Ratner, S. R. (2015). *The Thin Justice of International Law: A Moral Reckoning of the Law of Nations*, Oxford: Oxford University Press.

Saward, M. (2008). Representation and Democracy: Revisions and Possibilities. *Sociology Compass*, 2(3), 1000–13.

Shany, Y. (2012). Assessing the Effectiveness of International Courts, A Goal-based Approach. *American Journal of International Law*, 106(2), 225–70.

Shany, Y. (2014). *Assessing the Effectiveness of International Courts*, Oxford: Oxford University Press.

Statute of the International Court of Justice (adopted 29 June 1945; entered into force 24 October 1945), XV UNCIO 355.

Stokke, S. & Vidas, D., eds. (1998). *Governing the Antarctic: The Effectiveness and Legitimacy of the Antarctic Treaty System*, Cambridge: Cambridge University Press.

Stone, J. (1954). Fictional Elements in Treaty Interpretation – A Study in the International Judicial Process. *Sydney Law Review*, 1(3), 344–68.

Tams, C. & Tzanakopoulos, A. (2010). Barcelona Traction at 40: The ICJ as an Agent of Legal Development. *Leiden Journal of International Law*, 23(4), 781–800.

Underdal, A. (2004). Methodological Challenges in the Study of Regime Effectiveness. In Underdal, A. & Young, O. R., eds., *Regime Consequences: Methodological Challenges and Research Strategies*. Dordrecht, Boston, London: Kluwer, DOI: 10.1007/978-1-4020-2208-1_2, 27–48.

United Nations Framework Convention on Climate Change (UNFCCC) (adopted 9 May 1992; entered into force 21 March 1994), 1771 UNTS 107.

United Nations General Assembly (UNGA). (1948). *Universal Declaration of Human Rights*. Resolution 217A (III). UN Doc. A/810 at 71. Available at: www.ohchr.org/en/resources/educators/human-rights-education-training/universal-declaration-human-rights-1948.

UN General Assembly (2022). *The Human Right to a Clean, Healthy and Sustainable Environment*. Resolution adopted by the General Assembly, UN Doc. A/76/L.75.

UN General Assembly (UNGA). (2023). *Request for an Advisory Opinion of the International Court of Justice on the Obligations of States in Respect of Climate Change*. Resolution of the General Assembly. UN Doc. A/RES/77/276.

United Nations Office of the High Commissioner (OHCHR). (1996–2024). *Committee on the Rights of the Child* (OHCHR). Available at: www.ohchr.org/en/treaty-bodies/crc.

Uwasu, M., Kishita, Y., Hara, K. & Nomaguchi, Y. (2020). Citizen-Participatory Scenario Design Methodology with Future Design Approach: A Case Study of Visioning of a Low-Carbon Society in Suita City, Japan. *Sustainability*, 12(11), 4746. https://doi.org/10.3390/su12114746.

Vanderheiden, S. (2008). *Atmospheric Justice: A Political Theory of Climate Change* (online ed.), New York: Oxford Academic. https://doi.org/10.1093/acprof:oso/9780195334609.001.0001.

Wewerinke-Singh, M. (2019). *State Responsibility, Climate Change and Human Rights under International Law*, Oxford: Hart.

5

Lessons from Existing International Institutions to Represent Vulnerable Groups

5.1 Introduction

We have argued for a normative framework (Chapters 2 and 3) to justify the representation of future generations in the international legal order that is anchored to a threshold or subsistence concept of intergenerational justice and linked to the concept of solidarity. This implies that no one should fall below a minimum enjoyment of human rights necessary for a decent life and that special attention should be given to the vulnerable. We have noted that climate change exposes groups of people to vulnerability. Proxy representation of future generations is justified on the basis that it gives a voice to the vulnerable, with representation of the vulnerable being a key dimension in democratic theory. In this chapter, we enrich this argument with lessons from history. International mechanisms to protect particularly vulnerable groups have developed since the United Nations General Assembly (UNGA) adopted the UN Charter in 1945 and the Universal Declaration of Human Rights in 1947 (UN General Assembly 1948). This process has involved the adoption of a raft of human rights treaties which spell out the content of rights and corresponding obligations on governments with respect to particularly vulnerable groups, including the poor, minorities, those subject to racial discrimination, women, children, the elderly, Indigenous persons, and disabled persons (Spijkers 2011). This list is, of course, not comprehensive.[1]

The key point here is that the vulnerabilities of these groups – which relate to their interaction with broader society – have given rise to claims for separate and distinct international legal frameworks, as well as institutions to help enforce those frameworks. These claims form part of a historical process. The historical study of political and legal institutions that aim to protect vulnerable people or groups or improve their situation shows that the emergence and further development of

[1] This chapter is based on research undertaken by Peter Lawrence with support from Marcus Düwell's *Human Dignity as a Basis of Human Rights?* project, with funding by the Dutch Research Council.

these institutions is, itself, a political process. These institutions were established at certain points in time and have been constantly developed since. It is precisely from this historical perspective that the need arises to constantly refocus on who is particularly vulnerable and, if necessary, develop new institutions for them.

In Section 5.2 of this chapter, we present three case studies of international legal norms and institutions that relate to three vulnerable groups: children (Section 5.2.1), disabled persons (Section 5.2.2), and women (Section 5.2.3). We note at the outset that the treaty body mechanisms examined in our case studies were not established as representative institutions but, rather, as institutions that could support compliance with the obligations of a particular treaty. Nevertheless, these bodies, such as the UN Human Rights Committee, have played a representative function in the sense of giving the vulnerable group a voice through their concerns being taken up in the particular complaints mechanism, through participation as expert members of the Committee itself, and through the Committee's decisions. Thus, we argue, these mechanisms fall squarely within the concept of proxy compliance functions (as defined in Chapter 2), with the proxy mechanism aimed at securing compliance with the relevant international legal norm. In addition, however, we argue that these mechanisms de facto fall within the definition of representative proxy representation, where the mechanism also functions to represent the vulnerable group, in a more general sense, in articulating their interests. Proxy representation is involved to the extent that the group in question is incapable of having a voice. In terms of the three vulnerable groups considered here, this would only apply strictly to profoundly disabled persons who are unable to communicate. In this chapter, we examine the representational elements involved in each case study by exploring how the mechanisms work in relation to each group. This involves an examination of whether there are international rules which reflect their interests. Where there are such rules, we examine their scope and international institutions established to pressure and assist governments in the implementation of those rules, for example, the UN Human Rights Committee and Special Rapporteurs.

We then examine the normative underpinnings behind these international regimes with a view to analysing which normative arguments have gained political traction in the efforts to establish each of these treaties and related institutions (Section 5.3). A brief analysis of the effectiveness of these international legal rules and institutions, limited to the complaints mechanisms involved and not including the full range of decision-making mechanisms or secretariats of the relevant treaty bodies, follows. There are clearly methodological difficulties in making such assessments, given the difficulty of demonstrating clear links between law and behaviour, and the assessments made of effectiveness are very much preliminary. We also acknowledge that these case studies are only mapped out briefly, and that further case studies of other vulnerable groups are required. Moreover, some of the institutions we refer to have been established only very recently (for example, in relation to disabled persons), so only limited conclusions may be drawn in relation to these.

Our argument is based on political–legal coherence. If we accept that the vulnerability of groups (here, children, disabled persons, and women) justifies specialist treaties and institutions to protect their interests, then future generations – who are equally, if not more, vulnerable than these groups – also deserve specialist institutions to protect their interests. We apply this method to argue that the vulnerability of future generations entitles them to international institutions to protect their interests in the same way that the vulnerability of children, disabled persons, and women justifies institutions aimed at protecting their respective interests. Indeed, past extensions of human rights have often proceeded through this kind of analogous reasoning (Smith 2019). While there are important differences with respect to future generations – specifically, for example, the fact that they do not yet exist – we argue that these differences do not undermine the moral claim of future generations, which rests equally strongly on the notion of human dignity and human rights. According to our argument, the differences between existing vulnerable groups and future generations might affect the modalities (in terms of which institutions will be most fit for purpose) but do not undermine the rationale for establishing such institutions in the first place. Put simply, political–legal coherence requires support for institutions for future generations. Moreover, supporting international institutions for other vulnerable groups (such as children, disabled persons, and women) but not supporting institutions for future generations is incoherent.

We note that, in this argument, representation of future generations can necessarily only be by proxy (see Chapter 2). This is not the case with at least some of the vulnerable groups analysed in our case studies, who can exercise representation on an agency basis. The extent to which this will affect the rationale for representative-style institutions for future generations is examined.

5.2 Case Studies

Each of our case studies seeks to address five key questions. First, how is the vulnerable group defined? Second, what features of this particular group, and other factors, led to the creation of specialist representative institutions at the international level? Third, what is the nature of the form of representation (for example, individual complaints mechanism, international committee) assessed against the concepts of representation set out in Chapter 2? Fourth, what are the normative underpinnings behind the international mechanism and why did these normative discourses gain traction in the movement to establish each treaty and related mechanisms (for example, a particular notion of human rights linked to human dignity, inclusion, vulnerability, and so on)? Fifth, how effective is the institution?

5.2.1 Case Study 1: Children

The vulnerability of children began to find expression in the international legal order in the years just after the First World War, with the International Labour Organization (ILO) adopting conventions that involved the first steps in regulating child labour.[2] The Second World War inflicted acute suffering of children, which led to the 1959 UN Declaration of the Rights of the Child (UNGA 1959), the predecessor to the UN *Convention on the Rights of the Child* (CRC) (1989). In the decades after the Second World War, we see a progression from a sentimental view of the child as an object that deserves special protection to a view of the child as an imminent adult, possessing autonomy and rights deserving of protection, as reflected in the CRC. Anna Holzscheiter (2010: 2) eloquently expresses this transformation in perceptions of children from 'mute and helpless objects of charity and protection' to 'speaking and, accordingly, also "reasoning" social agents who should be actively involved in the shaping of their own destiny'. Crucially for the first time in international law, the CRC enshrined the right of the child to express her or his own views, to be listened to, and to participate in decisions. Thus, under Article 12(1) of the CRC, state parties 'shall assure to the child who is capable of forming his or her own views the right to express those views freely in all matters affecting the child in accordance with the age and maturity of the child'. In addition, Article 12(2) gives children the opportunity to be heard in judicial or administrative proceedings affecting them, either directly or through a representative.[3]

Given these provisions, it is ironic that children were given virtually no voice in the CRC negotiations.[4] Indeed, it is only since 1999 that the UN Committee on the Rights of the Child has taken steps to consult with children in its deliberative processes (Holzscheiter 2010). The Committee undertook an extensive consultative process involving children and youth organisations leading up to General Comment No. 26 on children's rights and climate change adopted by the Committee in 2023 (UN Committee on the Rights of the Child 2023).

[2] See, for example, *International Labour Organization Convention (No. 5) Minimum Age (Industry) Convention* (ILO) (1919). See discussion of these conventions in Buck (2011: 178).

[3] For discussion of childhood vulnerability, see Andresen (2014: 699–713), Bagattini (2014: 163–86), Feinberg (1980: 124–53), and Graf & Schweiger (2017).

[4] Introduction by Adam Lopatka, Chairman/Rapporteur of the Working Group on a draft convention on the rights of the child, Office of the United Nations High Commissioner for Human Rights (2007: XI). In the negotiation process, there was no formal consultation with children; delegates of a few states referred to opinions held by children and youth organisations in the countries they represented.

The negotiation of the CRC and its widespread ratification (with the notable exception of the United States) can be interpreted as the gradual globalisation of a Western concept of childhood. The concept of childhood as a separate phase of life is recent, emerging in nineteenth-century practices of the European bourgeoisie, and with roots in philosophical, economic, and medical advances dating from the sixteenth century (Holzscheiter 2010: 99). Concepts of unrestricted paternalism – going back to Roman times – were gradually replaced during the Enlightenment period by a concept of childhood as a protected sphere and the perception that children deserve special assistance because of their vulnerability. Childhood thus evolved into a liberal concept comprising love, care, education, and play, with the state intervening to ensure the child's protection (Fass 2011: 19). Crucial in the discourse underpinning the push for the CRC was the articulation of children's 'needs and rights in universal terms', meaning that not just privileged children, but *all* children in a particular nation, should be 'brought up to a basic level' and, internationally, that all children on a global level were equally entitled to basic rights (Fass 2011: 19).

The widespread suffering of children in the Second World War, both as victims of warfare and famine, forms a crucial part of the backdrop of the negotiation of the CRC. Holzscheiter, in her detailed study of the dominant discourses in the negotiation of the CRC, observes that 'the image of the child as an especially vulnerable (if not the most vulnerable) and innocent part of humanity was prevalent all throughout the drafting process' (Holzscheiter 2010: 161). Children were characterised as being vulnerable to a range of immoral harms inflicted upon them by adults, as is evident in this particularly emotive statement from one of the CRC negotiators. 'They were the children of famine, malnutrition and illiteracy, the children of millions of refugees, victims of armed conflict and concentration-camp inmates who were counting on international solidarity to help them out of their desperate situation.' (Konate (Senegal) ECOSOC, 1985: para 113 (Holzscheiter 2010: 161).

In this statement, we can see a strong link between solidarity and vulnerability with clear parallels to the normative framing of this book. There are strong parallels between warfare exposing the vulnerability of children and climate change similarly exposing the vulnerability of children (Schweiger & Graf 2017).

Interestingly, during the CRC negotiations, promoting children's rights was framed not in terms of individual human rights but, rather, in terms of the moral rights of younger generations *against* adult humanity as a whole, thus reflecting then-dominant welfarist and paternalistic discourses (Holzscheiter 2010: 163).

An important strand of the discourse in the development of the CRC was the notion that progress, and development of the society, was inexorably linked to progressive education and progressive childhood (Holzscheiter 2010: 21). So, the 'development' strand here included both the development of the individual and ensuring productive young citizens – combined with nationalism – as the key to a nation's future (Holzscheiter 2010: 19, 21). This was expressed through the idea of the 'imminent child'; in other words, the idea of the child as a future adult, whose development should be advanced to ensure the advancement of humanity and civilisation, and who would possess a range of qualities (including being 'morally and socially responsible') that should be encouraged (Holzscheiter 2010: 166).

Tensions emerged between individualistic, Western concepts of children's rights, and those of countries in Asia and Africa (that asserted that protection of children should be conditional on freedom of religion and cultural practices), which found expression in reservations being made to the CRC. Ratification of the CRC has also been accompanied by a discourse of perceiving human rights obligations in the CRC as consistent with Islam (George 2019: 163–82).

In summary, then, the core normative concepts that underpin the CRC regime include a universal idea of all children being entitled to basic rights, with children deserving of their own treaty and committee by reason of their vulnerabilities. In addition, the CRC encapsulates an idea of autonomy – albeit on a sliding scale – as children grow in maturity. It also incorporates the idea of the state intervening to ensure protection of the child; for example, against abusive parents (see Article 19; Gutwald & Reder 2023). In addition, protection of children is seen as interdependent with protection and flourishing of the family. Indeed, the whole treaty rests on the bedrock that all children are equally entitled to enjoy human dignity. Further, the flourishing of societies as whole requires the protection of children's rights: children are conceived of as citizens of the future.

In 2011, an *Optional Protocol to the CRC on a Communication Procedure*[5] was adopted, which entered into force in 2014 (Optional Protocol to the CRC 2011). This instrument allows for individual complaints to be brought to the UN Committee on the Rights of the Child, where parties to the CRC fail to meet their obligations. It is clear from the preamble of this protocol that the instrument aims to 'enhance the implementation of the Convention' (Optional Protocol to the CRC 2011: preambular para 10) and complement national mechanisms which 'enable a child whose rights have been violated to have access to effective remedies' (Optional Protocol to the CRC 2011: preambular paras 8, 10). The views of the Committee are expressed in the form of recommendations and are not strictly binding on the state involved. In practice, however, the Committee has taken on a quasi-judicial role, with its published case law and General Comments being highly influential in terms of how state parties to the CRC interpret and implement the treaty (Tomuschat 2014: 267, 269). Importantly, Article 5 of the Optional Protocol

[5] As of 23 December 2024, this optional protocol had 54 parties (United Nations Treaty Collection 2024).

allows for communications to be brought 'by or on behalf of an individual or group of individuals, within the jurisdiction of a State party, claiming to be victims of a violation by that State party of any of the rights set forth … in the Convention' or optional protocol relating to the sale of children, optional protocol on child prostitution and child pornography or optional protocol on children in armed conflict. Article 5(2) further provides that 'where a communication is submitted on behalf of an individual or group of individuals, this shall be with their consent unless the author can justify acting on their behalf without such consent'. These provisions, read together, seem to open the possibility of proxy-style representation in which the person bringing the claim on behalf of children does not have their consent but makes reasonable assumptions about their interests.

The case of *Sacchi et al.* (further analysed in Chapter 7; see also Dijk 2021a), which involved a claim brought by a number of young people, illustrates how these provisions operate in the climate context. In the petition in that case, the petitioners pointed to actual harm they were suffering because of climate change impacting their rights to health, culture, and other rights under the CRC. Some of the language in the petition can be construed as framing the claim on behalf of *all* children impacted by climate change now and in the future, thus implying that, in this respect, the petitioners were acting as proxy representatives for future children, in addition to acting on their own behalf.

5.2.2 Case Study 2: Disabled Persons

The movement to develop a discrete convention setting out the rights of disabled persons was linked to an understanding that disabled persons included some of the most vulnerable members of society and that, globally, most of these persons lived in developing countries (Kayess & French 2008).[6] In 2001, Mexico spear-headed a push to negotiate a disability human rights convention; the issues were framed in terms of social development, with an argument that the World Health Organization's Millennium Development Goals (MDGs) ignored this particular group. Support from developing countries was crucial in this campaign (Kayess & French 2008: 17). The UN *Convention on the Rights of Persons with Disabilities* (CRPD) (2006)[7] was the result of a long process, beginning with the United Nations' 1981 World Programme of Action concerning Disabled Persons and involving various Reports of Special Rapporteurs on Disability pursuant to

[6] Kayess & French (2008) cite a 2006 World Health Organization (WHO) report, which states that 80 per cent of the world's 650 million disabled persons were living in developing countries; most were poor and had limited access to health services.

[7] The CRPD entered into force in 2008; as at 23 December 2024 it had a total of 191 parties (United Nations Treaty Collection 2024).

Commission on Human Rights resolutions in 1998, 2000, and 2002 (Office of the Commissioner for Human Rights (OHCHR) 2010: 12).[8]

The development of the CRPD coincided with an approach that conceptualised the needs of disabled persons in a human-rights (rather than a medical or welfare) framework. The official view is that the Convention did not create human rights in relation to disabled persons; rather, it confirmed that disabled persons enjoyed existing, well-established human rights on equal terms (OHCHR 2010: 20). However, this view does not stand up to scrutiny and the Convention did, in fact, create several new rights (OHCHR 2010: 32).

The key normative underpinnings of the CRPD and its individual complaints procedure involve the concepts of human dignity, individual autonomy, effective participation and inclusion, equality of opportunity, gender equality, respect for difference, and accessibility, as set out in Article 3 of the Convention – which one observer described as the Convention's 'moral compass' (Kayess & French 2008: 27). The notion of the inherent human dignity of all persons is reflected in Article 1 of the Convention, which states that its purpose is to 'promote, protect and ensure the full and equal enjoyment of all human rights and fundamental freedoms by all persons with disabilities, and to promote respect for their *inherent dignity*' (emphasis added).

Interestingly, the CRPD does not contain a definition of disability. Rather, it acknowledges that disability is an evolving concept which, in the words of the Preamble, 'results from interaction between persons with impairments and attitudinal and environmental barriers that hinders their full and effective participation in society on an equal basis with others' (CRPD 2006: preambular para 5). Article 1 of the Convention refers to persons with disabilities as 'include[ing] those who have long-term physical, mental, intellectual, or sensory impairments which in interaction with various barriers may hinder their full and effective participation in society on an equal basis with others'. Thus, the Convention embodies a social rather than functional notion of disability equated with 'functional limitations'.[9] An advantage of this approach is that it places responsibility on the state and society to remove barriers and ensure the enjoyment of universal human rights, rather than placing responsibility on the individual. In addition, under this approach, recognition of difference becomes the 'gateway' to accessing human civil rights rather than segregation and stigmatisation (Morris 2001: 1).

[8] Important in this process were a number of UN General Assembly resolutions, including the 1975 Declaration on the Rights of Disabled Persons (UNGA 1975), the 1991 Principles for the Protection of Persons with Mental Illness (UNGA 1991), and the 1993 United Nations Standard Rules on the Equalisation of Opportunities for Persons with Disabilities (Standard Rules) (UNGA 1993), which made the case for a specific instrument on disabilities and drew connections with other thematic treaties on other vulnerable groups (Quinn & Degener 2002: 297).

[9] There are exceptions, however (Kayess & French 2008: 21).

Traditional notions of vulnerability focused on the individual's impairment, often linked to the individual's responsibility to manage an impairment and accept blame for its consequences. In contrast, the social/human rights model of disability reflected in the CRPD (as something that arises from the interaction of impairment with social barriers) goes hand in hand with the notion that it is the responsibility of the state and society to remove barriers and ensure universal rights enjoyment.[10] While disability rights scholars and activists have been reluctant to invoke 'vulnerability' – lest it reinforce disempowerment and denial of the rights of people with disabilities (Clough 2017: 469) – the argument that a specific treaty focusing on disabled persons' particular needs and the corresponding obligations of states has gained traction (Morris 2001). A strategic dimension in this debate is the argument that the efforts of non-governmental organisations (NGOs) advocating for the rights of disabled persons could be channelled into one treaty regime, rather than being diluted across the gamut of UN human rights treaty mechanisms (Quinn & Gerard 2002: 297).

The development of the CRPD was characterised by what is regarded as the most intense participation in history by civil society groups (overwhelmingly of persons with disability and disabled persons' organisations) in the development of any human rights treaty. The rejection of paternalism (for example, in the form of coercive treatment) by disabled persons was reflected by their demands (individually or through representative organisations) to participate in the negotiation process (de Beco 2021), and also by substantive norms in a global instrument that reflected rights to participation. These demands were captured well in the credo 'nothing about us without us' which can be considered the 'virtually universal claim of the disability rights movement internationally' (Kayess & French 2008: 12). Interestingly, this credo might also be considered a variant of the All Affected Principle (AAP) (see Chapter 2), which constitutes a golden thread running through theories of democracy.

The CRPD represents the interests of disabled persons by establishing a strong and comprehensive normative framework in terms of specific rights of disabled persons and corresponding obligations on governments to ensure that these rights are respected. The obligations are contained in a treaty that is binding under international law, thus moving beyond the earlier non-binding (soft law) instruments. In addition to this normative framework, which provide the basis for parties to the Convention to implement their own national legislation and policies related to disabled persons, an individual complaints mechanism was established by the Optional Protocol in 2006 and entered into force in 2008.[11] The individual

[10] Thank you to Yvette Maker for pointing this out.

[11] This Optional Protocol, as of 23 December 2024, had 107 parties (United Nations Treaty Collection 2024).

complaints mechanism allows an individual disabled person in a state party to the CRPD to bring a claim against their government to the Committee on the Rights of Persons with Disabilities in Geneva for adjudication (OHCHR) (2024). Prior to bringing such a claim, the claimant must exhaust possible remedies in the particular state. Decisions of the Human Rights Committee in response to such claims are not legally binding, but are, nevertheless, considered highly persuasive: we can point to examples where member states have changed their legislation policies in response to such decisions; for example, *Noble v Australia* (CRPD 2016).[12]

It is important to note that this committee was not established with the aim of creating a representative institution for disabled persons in the sense of providing a forum for disabled persons to feed into policy- or law-making decisions. Rather, the overarching focus of the committee is implementation and compliance: with a mandate to hear individual complaints in terms of violations of the CRDP and to consider national reports on individual states' progress in implementing the Convention. Nevertheless, to the extent that the individual complaints mechanism involves articulating disabled persons' interests, it does have a broader representative proxy compliance function (as defined in Chapter 2). This broader representative function is also underscored by the composition of the Committee itself. Article 34(4) invites states to consider the participation of experts with disabilities; to date, almost all members of the committee have been people with disability. In addition, Article 33 directs states to involve people with disability and their representative organisations 'fully in the monitoring process'.[13]

5.2.3 Case Study 3: Women

In feminist research, and feminist philosophy, scholars have been thinking for four decades about whether, and to what extent, vulnerability is an appropriate category to address gender inequalities – ethically, as well as politically. Authors such as Judith Butler stand paradigmatically for this. In doing so, these researchers emphasise that the general-human, and at the same time, very concrete (bodily) vulnerability of all human beings is further amplified for women by social, political, or economic mechanisms: they are made into particularly vulnerable groups. This manifests itself in systematic discrimination against women in the

[12] Note that in this case, legislative reform in Australia has only addressed some of the concerns raised by the committee. See *Noble v. Australia* (CRPD 2016); see also Australian Government (2017).

[13] The indicators to guide national implementation of monitoring of the CRDP produced by the Office of the United Nations High Commissioner for Human Rights include establishing mechanisms for the involvement of persons with disabilities and their representative organisations in monitoring implementation of the Convention, including financial support for strengthening such organisations (OHCHR 2020: 2).

workplace,[14] political life, and in the home in all countries around the world. While there have been some improvements in recent decades, women remain significantly under-represented in national parliaments.[15] Moreover, sexual violence against women remains an intractable problem across the world,[16] and occurs at alarming levels, even in wealthy countries such as the United States (Nussbaum 2015: 591) and Australia.[17] Against this backdrop, many feminist researchers have considered the extent to which group identity (being a woman) gives rise to a particular claim to representation to meet the inclusive and egalitarian ideal of democracy. Iris Marion Young (2000) and Anne Phillips (1993) have made seminal arguments in this regard, which might also be important for thinking about the international representation of women in legal institutions.

The international women's movement emerged after the Second World War but had its origins in the late nineteenth century (Rupp 1998). In the post-war era, an international legal structure developed aimed at ending discrimination against women and furthering their empowerment. The *International Covenant on Civil and Political Rights* (ICCPR) (1966) and *International Covenant on Economic, Social and Cultural Rights* (ICESCR) (1966) prohibit discrimination against women (ICCPR 1966: art. 26; ICESCR 1966: art. 2 (3)). These obligations were further elaborated in the 1967 UN Declaration against Discrimination against Women, which proclaims that 'discrimination against women is an offence against human dignity' (UNGA 1967: art. 1).

In 1979, the *Convention on the Elimination of All Forms of Discrimination against Women* (CEDAW) (1979) was adopted.[18] This Convention elaborates specific and binding obligations on states to eliminate discrimination against women in political, social, economic, and cultural fields, covering both civil and political rights (such as the right to vote, participate in public life, and retain/change their

[14] While there has been some improvement in women's participation in the workforce, on average around the world, women remain much less likely to participate in the labour market than men. The current global labour force participation rate for women is just under 47 per cent compared with 72 per cent for men, a difference of 25 percentage points, with some regions facing a gap of more than 50 percentage points (ILO 2021).

[15] As of 1 October 2022, the global average for participation of women in national parliaments was only 26.3 per cent (IPU 2022).

[16] The World Health Organization estimates that globally about 30 per cent of women worldwide have been subjected to either physical and/or sexual partner violence or non-partner sexual violence in their lifetime (WHO 2021a, 2021b).

[17] According to the Australian Bureau of Statistics, '2.2 million women (23%) and 718,000 men (8.0%) aged 18 years and over have experienced sexual violence in their lifetime, including childhood sexual abuse and/or sexual assault since the age of 15' (ABS 2021).

[18] CEDAW requires state parties to submit reports and establishes a compliance monitoring system, including a Committee, to monitor these reports. State parties agree to enact legislation implementing their obligations under CEDAW. This reporting system 'lacks teeth': no sanctions can be imposed and Committee's findings only have the status of recommendations. In 1999, an Optional Protocol to CEDAW was concluded which allows individual complaints to be made from countries party to CEDAW (Optional Protocol to CEDAW 1999). As of 23 December 2024, there were 115 parties to the Optional Protocol and 189 State parties to CEDAW (United Nations Treaty Collection 2024).

nationality, as well as the right to equality before the law, and freedom of movement) and economic, social, and cultural rights (such as the right to education, work, health, and financial credit).

CEDAW came out of the recommendation of the first UN Conference on Women convened in Mexico City in 1975 (UN 1976). At this conference, many countries argued that overcoming discrimination against women was required both by the normative demands of equal enjoyment of human dignity,[19] as well as the demands of development. Many countries at this conference argued that overcoming discrimination against women was inexorably linked to advancing social development more generally, both within national societies and internationally. Thus, the report of the conference stated that: 'national and international development was not possible without the full participation of women' (UN 1976: para 75). To this end, many countries argued that inequality between countries of the Global North and South needed to be addressed by constructing a New Economic Order as a precondition for advancing the condition of women (UN 1976: paras 66–94). Importantly, CEDAW embodies the concept of substantive – rather than merely formal – equality. In other words, striving for equality of outcomes is the goal and this can require affirmative action-type programmes, such as quotas (CEDAW 2004: para 7ff).

Framing issues of women's rights as a development issue is likely to have had a substantive role in garnering support for CEDAW, with a substantial number of developing countries regarding full participation of women in the workplace as a precondition for economic development – albeit where 'development' is defined by men. Other factors were also clearly involved, including the internationalisation of the feminist movement through globalisation (Ishay 2004: 297).[20]

Importantly, some scholars have argued that creating a specialist international institutional framework devoted to women's human rights carries with it the risk of creating human rights 'ghettos' in the sense of further marginalisation, particularly if the institutional bodies concerned have lesser resources than other human rights bodies dealing, for example, with racial discrimination, which seems to be the case (Charlesworth 1994: 59, 66). This contains an important lesson in terms of institutions for future generations: institutions must be properly resourced to avoid being token.

A particular international mechanism related to violence against women – Special Rapporteurs – seems to have had some modest success in this difficult area. From 1993 onwards, the UN appointed a succession of Special Rapporteurs on Violence against Women (OHCHR 2022). Their function has been to undertake

[19] The 'equality' concept has been criticised, however, as entailing a male-dominated construct, given the assumption that women 'conform to a male model' (Charlesworth 1994: 64).

[20] For an account of the history of CEDAW, see Schoepp-Schilling (2007).

country visits 'to examine the situation of women in specific contexts and make recommendations for eliminating violence as well as its root causes; to receive individual complaints and transmit them to the governments concerned: and prepare thematic reports relevant to the mandate' (Ertürk & Purkayastha 2012: 145). Yakin Ertürk and Bandana Purkayastha sum up well the value of the Special Rapporteurs' work in implementing a mandate which 'communicates the voices of the most vulnerable women and acts as a channel to access justice and accountability when national systems of justice are not well developed or when they fail to respond' (Ertürk & Purkayastha 2012: 145). Yet, the immensity of the problem to be addressed remains, and serious problems of implementation continue (Ertürk & Purkayastha 2012: 145).

The individual complaints mechanism of CEDAW is based on the general principle that only individual women whose rights have been violated under CEDAW are permitted to bring communications. Nevertheless, as with the provision referred to above in relation to the CRC, an important exception is that communications can also be 'submitted on behalf of individuals or groups of individuals, with their consent unless the author can justify acting on their behalf without such consent' (CEDAW 1979: art. 2). Christian Tomuschat (2014: 252) argues that the reference to 'groups of persons' represents a softening of the victim requirement – the requirement that a person bringing a claim must be a victim of the violation. This view is supported with reference to cases being brought where it was sufficient for groups of women to point to a 'legislative act or a general administrative measure' which impacted this group with 'some kind of general discrimination'. Moreover, in proceedings against Austria, the CEDAW Committee overseeing the complaints mechanism concluded that the language of Article 2 was sufficiently broad to grant standing to a human rights organisation. In this case, a women's rights organisation had taken up as guardians of those rights in cases where the victims themselves could not raise their voices: women who were killed by their husbands in a context where the authorities failed to take action in the face of evidence of serious threats to the victims (Tomuschat 2014: 252).[21] This case should be seen in the broader context of barriers faced by women victims of sexual assault in obtaining justice, who are often re-traumatised should they proceed to use the justice system (Clark 2010: 28).

The Austrian case certainly represents a type of proxy compliance representation (as defined in Chapter 3), with the human rights organisation asserting rights in relation to the victim women who were no longer alive at the time of the complaint. This is unproblematic in the sense that the failure of the state to protect

[21] See also *Vienna Intervention Centre against Domestic Violence and Association for Women's Access to Justice*, cases 5/2005 and 6/2005, 6 August 2007, cited in Tomuschat (2014: 252).

the rights of the women in question was well grounded. In addition, the human rights organisation in protecting the women was presumed to be legitimate, even though standing was not explicitly discussed in the case. The aim of the claim was to ensure that Austria complied with its obligation under CEDAW, and, in this sense, fits within the scope of compliance-style proxy representation (set out in Chapter 2). Moreover, it could also be argued that, to the extent the case involved the articulation of women's interests at a more general level, it also consists more broadly of an example of representative proxy representation as defined in Chapter 2.

Measuring the effectiveness of CEDAW, its Optional Protocol, and the other UN mechanisms relating to the protection of women's rights is extremely difficult. As Martha Nussbaum (2015: 594–6, 616) points out, there are inherent methodological difficulties in measuring the impact of law in deterring violent behaviour against women. Nevertheless, the international human rights regime for women gives women who are widely dispersed in many countries leverage in pressuring governments to comply with their obligations and address ingrained cultural practices of discrimination (Dairiam 2015).

In summary, then, we can see that detailed obligations relating to woman are spelt out in the global human rights treaties with various options for enforcement in the form of Special Rapporteurs and an individual complaints mechanism. These mechanisms do not involve representation of women, as such, but nevertheless provide women with a voice to pressure national institutions to protect women's rights. The normative underpinnings behind the UN international legal regime relating to protecting women's rights thus rest on a human rights approach linked to equal enjoyment of human dignity and strongly linked to concepts of social development, both within societies and internationally. Furthermore, CEDAW enshrines substantive rather than merely formal equality. A concept of procedural justice emphasises the importance of striving for equality for women in all levels of the political process.

The institutions described earlier are constantly in need of re-evaluation and improvement in terms of whether they sufficiently address the vulnerability of the groups they aim to serve. Politically, this potential for self-critical further development must be recruited from within the institutions themselves. Just as important, however, is the political pressure of social movements from outside. Often, it is only through such external pressure that institutions are made aware that they are not directing sufficient attention to certain forms of vulnerability. The diverse climate protests – particularly the youth climate protests – are an important example of this: by focusing attention on the next generation (broadly conceived), they indirectly provide necessary momentum for developing new institutions to represent future generations.

5.3 Analysis and Comparison with Institutions Designed to Represent Future Generations

5.3.1 Normative Justifications

In this section, we draw lessons from the case studies about the normative justifications successfully used to ground the international institutions. This will be instructive in terms of assessing which normative arguments used to justify institutions to protect future generations are likely to gain political traction. As we have seen, some of the normative justifications involve notions of reciprocity which, by definition, cannot apply in relation to future generations. Nevertheless, it is striking how many of the normative underpinnings of existing global representative institutions in relation to vulnerable groups rely on normative arguments that are equally appropriate in relation to institutions to represent future generations – and that mesh well with the arguments presented in Chapter 3. Political–legal coherence suggests that these normative arguments or considerations point in the direction of establishing some type of international institution (or institutions) to represent future generations.

In comparing the UN treaty regimes relating to children, persons with a disability, and women in terms of their normative underpinning, with the normative underpinnings for representative institutions for future generations, we can see the following points of similarity and difference.

There is no universally accepted definition of future generations.[22] If, however, future generations are defined as all persons born in the future, then there is at least clarity in terms of the scope of this definition, putting aside the contentious issue of whether a child in utero constitutes a person. As discussed earlier, climate change and ecological disaster involve a spectrum in terms of the vulnerability of future generations, with future people living in poverty likely to be the most seriously affected. Moreover, the inability of future generations to have a say in decisions affecting them involves a particular vulnerability. Underlying the *Convention on the Rights of the Child* was the idea that children individually, and as a group, are exposed to vulnerabilities, particularly those related to violence, war, and famine. During the CRC negotiations, there was some disagreement among states about precisely when childhood begins and ends, while some countries (for example, in the Africa group) emphasised the responsibility of children, and not just their rights. Nevertheless, the negotiations demonstrated the support of countries for the idea that the particular vulnerabilities of children required their rights to be spelt out in an international instrument, as well as a compliance mechanism involving a specialist committee – although, to date, only about one-quarter of the

[22] See the discussion in Tremmel (2009: 19–20).

international community has signed on to the individual complaints mechanism (Optional Protocol to the CRC 2011).[23]

The risk of catastrophic climate change potentially impacts all future generations, while within the category 'future generations', there is a range of vulnerabilities (Dijk 2021b). As we have seen, the Committee on the Rights of the Child has recognised the vulnerability of children in relation to climate change. In addition, we have seen that, during the negotiations of the *Convention on the Rights of Persons with Disabilities* (CPDR 2006), agreement on a definition of 'disabilities' proved elusive – and remains highly contentious. Nevertheless, parties agreed that there is a spectrum of levels of vulnerability linked to disabilities, in which interaction between disabilities and a range of other factors (including socio-economic level, gender, and age, for example) plays an important role. Specific vulnerabilities lead to specific modes of protection.

The social notion of disability involves the idea of impairment of human rights arising through the interaction between a disabled person and society. Does such an interactional concept have any parallel in terms of institutions to represent future generations? While there is only a one-way interaction between current and future generations (with current inaction on climate change negatively impacting future generations, for example), there is nevertheless a strong parallel here in the sense that the vulnerability of future generations arises due to the failure to factor their human rights (whether actual or contingent) into current political institutions and rule-making.

Another common thread running through these case studies is the human dignity/human rights framing of the issues. As we have seen, both the CRC and the *Convention on the Elimination of All Forms of Discrimination against Women* (CEDAW) were established on a human rights normative framework that rests on human dignity; as argued earlier, such a normative framework, combined with solidarity and vulnerability, also provides a convincing normative basis for institutions designed to represent the interests of future generations. The Preamble to the CRDP (2006: para a) reaffirms the 'inherent dignity' of 'all members of the human family', while Article 1 promotes respect for the 'inherent' dignity of 'all persons with disabilities'.

The Optional Protocol extends the CRDP's elucidation of how human rights obligations apply to persons with disabilities by facilitating the development of jurisprudence that clarifies, with greater precision, exactly how these human rights apply. There is an interesting analogy here with representation of future persons, which, again, can be considered to occur through an extension of existing human

[23] As of 23 December 2024, there were 52 parties to the Optional Protocol to the CRC (United Nations Treaty Series 2024).

rights, but this time extended to apply to a particular category of persons; namely, those born in the future. While contemporary institutions in their decision-making in relation to future generations should not be required to treat future and currently living people on an equal footing, there is an imperative, as explained earlier, to treat the generic rights of future generations as a constraint on current policymakers.

In the disability treaty regime, non-discrimination is also crucial: Articles 4 and 5 of the CRPD prohibit discrimination against persons based on their disability. While there is no temporal element involved here, there is nevertheless an analogy to be drawn, in that, in both cases, the underlying normative position is that discrimination based on the characteristic (time of being born, cf. disability) is prohibited.

The Convention recognises that formal equality is insufficient: it is often not equal treatment that is required but accommodation of difference; in other words, 'different' treatment. This is captured in the notion of 'substantive equality' which includes the notion of modifying a particular norm to consider human diversity (Kayess & French 2008: 8; CRPD 2018: para 10, page 3). In the disability context, this can involve the requirement to make reasonable accommodation to consider disability-related needs; for example, flexible work hours to accommodate mobility restrictions.[24]

When we compare this type of process with institutions to represent future generations, two points become apparent. First, institutions to represent future generations cannot operate in an interactive manner with individual members of future generations. Nevertheless, as explained in Chapter 3, the interests of future generations should operate as a constraint on contemporary decision-making. This does not require future and contemporary people to be treated on an equal footing but does require that decisions made now do not have a negative impact on future generations' human rights that are necessary for a decent life. A proxy representative of future generations should be able to challenge an existing norm, if the norm clearly violates the minimal requirements for intergenerational justice set out in Chapter 3. And, as we have seen, giving a voice to proxy representatives in this manner meshes with the democratic ideal embodied in the AAP.

Representation of future generations is often rejected on the basis that the future is characterised by a great deal of uncertainty. We do not know the exact political, economic, or cultural contexts in which future people will live, nor can we

[24] This corresponds to the obligation in Article 27 (1)I of the CRPD. As Kayees & French (2008: 9) observe, the obligation here 'operates on the bilateral basis between a person to be accommodated and the person or institution required to make the accommodation'. They cite the example of an Australian case in which a blind person sought to have the 2000 Olympics website adjusted so that it would be accessible for blind persons. This challenge resulted in a modification of the norm, with many other public websites in both the government and private sectors subsequently being modified.

accurately predict their technical capabilities (for climate mitigation) or their interests in a detailed way. But this is not a valid argument for ignoring these interests entirely. While uncertainty about the future makes it difficult to elaborate detailed obligations in relation to future generations, it is feasible for governments to take on obligations to curb action which is highly likely to result in harm to the human rights of future generations necessary for them to enjoy a decent life.

Support for the international mechanisms relating to women and disabled persons partly reflects the strong link made between these issues and development concerns of developing countries. Thus, for example, we saw that Mexico took up the concern of disabled persons, which had been neglected in the WHO Millennium Development Goals. Similarly, strong links were made between social development – both national and international – which played a crucial role in developing countries' support for CEDAW. In relation to the CRC, there was a strong discourse of protecting children based on their role as future citizens, with the development of nations, societies, and humanity seen as inexorably connected to the development of children, individually and as a group. Yet, tensions remain as to whether the CRC regime unduly reflects Western conceptions of childhood by, for example, underplaying the responsibility of children towards adults, which has considerable emphasis in much of Africa and Asia (Holzscheiter 2010: 224).[25]

5.3.2 Effectiveness

In relation to the CRC regime, there is no doubt that this treaty has had a significant impact; yet, issues of non-compliance remain problematic. The situation is encapsulated by Olga Khazova, who observes that the CRC has helped bring about a change in mindset around the world: A child is now more often perceived as an autonomous person and not the property of its parents. But there is still much to be done: despite an increase in legislation enshrining children's rights, this is 'still limited or fragmented in many countries' (Khazova 2021: 5).

In relation to women's rights, the international legal norms and representative institutions represent a step forward, but implementation remains problematic. It is too early to assess thoroughly the effectiveness of the CRPD and its Optional Protocol, but there is no doubt that, together, these instruments have been an important catalyst for disability law and public policy reform in many countries.[26]

[25] Holzscheiter (2010) points out that the Asian and African views on family structures, privacy, interdependence, and child rearing practices were marginalised in the CRC negotiations.

[26] Brazil, for example, has overhauled its domestic legislation to comply with the provisions of the Convention. While the UN Committee on the Rights of Persons with Disabilities commented positively on these changes, it also pointed to other areas where much work remained to be done (CRPD 2016). Since 2013, the European Union, as a party to the CRPD, has had in place a framework for the Convention's implementation (European Union Agency for Fundamental Rights 2013). See also Degener (2017: 152).

The effectiveness of institutions to represent future generations may be difficult to assess, as we will only know in the future what the impact of such institutions will be. But this is true of very many democratic institutions and their work along the normative ideals outlined. Thus, this challenge can be overstated. It is possible to assess now, for example, whether such an institution is highlighting or factoring the interests of future generations into contemporary policy-making.

5.4 Conclusion

An important lesson from the case studies – of children, disabled persons, and women – outlined in this chapter is that support from developing countries is crucial for establishing international institutions to represent vulnerable groups. This involves not just a normative discourse in which development concerns feature prominently, but also a perception that any new institution does not interfere with legitimate concerns of developing countries in terms of their sovereign right to development (Marong 2010). This is borne out in the history of the proposal for a UN High Commissioner for Future Generations, which was narrowly defeated at the Rio +20 UN conference due to concerns from developing countries that such a mechanism would be overly intrusive and interfere with their development aspirations (Lawrence 2014: 17). The Mary Robinson Foundation proposed, as a way of addressing this concern, to institute a commission – rather than individual commissioner – for future generations that would involve participation by developing and developed country representatives. We discuss how this issue has been addressed in relation to mechanisms considered at the United Nations 2024 Summit of the Future (UNGA 2022) in Chapter 8.[27]

In short, our three case studies, while inherently limited, point in the direction of reforming international institutions to represent future generations in some way or another. The systematic injustice against future generations is comparable to the systematic injustice against children, disabled persons, and women, which points to the need for an international institutional response entailing the representation of future generations. Recall that the normative basis for representation of future generations we argue for here (see Chapter 3) rests on a subsistence threshold concept of intergenerational justice, combined with a concept of intergenerational solidarity that aims to address the needs of the most vulnerable. While the language is not exactly the same, some common threads can be identified between these

[27] As this book went to press, the United Nations Summit of the Future on 22 September 2024 adopted *The Pact for the Future*, para 32 of which noted the proposal for an Envoy for Future Generations but did not agree to create one. For all outcomes of this summit – including the *Pact for the Future* – see United Nations (2024). In October 2024 it was reported that a senior UN official had announced at a major international conference that the Secretary-General was intending to proceed to create such an envoy (Day 2024).

normative arguments and the normative discourses used historically to justify various international institutions regarding children, disabled persons, and women. We saw, for example, that the concept of social development played a key role in normative claims relating to children, disabled persons, and women.

There is no single concept of development, but an important discourse involves ensuring that all persons are raised above a certain threshold. This, in turn, can be expressed in terms of solidarity between generations. In relation to children, we saw that, in the push to establish global legal norms and institutions to protect children, there was a powerful discourse of universality: the idea that all children were entitled to threshold rights. Similarly, in the disability context, the CRPD strongly reflects the idea that human dignity is universal. This universality has strong parallels with the concept of intergenerational justice elaborated in Chapter 3, which involves the key idea that all persons – regardless of when and where they are born – are entitled to human rights necessary for the enjoyment of a decent life. In addition, the subsistence concept of intergenerational justice we argue for is justified as an expression of intergenerational solidarity. As we saw earlier, intergenerational solidarity, in the sense of the bond between adults and children, played a role in some of the normative arguments underlying the CRC.

The three case studies involve areas where there are now detailed rights, with corresponding duties on governments spelt out in a particular treaty regime in relation to the vulnerable group in question. This is in stark contrast to future generations, where – as discussed earlier – the current global legal regime is rather weak. While the effectiveness of all three treaty regimes discussed in this chapter is mixed, there is no doubt that all three have had at least some positive impact on each of the vulnerable groups concerned. This would suggest the need to elaborate detailed obligations in a legally binding instrument relating to future generations (see Chapter 8).[28]

The other imperative arising from this analysis is the need to strengthen the global climate regime. Various strategies are possible here, one of which involves making the Nationally Determined Contributions (NDCs) under the *Paris Agreement* legally binding (Lawrence & Wong 2017). A further option is elaborating equity-based criteria in the Paris stocktake process, which involves a review of the level of ambition under the *Paris Agreement* at five-yearly intervals (Lawrence & Reder 2019).

The case studies also suggest, both in terms of legitimacy and political feasibility, that it is essential to link institutions for representing future generations to the development aspirations of developing countries. Thus, the concept of sustainable development should be included in the normative underpinnings for an institution

[28] This is not a novel idea. See the proposal by Edith Brown Weiss (1989).

to protect future generations, both for reasons of principle and of pragmatic political feasibility. Development, however, needs to be combined with the requirements of intergenerational justice through the concept of sustainable development, defined in a way that preserves a specific quality or standard of nature (Klauer et al. 2017: 28): 'strong sustainability' is required to avoid misuse of the concept of sustainable development to justify economic development at the expense of the environment, as has occurred in the past (Pickering & Dryzek 2019: 58). In addition, the case studies show that concepts of human rights based on human dignity, given the universality of this discourse, have great advantages.

The case studies analysed in this chapter provide valuable insights into which types of normative justifications are likely to find support in the political process of justifying institutions to represent future generations. An important caveat here is that some of the normative justifications presented in relation to these vulnerable groups do not map into the intergenerational context. Thus, for example, normative principles in relation to disabled persons based on reciprocity – involving a two-way interaction between disabled persons and society – cannot operate in the context of future generations, given the necessarily one-way relationship between persons alive now and future generations.

Despite this caveat, legal–political coherence suggests that – given a commitment to human dignity and human rights provides a normative basis for specialist international institutions aimed at protecting children, disabled persons, and women – the same principles require establishing international mechanisms to protect future generations. Put the other way around, it would be logically incoherent, given a commitment to human rights and human dignity, to establish specialist institutions in relation to children, disabled persons, and women, but not to establish an institution devoted to protection of future generations. In this argument, we use the term 'protection', not 'representation'. As discussed at the beginning of this chapter, the case studies canvassed here all involve treaty compliance mechanisms – such as individual complaints to the Committee on the Rights of the Child – but de facto such bodies play a role as representational bodies in giving members of the vulnerable group in question a voice, both individually and collectively. Thus, all mechanisms canvassed in the case studies involve primarily proxy compliance functions but also de facto representative proxy representation (as defined in Chapter 2).

In the negotiation of the CRC, children were seen as particularly vulnerable to harms inflicted on them by adults, thus justifying a treaty regime that enshrined children's rights with corresponding obligations on the state to ensure the respect of these rights. This was combined with a 'development discourse' which included both individual development and the development of the nation and humanity.

The relatively new global disability regime under the CRPD was also justified on the human rights and human dignity bedrock, with a strong concept of substantive equality. While the interactive concept of social disability does not map onto the intergenerational context, the concept of equality does. Indeed, in Chapter 3, we saw that a key basis for proxy representation of future generations was the idea that all persons, regardless of where and when they are born, possess certain generic rights linked to a threshold concept of intergenerational justice that is based on human rights necessary for the enjoyment of a decent life.

The case study relating to the protection of women's rights shows that, in this area, there is a well-developed international legal regime, even though serious problems of implementation remain. The normative basis for this regime rests on a human rights approach founded on a commitment to human dignity. Procedural justice is also a key notion in this regime, involving the idea of equality for women in the political process, for example. Similarly, proxy representation of future generations remains a key vehicle for ensuring this group's indirect participation in contemporary decision-making. In responding to violations of women's rights, the legal system tends to focus on discrimination and crimes that have already been committed, whereas proxy representation of future generations would necessarily involve preventive action.[29]

A golden thread running through all three case studies is the notion of development. Protection of the rights of children, disabled persons, and women is argued to be essential for development – understood not just within a nation or society but also between countries. In the CRC context, this is combined with an emphasis on individual development. These normative discourses meshed with the aspirations of developing countries, whose support was key to establishing institutions that give the relevant vulnerable group a voice. This is a vital lesson in establishing a stronger international legal framework for future generations. Success in achieving such reforms would necessarily depend upon both broad-ranging support from all countries – including developing countries, which comprise an overwhelming majority of the international community – and a conviction that future generations are vulnerable and deserving of protection, for the same reasons that apply to other vulnerable groups.

References

Andresen, S. (2014). Childhood Vulnerability: Systematic, Structural, and Individual Dimensions. *Child Indicators Research*, 7(4), 699–713.

Australian Bureau of Statistics (ABS). (2021). *Sexual Violence: Victimization*. Available at www.abs.gov.au/articles/sexual-violence-victimisation.

Australian Government, Attorney General's Department. (2017). *Noble v Australia (7/2012) Australian Government Response*. Available at www.ag.gov.au/rights-and-protections/publications/noble-v-australia-72012-australian-government-response.

[29] Thank you to Anne Meuche for this observation.

Bagattini, A. (2014). Child Well-Being: A Philosophical Perspective. In Ben-Arieh, A., Casas, F., Frønes, I. & Korbin, J. E., eds., *Handbook of Child Well-Being: Theory Indicators, Measures and Policies*. Dordrecht /New York: Springer, 163–86.

Brown Weiss, E. (1989). *In Fairness to Future Generations: International Law: Common Patrimony, and Intergenerational Equity*, Tokyo: The United Nations University; Dobbs Ferry, NY: Transnational Publishers.

Buck, T. (2011). *International Child Law*, 2nd ed., London: Routledge.

Charlesworth, H. (1994). What are 'Women's International Human Rights'? In Cook, R. J., ed., *Human Rights of Women, National and International Perspectives*. Philadelphia, PA: University of Pennsylvania Press, 58–84.

Clark, H. (2010). What Is the Justice System Willing to Offer? *Australian Institute of Family Studies, Family Matters*, 85, 28–37.

Clough, B. (2017). Disability and Vulnerability: Challenging the Capacity/Incapacity Binary. *Social Policy and Society*, 16(3), 469–81.

Convention on the Elimination of All Forms of Discrimination against Women (CEDAW) (1979) (adopted 18 December 1979; entered into force 3 September 1981), 1249 UNTS 13.

Convention on the Rights of Persons with Disabilities (CPDR) (2006) (adopted 12 December 2006 in UNGA resolution A/RES/61/106; entered into force 3 May 2008), 2515 UNTS 3.

Convention on the Rights of the Child (CRC) (1989) (adopted 20 November 1989; entered into force 2 September 1990), 1577 UNTS 3.

Dairiam, M. S. (2015). CEDAW, Gender and Culture. In Baksh, R. & Harcourt, W., eds., *The Oxford Handbook of Transnational Feminist Movements*. Oxford: Oxford University Press, 367–93.

Day, R. (2024). Coming Soon A UN Envoy for Future Generations, United Nations University (October 9, 2024). Available at: https://unu.edu/cpr/blog-post/coming-soon-un-envoy-future-generations.

De Beco, G. (2021). Nothing about Us without Us. In de Beco, G., ed., *Disability in International Human Rights Law*. Oxford: Oxford University Press, 159–C9.N79. https://doi.org/10.1093/oso/9780198824503.003.0010.

Degener, T. (2017). 10 Years of Convention on the Rights of Persons with Disabilities. *Netherlands Quarterly of Human Rights*, 35(3), 152–157. https://doi-org/10.1177/0924051917722294.

Dijk, N. van. (2021a). From Exacerbating the Anthropocene's Problems to Intergenerational Justice: An Analysis of the Communication Procedure of The Human Rights Treaty System. *Earth System Governance*, 10(100123), 1–10. https://doi.org/10.1016/j.esg.2021.100123.

Dijk, N. van. (2021b). The Capability Approach as a Road Map for Re-thinking Intergenerational Justice. In Linehan, J. & Lawrence, P., eds., *Giving Future Generations a Voice: Normative Frameworks, Institutions and Practice*. Cheltenham/Camberley: Edward Elgar, 42–61.

Ertürk, Y. & Purkayastha, B. (2012). Linking Research, Policy and Action: A Look at the Work of the Special Rapporteur on Violence against Women. *Current Sociology*, 60(2), 142–60.

European Union Agency for Fundamental Rights. (2013). *EU Framework for the UN Convention on the Rights of Persons with Disabilities*. Available at http://fra.europa.eu/en/cooperation/eu-partners/eu-crpd-framework.

Fass, P. S. (2011). A Historical Context for the United Nations Convention on the Rights of the Child. *The Annals of the American Academy of Political and Social Science*, 633, 17–29.

Feinberg, J. (1980). A Child's Right to an Open Future. In LaFollette, H. & Aiken, W., eds., *Whose Child? Parental Rights, Parental Authority and State Power*. Totowa, NJ: Rowman and Littlefield, 124–53.

George, R. A. (2019). Islam and UN Human Rights Treaty Ratification in the Middle East. In Quataert, J. & Wildenthal, L., eds., *The Routledge History of Human Rights*. London: Routledge, 163–82.

Graf, G. & Schweiger, G. (2017). *Ethics and the Endangerment of Children's Bodies*, Basingstoke: Palgrave Macmillan.

Gutwald, R. & Reder, M. (2023). How to Protect Children? A Pragmatistic Approach on State Intervention and Children's Welfare. *The Journal of Ethics*, 27, 77–95.

Holzscheiter, A. (2010). *Children's Rights in International Politics, The Transformative Power of Discourse*, London: Palgrave Macmillan.

International Covenant on Civil and Political Rights (ICCPR) (1966) (adopted 16 December 1966; entered into force 23 March 1976), 999 UNTS 171.

International Covenant on Economic, Social and Cultural Rights (ICESCR) (1966) (adopted 16 December 1966; entered into force 3 January 1976), 993 UNTS 3.

International Labour Organization (ILO). (2021). *Info Stories: The Gender Gap in Employment: What's Holding Women Back?* Available at www.ilo.org/infostories/en-GB/Stories/Employment/barriers-women#global-gap.

International Labour Organization Convention (No. 5) Fixing the Minimum Age for Admission of Children to Industrial Employment (*Minimum Age (Industry) Convention*) (ILO) (1919) (adopted 28 November 1919; entered into force 13 June 1921) 1197 UNTS 424.

International Parliamentary Union (IPU). (2022). *Global and Global and Regional Averages of Women in National Parliaments*. Available at https://data.ipu.org/women-averages?month=10&year=2022.

Ishay, M. R. (2004). *The History of Human Rights*, Oakland, CA: University of California Press.

Kayess, R. & French, P. (2008). Out of Darkness into Light? Introducing the Convention on the Rights of Persons with Disabilities. *Human Rights Law Review*, 8(1), 1–34.

Khazova, O. (2021). How to Ensure Wider Implementation of the CRC. In Marrus, E. & Laufer-Ukeles, P., eds., *Global Reflections on Children's Rights and the Law 30 years after the Convention on the Rights of the Child*. New York: Routledge, 3–16.

Klauer, B., Manstetten, R., Petersen, T. & Schiller, J. (2017). *Sustainability and the Art of Long-Term Thinking*, New York: Routledge.

Lawrence, P. (2014). *Justice for Future Generations, Climate Change and International Law*, Cheltenham: Edward Elgar.

Lawrence, P. & Reder, M. (2019). Equity and the Paris Agreement: Legal and Philosophical Perspectives. *Journal of Environmental Law*, 31(3), 511–31.

Lawrence, P. & Wong, D. (2017). Soft Law in the Paris Climate Agreement: Strength or Weakness? *Review of European, Comparative & International Environmental Law*, 26(3), 276–86.

Marong, A. (2010). Development, Right to, International Protection. In Peters, A. & Wolfrum, R. eds., *Max Planck Encyclopaedia of International Law*. Oxford: Oxford University Press.

Morris, J. (2001). Impairment and Disability: Constructing an Ethics of Care That Promotes Human Rights. *Hypatia*, 16(4), 1–16.

Noble v Australia (CRPD, 2016). Remedy Australia. (2016). Available at https://remedy.org.au/cases/40.

Nussbaum, M. (2015). Women's Progress and Women's Human Rights. *Human Rights Quarterly*, 38(3), 589–622.

Office of the High Commissioner for Human Rights (OHCHR). (2010). *Monitoring the Convention on the Rights of Persons with Disabilities, Guidance for Human Rights Monitors*, Professional Training Series No. 17, New York/Geneva: United Nations.

Optional Protocol to the Convention on the Elimination of All Forms of Discrimination against Women (Optional Protocol to CEDAW) (1999) (adopted 6 October 1999; entered into force 22 December 2000), 2131 UNTS 83.

Optional Protocol to the Convention on the Rights of Persons with Disabilities (Optional Protocol to the CRPD) (2006) (adopted 13 December 2006; entered into force 3 May 2008), 2518 UNTS 283.

Optional Protocol to the Convention on the Rights of the Child on a Communications Procedure (Optional Protocol to the CRC) (2011) (adopted 19 December 2011; entered into force 14 April 2014), 2983 UNTS 135.

Phillips, A. (1993). *Democracy and Difference*, University Park, PA: Pennsylvania State University Press.

Pickering, J. & Dryzek, J. (2019). *The Politics of the Anthropocene*, Oxford: Oxford University Press.

Quinn, G. & Degener, T. (2002). *Human Rights and Disability, the Current Use and Future Potential of United Nations Human Rights Instruments in the Context of Disability*, New York/Geneva: OHCHR. Available at: www.ohchr.org/sites/default/files/Documents/Publications/HRDisabilityen.pdf.

Rupp, L. J. (1998). *Worlds of Women, The Making of an International Women's Movement*, Princeton, NJ: Princeton University Press.

Schoepp-Schilling, H. B. (2007). The Nature and Scope of the Convention. In Schoepp-Schilling, H. B., ed., *The Circle of Empowerment, 25 years of the UN Committee on the Elimination of Discrimination against Women*. New York: The Feminist Press at The City University of New York, 10–30.

Schweiger, G. & Graf, G. (2017). Ethics and the Dynamic Vulnerability of Children. *The Ethics Forum*, 12(2–3), 243–61.

Smith, R. A. (2019). *Extending International Human Rights Protections to Vulnerable Populations, Abingdon*, Oxford/New York: Routledge.

Spijkers, O. (2011). *The United Nations, The Evolution of Global Values and International Law*, Cambridge: Intersentia.

The Pact for the Future, contained in UNGA resolution A/RES/79/1 (22 September 2024).

Tomuschat, C. (2014). *Human Rights, between Idealism and Realism*, Oxford: Oxford University Press.

Tremmel, J. C. (2009). *A Theory of Intergenerational Justice*, Oxford: Earthscan.

UN Committee on Economic, Social and Cultural Rights (CESCR). (2002). *General Comment 15, article 11, 12 (The Right to Water)*, 20 January 2002, ESCOR, CESCR, 29th session, Agenda item 3 UN Doc. E/C/12/2002/11 at para 11. Available at: https://digitallibrary.un.org/record/486454.

UN Committee on the Elimination of Discrimination Against Women (CEDAW). (2004). *General Recommendation No. 25, on article 4, paragraph 1, of the Convention on the Elimination of All Forms of Discrimination against Women, on temporary special measures*. Available at: www.un.org/womenwatch/daw/cedaw/recommendations/General%20recommendation%2025%20(English).pdf.

UN Committee on the Rights of Persons with Disabilities (CRPD). (2016). *Committee on the Rights of Persons with Disabilities considers initial report of Brazil*, 26 August 2015. Available at: www.ohchr.org/EN/NewsEvents/Pages/DisplayNews.aspx?NewsID=16348&LangID=E.

UN Committee on the Rights of Persons with Disabilities (CRPD). (2016). *Views Adopted by the Committee under Article 5 of the Optional Protocol, Concerning Communication No. 7/2012*, 1. UN Doc. CRPD/C/16/D/7/2012 (Noble v. Australia).

UN Committee on the Rights of Persons with Disabilities (CRPD). (2018). *Convention on the Rights of Persons with Disabilities, General Comment No. 6* (2018) on equality and non-discrimination, UN Doc. CRPD/C/GC/6. Available at: www.ohchr.org/en/documents/general-comments-and-recommendations/general-comment-no6-equality-and-non-discrimination.

UN Committee on the Rights of the Child. (2016). *Report of the 2016 Day of General Discussion on Children's Rights and the Environment*. Available at: www.ohchr.org/sites/default/files/Documents/HRBodies/CRC/Discussions/2016/DGDoutcomereport-May2017.pdf.

UN Committee on the Rights of the Child. (2019). *Sacchi et al. v. Argentina, et al.* 23 September 2019, available at: http://climatecasechart.com/climate-change-litigation/wp-content/uploads/sites/16/non-us-case-documents/2019/20190923_Communication-No.-1042019-Argentina-Communication-No.-1052019-Brazil-Communication-No.-1062019-France-Communication-No.-1072019-Germany-Communication-No.-1082019-Turkey_petition.pdf. (Sacchi Communication).

UN Committee on the Rights of the Child. (2021). *Decision Adopted by the Committee on the Rights of the Child under the Optional Protocol to the Convention on the Rights of the Child on a communications procedure in respect of Communication No. 104/2019.* UN Doc. CRC/C/88/D/104/2019.1

UN Committee on the Rights of the Child. (2023). *General Comment No. 26 (2023) on children's rights and the environment with a special focus on climate change*. UN Doc. CRC/C/G C/26.

UN General Assembly (UNGA). (1959). *Declaration of the Rights of the Child*. Resolution adopted by the UN General Assembly (20 November 1959) UN Doc. A/RES/1386 (XIV).

UN General Assembly (UNGA). (1967). *Declaration on the Elimination of Discrimination against Women*. Resolution adopted by the UN General Assembly 2263 (XXII). UN Doc. A/RES/22/2263.

UN General Assembly (UNGA). (1975). *Declaration on the Rights of Disabled Persons*. Resolution adopted by the UN General Assembly 3447/30 (9 December 1975) UN Doc. A/RES/3447.

UN General Assembly (UNGA). (1991). *Principles for the Protection of Persons with Mental Illness*. Resolution adopted by the UN General Assembly 46/119 (17 December 1991) UN Doc. A/RES/46/119.

UN General Assembly (UNGA). (1993). *United Nations Standard Rules on the Equalisation of Opportunities for Persons with Disabilities (Standard Rules)*. Resolution adopted by the UN General Assembly (20 December 1993), UN Doc. A/RES/48/96, Supp. No. 49, Annex. at 202-11.

UN General Assembly (UNGA). (2022). *Modalities for the Summit of the Future*. Resolution of the General Assembly, UN Doc. A/RES/76/307.

UN General Assembly. (1948). *Universal Declaration of Human Rights*, 10 December 1948, 217 A (III). Available at: www.refworld.org/docid/3ae6b3712c.html.

UN Human Rights Committee (HRC). (2019). *General Comment No. 36, Article 6 (Right to Life)*, 3 September 2019, CCPR/C/GC/35. Available at: www.refworld.org/docid/5e5e75e04.html.

UN Office of the High Commissioner for Human Rights (OHCHR). (2021). *General Comment No. 26 on children's rights and the environment with a special focus on climate change*. Issued by Committee on the Rights of the Child.

UN Office of the High Commissioner for Human Rights (OHCHR). (2007). *Legislative History of the Convention on the Rights of the Child*, Vol. 1, New York/Geneva: United Nations, xxxvii.

UN Office of the High Commissioner for Human Rights (OHCHR). (2010). *Monitoring the Convention on the Rights of Persons with Disabilities, Guidance for Human Rights Monitors*, Professional Training Series No. 17, New York/Geneva: United Nations.

UN Office of the High Commissioner for Human Rights (OHCHR). (2020). *Article 33: List of administrative indicators on national implementation and monitoring*. Available at www.ohchr.org/sites/default/files/article-33-indicators-en.pdf.

UN Office of the High Commissioner for Human Rights (OHCHR). (2022). *Report of the Special Rapporteur on Violence against Women Its Causes and Consequences*. Available at: www.ohchr.org/en/special-procedures/sr-violence-against-women.

UN Office of the High Commissioner for Human Rights (OHCHR). (2024). *Individual Communications, Committee on the Rights of Persons with Disabilities*. Available at: www.ohchr.org/en/treaty-bodies/crpd/individual-communications.

United Nations. (1976). *Report of the World Conference of the International Women's Year*, Mexico City, 19 June–2 July 1975, New York, UN Doc E/CONF.66/34. Available at: www.un.org/womenwatch/daw/beijing/otherconferences/Mexico/Mexico%20conference%20report%20optimized.pdf.

United Nations. (2024). *Summit of the Future, Our Common Agenda*. Available at: www.un.org/en/summit-of-the-future/pact-for-the-future.

United Nations Economic and Social Council (ECOSOC). (1985). Commission on Human Rights, 'Summary Records of the Meetings of the Commission on Human Rights at its 41st Session. Question of a Convention on the Rights of the Child (Agenda Item 13)', UN Doc. E/CN.4/1985/SR53, add.1, 26 March 1985.

United Nations Treaty Collection. (2024). *Status of the Optional protocol to the Convention on the rights of the Child on a communication procedure*.

World Health Organization (WHO). (2006). *Global Programming Note 2006-2007: Call for Resource Mobilisation and Engagement opportunities: Disability and Rehabilitation*. Available at: www.who.int/nmh/donorinfo/vip_promoting_access_healthcare_rehabilitation_update.pdf.pdf.

World Health Organization (WHO). (2021a). *Violence against Women*. Available at: www.who.int/news-room/fact-sheets/detail/violence-against-women#:~:text=Estimates%20published%20by%20WHO%20indicate,sexual%20violence%20in%20their%20lifetime.

World Health Organization (WHO). (2021b). *Violence against Women Prevalence Estimates, 2018: Global, Regional and National Prevalence Estimates for Intimate Partner Violence against Women and Global and Regional Prevalence Estimates for Non-Partner Sexual Violence against Women*. Geneva: World Health Organization. Available at: https://apps.who.int/iris/handle/10665/341337.

Young, I. M. (2000). *Inclusion and Democracy*, Oxford/New York: Oxford University Press.

Part III

Case Studies

6

The ICJ Advisory Opinion on Climate Change and Proxy Representation of Future Generations

6.1 Introduction

In March 2023, the United Nations General Assembly (UNGA) passed a resolution requesting the International Court of Justice (ICJ) to provide an advisory opinion on states' international legal obligations in relation to climate change, including their obligations in relation to both current and future generations (UNGA 2023). This resolution was the culmination of a long civil society campaign spearheaded by youth climate justice activists, Vanuatu, and the Pacific Island countries (Wewerinke-Singh & Hinge Salili 2020; Pacific Island Students Fighting Climate Change 2024). The inclusion of obligations towards future generations in this mandate reflects, *inter alia*, the concern of Pacific Island countries about climate change threats – to their lives now, and the lives of their future generations – as well as their capacity to maintain their culture into the future. This chapter assesses the potential for this ICJ advisory opinion to act as an effective proxy for future generations in the climate change context. We offer recommendations on how our proposed normative framework could feed into an ICJ advisory opinion to further international, intragenerational, and intergenerational justice, without undermining the legitimacy of the Court. Whether or not the ICJ advisory opinion is decided in the direction proposed here, the arguments we set out will remain relevant for other climate litigation processes.

This chapter rests on the normative assumptions laid out earlier in this book, including the definition of proxy representation, and assumptions about the role of international law and institutions, including the ICJ. In addition, the legitimacy criteria applicable to international institutions such as the ICJ (Chapter 4) are crucial, given the close link between legitimacy and effectiveness. We introduced the concept of *future legitimacy* as involving the idea of looking back at decisions to be taken by the ICJ now from the perspective of future generations, including a projected vantage point decades from now, when scientists predict many parts of the world will be increasingly negatively impacted by climate change (Section 4.3.2).

An important part of the context includes the role of ICJ advisory opinions. While such opinions of the ICJ are non-binding, they nevertheless have the potential to influence the direction of international law and are an important part of the international political process. Advisory opinions of the ICJ can feed into national litigation, as well as having an impact in raising awareness and global public opinion (Wewerinke-Singh, Aguon & Hunter 2021: 404). Even if, from this perspective, an ICJ advisory opinion can be interpreted as a form of representation of future generations, there are also tensions that need to be discussed.

One is the tension between the ICJ's role of providing clarity to states' existing international legal obligations, grounded on state consent, and the role of the Court (often unstated) as an agent for further development of international law, to meet the requirements of international, intragenerational, and intergenerational justice. Given there is already an elaborate climate change treaty regime, an advisory opinion that is overly prescriptive in terms of individual states' obligations would, on the one hand, run the risk of undermining this treaty regime and weakening the legitimacy of the Court (Bodansky 2017, 2022, 2023). On the other hand, an advisory opinion that is overly timid could be seen as missing a valuable opportunity to exert pressure on states to take action on climate change and provide crucial impetus for strengthening the existing treaty regime, in a context where the future of humanity – of which the international legal system is a part – is threatened. This chapter argues that the ICJ Advisory Opinion on Climate Change could further clarify existing international environmental law principles in ways which could strengthen the climate regime by providing greater specificity to states' international legal obligations.

A further tension running through the discussion in this chapter can be characterised through the differences between *inter* and *intra*generational and national and international (or transnational) justice. As mentioned in Chapter 2 (Section 2.5), the UN climate regime contains evidence of both an international and intergenerational justice framing. The former is embodied in the principle of 'common but differentiated responsibilities', which emphasises the duty of the developed countries to take the lead in addressing climate change. But the climate regime also contains evidence of intergenerational justice framings, with references to future generations contained, for example, in the 'Principles' section of the *United Nations Framework Convention on Climate Change* (UNFCCC) (1992), where Article 3 delineates principles to be considered in interpreting the UNFCCC and subsequent agreements, including the *Paris Agreement* (2015). The ICJ, in its advisory opinion will need to tread carefully in terms of these different dimensions of justice. On the one hand, if the Court overly focuses on obligations towards future generations, this could be perceived by developing states as exhibiting a bias towards the developed countries which have tended in the UN negotiations to emphasise the reduction of greenhouse gas emissions (mitigation), rather than adapting to climate change impacts (adaptation) (Humphreys 2022: 1067). On the other hand, the intergenerational justice dimension is an explicit part of the question put to the Court and a crucial part of the rationale to address climate change. The normative framing of this book emphasises the importance of all three key axes of justice – intragenerational, intergenerational, and international – with the focus on future generations.

This chapter is structured as follows. First, we explain how the ICJ advisory opinion came about and what it could achieve (Section 6.2). We then address how the proxy representation functions (elaborated in Chapter 3) apply in relation to the ICJ advisory opinion and recall our normative framework of justice, solidarity, and vulnerability (Section 6.3). We then analyse the references to future generations in the mandate of the advisory opinion (Section 6.4). The normative framework is then applied to inform proposals as to how the Court should interpret the principle of harm prevention (Section 6.5), and fallback options, involving an indirect obligation of future generations (Section 6.6). We then examine how the Court could approach the principle of intergenerational equity (Section 6.7); analyse the potential of *amicus curiae* briefs, and expert witnesses, to act as proxy representatives of future generations (Section 6.8); and assess the advisory opinion in terms of the criteria of legitimacy and effectiveness (Section 6.9); before drawing some conclusions (Section 6.10).

6.2 Origins and Functions of an Advisory Opinion on Climate Change

The United Nations General Assembly resolution establishing the request for an advisory opinion of the ICJ of March 2023 (UNGA 2023) was the culmination of a campaign led by Vanuatu and the Pacific Island countries (Stephens 2020), combined with a civil society campaign (Wewerinke-Singh & Hinge Salili 2020: 681 et seq.). This campaign had its origins in an initiative taken by law students at the University of the South Pacific in mid-2019, which became a regional and global campaign (Wewerinke-Singh, Garg & Agarwalla 2023: 14; Seneviratne 2023). Pacific Island countries were deeply concerned at the failure of the UN climate treaty process to deliver sufficiently strong action. For these countries, climate change constitutes an existential threat, as they face-ever increasing inundation from rising sea levels and more frequent and extreme weather events.[1]

In terms of a litigation strategy involving the ICJ, an advisory opinion is the most desirable route, as it avoids many of the difficult issues relating to causation and

[1] Under Article 96 of the *Statute of the International Court of Justice* (1945), an advisory opinion can be requested by the UN General Assembly on the basis of a majority vote or by a specialised agency, such as the World Health Organisation.

attribution of harm to individual states in the climate change context (Bodansky 2017; Sands 2016: 23 et seq.). Under Article 34(1) of the *Statute of the International Court of Justice* (ICJ Statute) (1945), the Court limits standing in contentious proceedings to states. While it is possible for states to bring claims on behalf of their citizens and future generations, arguably most states will continue to be reluctant to bring a case against high greenhouse gas emitting states due to concerns about potential negative impacts on their trade and investment – given the powerful fossil fuel-related vested interests in many states (Influence Map 2020). For this reason, an ICJ advisory opinion is seen as the most desirable strategy for states seeking to strengthen action on climate change.

The ICJ Advisory Opinion on Climate Change could perform a range of functions. First, it could increase pressure on states to ratchet up the level of their ambition in their Nationally Determined Contributions (NDCs) under the *Paris Agreement* (2015) (Bodansky 2017). Second, it could clarify customary international law principles that may be invoked in many ways in both international and national legal processes. Such clarification could bolster the bargaining power of states vulnerable to climate change in the ongoing international climate negotiations (Wewerinke-Singh & Hinge Salili 2020: 688). Finally, it could increase the legitimacy of climate science (Sands 2016: 29; see also the contrary view in Bodansky 2017). In this chapter, we do not address all these functions, but hone in on the issue of how the ICJ advisory opinion could act as vehicle for proxy representation of future generations, assessed in terms of our proposed effectiveness and legitimacy criteria (Chapter 4). This involves the second and third functions listed earlier; namely, clarifying the relevant rules of customary international law, and bolstering the legitimacy of climate science.

6.3 Proxy Representation and Its Normative Implications

As we explained in Chapter 2, proxy representation involves the representation of interests or persons who cannot speak for themselves. Current international institutions and rules manifest bias against the interests of future generations. This bias is evident in the climate change regime, which contains inadequate rules for future generations in terms of their stringency and bindingness. The failure of the *Paris Agreement* to include an effective enforcement regime, combined with developed countries' failure to contribute promised climate finance and the weak implementation of individual states' mitigation commitments (as contained in their NDCs), are further weaknesses (Stankovic, Hovi & Skodvin 2023; Torstad 2020).

Proxy representation is justified as an expression of the relation between current and future relations. The recognition of this relation and its political implications can be described as intergenerational solidarity. Proxy representation of future generations is justified as a means for addressing bias towards current generations within political and legal institutions, using a yardstick of intergenerational justice defined as requiring, as a minimum, the protection of the human rights of future generations necessary to lead a decent life (see Section 3.4.1). This normative benchmark for intergenerational justice is used as a springboard for further clarifying the international legal principle of intergenerational equity by linking it to human rights obligations (see later). This approach finds resonance in the recent European Court of Human Rights (ECtHR) 2024 decision in *Verein Klimaseniorinnen v Switzerland* (hereafter, *Verein Seniorinnen*); central to this decision was the connection between human rights protection and intergenerational justice (Nolan 2024). The Court emphasised that the 'damaging effects of climate change raise an issue of intergenerational burden sharing' (*Verein Seniorinnen* 2024: para 410), noting that 'future generations are likely to bear an increasingly severe burden of present failures and emissions to combat climate change' while having 'no possibility of participating in relevant current decision-making processes' (para 420). This was used by the Court, together with state's obligations under the UNFCCC Article 3 obligation to protect the climate system for the benefit of present and future generations (*Verein Seniorinnen* 2024: para 420), as the basis for deciding that the *European Convention on Human Rights* (ECHR) (1950) required certain minimal requirements in terms of contracting states' mitigation efforts (para 520).

Further elements of our normative framework involve the protection of the vulnerable (Section 3.4.3), combined with solidarity principles which emphasise the commonality of interest between current and future generations (Section 3.4.2). Our pragmatist methodology involves pointing out that these normative principles are already embedded in the international legal order in a range of UN instruments and the ECHR (Section 2.4) and formally endorsed by the international community. Given existing proxy-style mechanisms of representation in the international legal order for various vulnerable groups (Chapter 5), the proxy representation of future generations in the climate context is an incremental, rather than a radical, step in the process of international legal reform.

We use Rehfeld's audience-based concept of proxy representation, in which endorsement by the relevant audience of a proxy is a defining feature (Section 2.2). Proxy representation as a legal concept, as we have seen, involves authorisation by law to take on proxy functions (Section 2.2). We have explained that proxy representation in the international legal context can have a range of functions: representational, compliance, and norm entrepreneurial (Section 2.5). We define representation of future generations as having direct and indirect dimensions. Under this definition, indirect representation includes the situation where an international law rule embodies the interests of future generations (Section 2.4). Thus, the ICJ applying or interpreting a rule of international law which embodies or reflects the interests of future generations would fall within this definition, with the ICJ facilitating a form of proxy representation (Sections 2.4 and 2.5). We have also observed that discourses can capture the interests of future generations. Before applying these concepts to the ICJ advisory opinion, it is important to examine closely the questions put to the Court by the UN General Assembly.

If the ICJ is to facilitate a form of proxy representation, this would require it to recognise the outlined normative implications of representation more strongly than it has to date and to implement them both substantively in decisions and in the development of new mechanisms. In the following discussion, we show which conclusions can be drawn for the ICJ from the three normative heuristics as the basis for representation of future generations.

6.4 The Mandate of the Advisory Opinion and Future Generations

At this point, it is essential to consider with some precision the scope of the mandate for the advisory opinion.[2] The questions put to the ICJ by the UN General Assembly require the Court to determine:

(a) What are the obligations of states under international law to ensure the protection of the climate system and other parts of the environment from anthropogenic emissions of greenhouse gases for states and for present and *future generations*?

In addition, the ICJ is asked:

(b) What are the legal consequences under these obligations for states where they, by their acts and omissions, have caused significant harm to the climate system and other parts of the environment, with respect to:
(i) States, including, in particular, small island developing states, which due to their geographical circumstances and level of development, are injured or specially affected by or are particularly vulnerable to the adverse effects of climate change?
(ii) Peoples and individuals of the present and *future generations* affected by the adverse effects of climate change? (UNGA 2023) (emphasis added).

Part (a) involves analysis by the Court of the obligations of states to protect the climate system 'for States and for present and future generations'. One option is for the Court to refuse to answer this question on the grounds that it is too general (Mayer 2023: 48, 58, 78). However, refusing to answer this part of the question would undermine the Court's legitimacy. Furthermore, this question does not require assessment of states' obligations *directly* towards future generations. And

[2] This section draws on Lawrence (2024).

the way in which the question is framed also indicates that the interests of future generations, as well as people currently living, should be factored into the analysis of states' obligations in relation to protection of the climate system.

At first blush, the wording of part (a) of the mandate seems to break away from an anthropocentric approach, by asking the Court to examine states' obligations to ensure protection of the climate system. These obligations are to be assessed in terms of protecting this system for 'present and future generations' – which has an anthropocentric flavour, implying that it is the *benefit* of the climate system for present and future generations – presumably 'of human beings' – which is to be the benchmark. Given the dependency of human beings on a functioning climatic system, however, this distinction might, in fact, be less significant than it appears at first glance.

Part (b)(ii) requests the Court to assess 'the legal consequences under these obligations for States where they, by their acts and omissions, have caused significant harm to the climate system and other parts of the environment with respect to', *inter alia*, 'Peoples and individuals of the present and future generations affected by the adverse effects of climate change'. This requires the Court to consider what secondary obligations flow from states breaching their due diligence duty to avoid causing significant harm to the climate system, including to both '[p]eoples and individuals of the present and *future generations* affected by the adverse effects of climate change' (emphasis added). These secondary obligations could include, for example, obligations of restitution, including compensation (Dupuy & Viñuales 2018: 315–17).

As there is no definition of 'future generations' in the UN General Assembly's request, it will be interesting to see whether the Court defines this concept. The Court could avoid defining future generations. This may have some appeal from a pragmatic perspective, given the issue's complexity[3] (and see later). But not defining future generations would entail the court failing to accord sufficient weight to this part of the mandate, including Part (b). For the sake of clarity, it would be helpful if the Court defined 'future generations' as 'all persons born in the future, globally'. This would have the distinct advantage of keeping this concept separate from a more expansive definition which also includes younger persons alive now. As noted in the Introduction to this book (Section 2.1), young persons and future generations have overlapping, but not necessarily the same, interests. Defining future generations as persons born in the future carries the

[3] Regrettably, the UN Committee on the Rights of the Child (2023), in its 'General Comment no. 26 (2023) on Children's Rights and the Environment, with a Special Focus on Climate Change', recognised 'the principle of intergenerational equity and the interests of future generations' but no attempt was made to address the relationship between future generations', interests and those of current generations including children. See Nolan (2023).

risk that young people alive now (who presently cannot vote) could end up at a representational disadvantage vis-à-vis future generations, if the latter were to benefit from representational institutions that exclude young people alive now. However, young people alive now are already clearly defined as children by the United Nations *Convention on the Rights of the Child* (CRC) (1989: art 1). It would be helpful to keep these categories distinct; therefore, considerations of legal certainty point in favour of the narrower definition of future generations as persons born in the future. The European Court of Human Rights (ECtHR) in its decision in *Verein Klimaseniorinnen* (2024: para 419) designated future generations as people born in the future, rather than including existing rights holders, such as children (Nolan 2024).

The proposed definition of future generations could nevertheless give rise to some thorny issues. One concern is that this category is too vague because the composition of this group is constantly changing, with persons born every second (Humphreys 2022: 1066). Yet, other international legal concepts such as 'children' also include constantly changing members (CRC 1989: art. 1). A further concern is that the ICJ, by defining future generations as 'persons born in the future', would necessarily imply that they possess human rights, which is impossible if they are not yet born. The Court could, however, avoid this issue by focusing on the duties of states to take preventive action to ensure protection of the human rights of future generations upon being born. This would reflect the insight that the acquisition of human rights by persons *upon being born* is sufficient to ground normative duties towards future generations (Vanderheiden 2008: 137).

In answering these questions, the Court will need to assess the substance of international legal rules applicable in the climate context. To the extent that these rules embody the interests of future generations, they may constitute a form of indirect proxy representation of future generations within the definition we use in this book. To the extent that these rules fail to ensure that future generations will be able to enjoy the human rights necessary for a decent life (our touchstone for intergenerational justice), the Court should use the normative framing set out in this book – including the concept of intergenerational justice – as a guide for interpreting and further developing the rules of international law to meet this objective. The Court in this scenario would be acting as a vehicle for proxy representation of future generations. More specifically, this would entail the Court taking on a proxy representative *norm entrepreneurial role* in promoting the rules necessary to meet this yardstick. Importantly, however, there are legitimacy constraints in the Court taking on this role, which we discuss later.

To the extent that the existing international legal rules applicable to climate change meet the requirements of intergenerational justice, the Court may play a proxy compliance function in that its advisory opinion, while strictly non-binding, can provide the basis for increased pressure on states to meet their relevant international legal obligations.

A further possibility is that the Court itself may purport to act as a proxy or guardian for future generations. Justice Weeramantry has argued for this in several ICJ judgements, including in the 1974 *Nuclear Tests* case (ICJ 1974: 341). This proposal, however, faces the difficulty that it involves the Court taking on a role which is not specified either in its Statute or in the treaties it is applying. Reflecting this reality, the other judges of the ICJ have not taken up Justice Weeramantry's approach – with the exception of Justice Cançado Trindade in the 2014 *Whaling in Antarctica* (hereafter *Whaling* case), who came close to this view in urging the Court, in his Separate Opinion, to pronounce 'upon a system of collective regulation of the environment for the benefit of future generations' (*Whaling* case 2024: 381), noting the embodiment of intergenerational equity in a raft of international environmental treaties (140–44). Before considering further how the ICJ can utilise the concept of proxy representation, we turn to apply the normative framework set out above to the principle of harm prevention.

6.5 Normative Evaluation of the Principle of Harm Prevention

The UNGA resolution establishing the advisory opinion makes specific reference to 'the duty of due diligence' and 'the principle of prevention of significant harm to the environment' (UNGA 2023: chapeau and first operative paragraph), requiring the Court to examine states' international legal obligations to *prevent* harm to the global climate system, with reference to the impact this has on future generations (UNGA 2023: first operative paragraph).[4]

The principle of harm prevention is a rule of customary international law, according to which states have the responsibility to ensure that activities within their jurisdiction or control do not cause damage to the environment of other states or of areas beyond the limits of national jurisdiction. The principle has been affirmed by the ICJ as part of customary international law in the 1996 *Legality of Nuclear Weapons* case and the 1997 *Gabčíkovo-Nagymaros Project* case (para 140).[5] The International Law of the Sea Tribunal (ITLOS) in its 2024 *Request for an Advisory Opinion Submitted by the Commission of Small Island States on Climate Change and International Law* (ITLOS *Advisory Opinion on Climate Change*) highlighted that Article 192 of the *UN Convention on the Law of the* Sea (UNCLOS) (1992) reflected the customary international law principle of harm prevention, entailing a due diligence obligation on states applicable

[4] This section draws upon Lawrence and Köhler (2018).

[5] The ICJ has interpreted the principle of harm prevention as entailing duties to prevent harm in the *Certain Activities Case* (2015).

to marine pollution caused by anthropogenic greenhouse gas emissions (ITLOS *Advisory Opinion on Climate Change* 2024: para 250).[6]

Currently, there is uncertainty as to whether the principle of harm prevention involves an obligation of due diligence or is, rather, a rule of result.[7] The latter approach would foreclose application of the principle of harm prevention in relation to foreseeable harm likely to occur to future generations resulting from climate change, as proof of harm to future generations prior to its actually occurring could never be brought to a tribunal. The normative principles of this book could be invoked to argue that the ICJ should come down on the side of the 'due diligence' interpretation of the principle of harm prevention. Given conflicting authorities in this area and the duty of the Court to promote justice – extending to intergenerational justice – the Court should conclude that the principle of harm prevention establishes obligations on states in the climate change context to prevent foreseeable harm to future generations. This would be supported by the elements of the normative framework involving: (i) giving equal weight to current and future generations and (ii) the intergenerational justice requirement that future generations enjoy the human rights necessary to lead a decent life. Limiting the harm avoidance principle to cases where damage has already occurred – thus entailing the exclusion of future generations' interests – would run counter to these elements of the normative framework. This interpretation of the harm avoidance principle would also be consistent with an emphasis on the duty of states to proactively *prevent* damage to the environment and with the UN General Assembly resolution establishing the advisory opinion, which, as noted earlier, refers to the 'principle of prevention of significant harm to the environment' (UNGA 2023: first operative paragraph).

In this section, we make proposals as to how the ICJ could, in its advisory opinion, clarify the principle of harm prevention in the climate context in ways based on the normative principles outlined in this book. First, we argue that the principle is a rule of due diligence rather than a rule of result. Second, we argue that the scope of the principle of harm prevention should be extended to include harm to future generations. Third, we argue that the prevention of harm principle in the climate change context should be interpreted as requiring a threshold of harm linked to certain elements of the *Paris Agreement* (2015). In each of these arguments, the traditional sources of international law applied by the ICJ *are* applied

[6] ITLOS (2024: para 250) concluded that the level of due diligence required was 'as necessary to limit average global temperature rise to no more than 1.5°C'.

[7] The International Law Commission (ILC) in its '*Draft Articles on Prevention of Transboundary Harm from Hazardous Activities*', *with Commentaries* (ILC 2001: art. 3, 253) supported the 'due diligence' view. (These draft articles were adopted by the ILC at its 53rd session in 2001 and noted by the UNGA (2006).) However, the ICJ in the *Certain Activities Case* (2015: paras 196, 207, 213, 216–17) seems to support the 'rule of result' view. See Brent (2017).

in conjunction with the normative principles of this book. Before turning to these various elements, we introduce the principle of harm prevention.

An advisory opinion could also helpfully clarify that the principle of harm prevention extends to imposing an obligation on states to prevent foreseeable harm *to future generations*. Support for this conclusion can be found in three key sources. First, the Court could build on some of its previous pronouncements on sustainable development. Second, the Court could rely on the principle of intergenerational equity. Third, various elements of the normative framework set out in this book could be relied upon as entailing a duty on states to avoid harm to the human rights of future generations (Lawrence & Köhler 2018). Fourth, extension to future generations could also be grounded on the idea that this is a vital interest which the international community needs to protect. The 'future generations' referred to here would comprise the 'future generations of all states', reflecting the scientific reality that the harms caused by a failure to mitigate greenhouse gas emissions occur globally.

First, extension of the principle of prevention to include harm to future generations could be based on the ICJ's recognition of the principles of sustainable development and intergenerational equity.[8] The ICJ in the 1997 *Gabčíkovo-Nagymaros* case considered a dispute between Hungary and Slovakia relating to the construction of a hydroelectric facility by Hungary which impacted the environment of downstream Slovakia (*Gabčíkovo-Nagymaros Project* ICJ 1997). The majority judgement referred to 'new scientific insights and to a growing awareness of the risks for humankind – for present and future generations – of pursuit of interventions in nature' (*Gabčíkovo-Nagymaros Project* ICJ 1997: para 140). The judgement went on to recognise the development of 'new norms' which need 'to be taken into consideration … not only when states contemplate new activities but also when continuing with activities begun in the past. This need to reconcile economic development with protection of the environment is aptly expressed in the concept of sustainable development' (ICJ 1997: para 140). While the passage leaves unclear whether these new norms are binding, the sustainable development principle was integral to the Court's order instructing the parties to negotiate a solution to the volume of water issue, balancing environmental and economic considerations (ICJ 1997: para 140).

[8] Support for this argument could be based on the Separate Opinion of Justice Weeramantry in the *Legality of Nuclear Weapons Case* (ICJ 1996: 454), where he argued that the Court, in applying international law, must 'pay due recognition to the rights of future generations' (ICJ 1996: 454) and that the 'rights of future generations have … woven themselves into international law through major treaties, through juristic opinion and through general principles of law recognised by civilisations'. In the *Request for an Examination* case (ICJ 1995), Justice Weeramantry in his dissent referred to the 'concept of intergenerational equity' as 'an important and rapidly developing principle of contemporary environmental law' stating that, 'The rights of the people of New Zealand include the rights of unborn posterity', which New Zealand was entitled to assert in addition to the rights of its people presently in existence (ICJ 1995: 341).

Justice Cançado Trindade, in his strong dissent in the 2010 ICJ *Pulp Mills* case, concludes that intergenerational equity 'forms part of conventional wisdom of International Environmental Law' reflected in numerous treaties (*Pulp Mills Case* ICJ 2010: para 122) and that sustainable development is a general principle of international environmental law (para 183). He describes the principle of intergenerational equity as being linked to a concept of conservation involving a cultural manifestation of the integration of human beings with nature, in turn, linked to an obligation to other generations past and future (*Pulp Mills Case* ICJ 2010: para 114). Justice Cançado Trindade links the preventive character of environmental protection to other areas of international law including human rights, which he notes extend obligations into the future to 'potential or prospective victims' (ICJ 2010: para 116). The integration of the due diligence harm prevention principle with human rights benchmarks argued for in this chapter (see later) fits well with this approach.

First, Justice Cançado Trindade emphasises 'solidarity in time' between current and future generations as manifest in a number of decisions of the Inter-American Court of Human Rights (IACtHR)[9] which gave effect to the particular relationship of Indigenous people to their land, which includes a spiritual element essential for transmitting their cultural legacy to future generations (ICJ 2010: paras 128–31). This resonates with the solidarity element of the normative framework of this book.

Second, it could be argued that the principle of harm prevention must, in the climate context, be interpreted consistently with the principle of intergenerational equity, which should be interpreted by the ICJ as requiring states to take mitigation action to ensure that future generations enjoy human rights necessary to lead a decent life (see Section 6.7.3). The principle of intergenerational equity is a vital element of the principle of sustainable development which, as we have seen, has been recognised by the ICJ, and is also integrated into the UN climate regime (see Section 6.7). Indeed, extension of the principle of harm prevention to include an obligation to avoid harm to future generations could be seen as required by sustainable development. While sustainable development and intergenerational equity are indeterminate concepts in terms of specifying the exact weight to be accorded to future vis-à-vis current generations, excluding harm occurring to future generations *entirely* from the scope of the harm prevention rule would conflict with any minimal content of intergenerational equity.

Third, elements of the normative framework set out in this book would also support an extension of the principle of harm prevention to future generations. Extension of the principle of harm prevention to future generations could be seen

[9] *Community Mayagna (Sumo) Awas Tingni* (IACtHR) (2001); *Indigenous Community Yakye Axa* (IACtHR) (2006); *Indigenous Community Sawhoyamaxa*, (IACtHR) (2006).

as a vital expression of intergenerational solidarity and flowing from a recognition of the vulnerability of future generations. In addition, intergenerational justice grounded on a concept of equality – with the interests of future generations being given equal consideration to the interests of contemporaries. Excluding harm to future generations from the scope of the principle of harm prevention would cut across this normative requirement. Intergenerational justice is defined as entailing an obligation to ensure that future generations enjoy the human rights necessary to lead a decent life. Extension of the principle of harm prevention to future generations is required by this concept of intergenerational justice as, absent such an extension, international law would be permitting harm to occur to future generations.

Fourth, extension of the principle of harm prevention to future generations could be grounded on the idea that the interests of future generations are vital interests which the international legal order needs to protect. This is recognised in the UN General Assembly resolution establishing the mandate for the advisory opinion, which states that 'climate change is an unprecedented challenge of civilisational proportions and that the well-being of present and future generations of humankind depends on our immediate and urgent response to it' (UNGA 2023). This resolution, adopted by consensus, but strictly non-binding, would provide a basis for the Court to interpret the principles of international environmental law in a progressive manner which gives sufficient weight to the interests of future generations. Just as the principle of harm prevention was extended by the ICJ to include harm to areas outside national jurisdiction and the global commons, reflecting the value of the environment of these areas to the entire international community, extension of the principle of harm prevention to protect all future generations reflects an equally important value.

While, to date, the ICJ has not had the opportunity to proclaim in the climate change context on *erga omnes* based obligations owed to the whole international community (Tams 2005), the approach argued for here would mesh well with a step in this direction (Bodansky, Brunnée & Rajamani 2017: 51). The International Law Commission (ILC) has previously suggested that not preventing massive environmental harm to areas beyond national jurisdiction could constitute breach of *erga omnes* obligations, while in its recent reports relating to international law applicable to climate change, states pushed back against a suggestion that there were international legal obligations owed *erga omnes* in relation to the global atmosphere (United Nations Department for General Assembly and Conference Management 2021: 31). It has been pointed out that human beings' enjoyment of the right to life is dependent on preservation of the global climate system; it would therefore make sense for the ICJ to pronounce that preservation of the global climate system is an obligation owed *erga omnes* to the international community as a whole, given the crucial importance of this to the international community as a whole (Duvic-Paoli & Gervasi 2022: 232). The ICJ could, in making such a pronouncement, rely on various elements of the global climate regime, including the reference in the UNFCCC Preamble to 'change in the Earth's climate and its adverse effects are common concern of humankind' (UNFCCC 1992: first preambular paragraph).

Defining future generations as 'all persons born in the future globally', when combined with an extension of the principle of harm prevention in the climate context to include a responsibility on each state to avoid harm to the future generations of all states, would have complex ramifications.[10] One troubling ramification could be that this would entail placing responsibility on developing countries to prevent harm to the future generations of developed countries.

To address this concern, the Court could, first, clarify that, in the context of climate change, the principle of harm prevention needs to be interpreted in a manner which considers the principle of 'common but differentiated responsibilities' contained in the global climate regime (Rajamani 2016). As already mentioned, the interpretation of this principle is contentious, also within the philosophical discourse (Edenhofer et al. 2012: 312ff.). However, the Court could avoid this controversy by specifying that the principle of harm prevention in the climate change context must be interpreted with reference to *both* responsibility for climate emissions *and* capacity.

Second, the Court could point out that the principle of harm prevention has always entailed a due diligence duty on a state to take reasonable measures to prevent harm, considering its capacity, rather than a duty (of result) to stop any harm occurring (ILC 2001: 155). Third, given that the sources of greenhouse gas emissions in any one state contribute (in varying proportions) to climate change globally, it makes no sense to limit the principle of harm prevention to harm to the future generations of citizens of a particular state bearing that responsibility. Such an interpretation would be consistent with recent jurisprudence indicating that states' obligations in relation to the protection of human rights extend extraterritorially to include climate-related harms on citizens in other states, where there was a causal link to the harm and activities within the control of the source state.[11]

[10] The *Maastricht Principles on the Human Rights of Future Generations* (2023: art. 24 b) propose a duty on states not to cause impairment of human rights of future generations to be applied.

[11] The Inter-American Court on Human Rights (IACtHR) in its *Advisory Opinion OC-23/17* (2017: paras 140, 95–103, and s VIII.B.3) held that states had under the American Convention on Human Rights, combined with the customary international law due diligence obligation to prevent transboundary harm, an obligation to take measures to prevent harm or damage to the environment that may involve a violation of the rights to life and personal integrity. The Court went on to find that this duty extended to harm or damage which occurred in a neighbouring state, provided that it was causally linked to activities within the control of the origin state. A similar finding was made in the *Sacchi et al.* case by the UN Committee on the Rights of the Child (UNCRC) (2021: 11). But in the *Duarte Agostinho and Others* case, the European Court of Human

It would also mesh with the justice framework, with the principle of harm prevention modified to maximise both intragenerational and intergenerational justice. While each state would be responsible for its share of emissions, this would still leave thorny issues of attribution and causation (Nedeski, Sparks & Hernandez 2023: 312, 324–25).

The principle of harm prevention is vague in terms of the substantive threshold required to be met; the ICJ could make a distinctive contribution by clarifying this in the climate context. The advisory opinion could clarify the threshold of the principle of harm prevention in the climate context by drawing on certain elements of the *Paris Agreement* (2015) in a manner which supplemented, and did not undermine, the UN climate regime.

As Bodansky (2017: 20) argues, the ICJ could helpfully elaborate obligations of states 'to ensure that their greenhouse gas emissions do not cause serious damage to other states', which could exert pressure on countries to improve their implementation of the *Paris Agreement* in line with the effectiveness criteria set out above.

Indeed, the Court could go even further by deciding that due diligence in the climate change context entailed an obligation on each state to put in place:

> both long-term and interim climate mitigation targets – and policies and measures necessary to implement these targets – necessary to achieve the Paris Agreement objective of limiting global warming to 1.5°C or kept well below 2°C,[12] proportionate to the particular state's historic emissions and in light of their national circumstances, capacity, and consistent with the principle of common but differentiated responsibilities (cf. Voigt 2023: 241; Bodansky, Brunnée & Rajamani 2017: 45).

The connection to the principle of harm prevention entailed in this obligation is that, without these targets and supporting measures, each state is arguably not taking action to meet its responsibility to prevent harm to the environment of other states or in areas of national jurisdiction 'for present and future generations' (para (a) mandate) but is complicit in such harm.[13]

Rights (ECtHR) (2024: paras 181–213) rejected an argument that obligations under the ECHR applied to cover extraterritorial climate change-related damage.

[12] Article 2(1)(a) of the *Paris Agreement* requires '[h]olding the increase in the global average temperature to well below 2°C above pre-industrial levels and pursuing efforts to limit the temperature increase to 1.5°C above pre-industrial levels'. The IPCC in its 2023 Sixth Assessment Report (AR6) found that emissions must peak before 2025 and then be roughly halved by 2030 (cf. 2019 emission levels) to have a greater than fifty per cent chance of limiting global warming to 1.5°C (IPCC 2023: para B.6.1).

[13] The Court could take inspiration from the 2024 ECtHR decision in *Verein Klimaseniorinnen*, which decided that, in order for contracting states to be in compliance with the ECHR (rights to privacy and family life), and 'in order to avoid a disproportionate burden on future generations, immediate action needs to be taken and adequate intermediate reduction goals must be set for the period leading to net neutrality' (*Verein Klimaseniorinnen* 2024: para 549). Some parts of the judgement have a weaker version of this concept, for example: 'the Court will examine whether the competent domestic authorities, be it at the legislative, executive or judicial level, have had *due regard* to the need to: (a) adopt general measures specifying a target timeline for achieving carbon neutrality and … in line with the overarching goal for

The proposal sketched above would find justification in the normative framework set out in this book, in that, absent the benchmark specifying the content of the due diligence obligation, the interests of future generations would be negatively impacted by continuing greenhouse gas emissions. This would violate the equality principle which underpins intergenerational justice, as it would entail future generations being ascribed less value than people currently living, and would also be contrary to the principle of intergenerational solidarity (Section 3.4.2).

By referring to the 'principle of common but differentiated responsibilities' and both 'historic emissions' and 'capacity', the ICJ would recognise the greater responsibility of developed states to take action on climate change, while avoiding taking sides in the ongoing conflict between developing countries, on the one hand, who emphasise historic emissions as the basis for the responsibility of developed countries to take the lead in reducing emissions, and, on the other hand, the US and many developed countries, which argue that mitigation and adaptation action more appropriately should rest on the 'capacity to pay principle' (Vanderheiden 2008: 184; Shams 2023). Put simply, the ICJ would need to retain the ambiguous concept of 'differentiation' in the *Paris Agreement*.

A further concern is that the principle of harm prevention interpreted in this manner would be problematic from a developing country perspective: it would mean that developing countries owed duties to their own future generations that arise from impacts to which they have contributed very little. However, the proposal above makes clear that responsibility is proportionate to the state's historic emissions and capacity.[14]

The approach suggested here could be opposed on the basis that the climate regime is a *lex specialis* and therefore takes priority over more general

national and/or global climate-change mitigation commitments' (*Verein Klimaseniorinnen* 2024: para 550) (emphasis added). This would suggest that contracting states are only subject to a procedural obligation to give 'due regard to' adopting appropriate targets, but that the Court treats this as a substantive obligation in finding that Switzerland had failed to have in place regulatory targets for the period from 2024 (see *Verein Klimaseniorinnen* 2024: paras 561–62). The ECtHR was likely influenced by the German Constitutional Court decision in *Neubauer et al.* case (BVerfG 2021: 56) that the German government's failure to have interim targets meant that climate mitigation burdens were being unfairly shifted onto future generations.

[14] Emissions of fossil CO_2 – the largest driver to historical climate change – have generally continued to rise with economic growth in developing countries even after the establishment of the UNFCCC in 1992. On the other hand, fossil CO_2 emissions in developed countries have begun to decline after increasing throughout much of the industrial era since the mid-19th Century. National contributions to climate change are closely tied to cumulative emissions of CO_2 in the industrial era because a substantial fraction of emitted CO_2 remains in the Earth's atmosphere for centuries. Consequently, emissions from developed nations have contributed significantly to warming since the industrial revolution (Jones et al. 2023: 2).

These authors find that the list of top-10 contributors to the warming caused by total CO_2 emissions during 1851–2021 comprises USA, China, Russia, Brazil, Germany, Indonesia, India, UK, Japan, and Canada (Jones et al. 2023: p. 14).

customary international law obligations (Zahar 2014: 230). However, there is no inconsistency between the general customary international law obligations referred to above and the provisions of the *Paris Agreement* (Duvic-Paoli & Gervasi 2022: 229).

Nevertheless, the ICJ could have concerns that extending the prevention of harm principle to include an obligation to future generations would be beyond the scope of the Court's mandate. It is to this issue that we now turn.[15]

6.6 Fallback Options: An Indirect Obligation to Future Generations

The extension of the principle of harm prevention to include a duty to prevent harm to future generations could be argued to be beyond the scope of the advisory opinion mandate because, as pointed out above, the Court is not being asked whether states have a direct obligation to future generations. While the extension would be in the spirit of the mandate, critics might point out that the General Assembly could have specifically asked – if that was its intention – what obligations under international law were owed to future generations.

To address this concern, some fallback options might prove attractive to the Court. One such option would be to specify the duty of states to protect the climate system with reference to a threshold defined in terms of potential harm to future generations. Thus, the ICJ could specify that states must put in place laws and policies sufficient to ensure protection of the climate system and other parts of the environment at a level which ensures that current and future generations, who rely on this climate system, can enjoy human rights to lead a decent life. This would be consistent with the mandate and would avoid the Court examining whether states have a direct obligation towards future generations. However, this approach would still require the Court to define the threshold, which would inevitably lead us back into the complex definitional issues set out above.

In summary, the normative framework would provide a basis for the ICJ interpreting the principle of harm prevention as a rule of due diligence, extending to harm to future generations, and entailing certain substantive obligations on each state of sufficient stringency to ensure that it takes action to ensure that the overarching 1.5°C/2°C *Paris Agreement* target is met, in line with its historic responsibility/capacity and the principle of common but differentiated responsibility.

A further important principle of international environmental law which the Court will have to consider in its decision is the principle of intergenerational equity, to which we now turn.

[15] The next section draws on Lawrence (2024).

6.7 Intergenerational Equity

6.7.1 Intergenerational Equity: Introduction

Equity has become an important term in climate politics. And it is also an old philosophical term, in use since ancient times. Today, in the context of the global climate regime, equity is often used to refer to the overall fairness of the obligations placed on states under the *Paris Agreement*. Here, 'equity' is often used synonymously with justice or fairness (Tørstad & Sælen 2017). 'Equity' matters in this context because empirical studies in the field of international relations demonstrate that, without some minimal common understandings of 'equity', compliance and the ultimate effectiveness of global environment agreements are likely to suffer. Equity in this sense has, therefore, instrumental value in being a precondition for an effective agreement (Young 2014). The ICJ's consideration of states' international legal obligations in relation to both present and future generations would require an assessment of the principle of intergenerational equity in the climate change context.

6.7.2 Intergenerational Equity as a General Principle of Law

One option is that intergenerational equity constitutes a rule or principle of customary international law which directly binds states in the climate change context. A rule or principle that is repeated in global treaties may enter customary international law, if it is sufficiently precise and states have manifested the necessary *opinio juris* in relation to the rule; namely, a conviction that the rule is binding under international law (*North Sea Continental Shelf* ICJ 1969: paras 41–42; UNGA 2018: 66).[16] The principle of intergenerational equity has been embodied in a range of global environmental treaties, ranging from whaling and biodiversity to the protection of the world heritage; however, the content of these treaties is insufficiently uniform to constitute a binding rule of custom (Lawrence 2014: 114).

The ICJ has, to date, refrained from endorsing intergenerational equity as a principle of international law capable of deciding cases (Scholtz 2021: 342). It has, however, made some pronouncements suggesting that intergenerational equity is a guiding principle with some normative force as part of sustainable development (Scholtz 2021: 342).[17] In the 1966 ICJ decision on the *Legality of Nuclear Weapons* (ICJ 1966: 405), Justice Weeramantry went further, taking the view that intergenerational equity is a general principle of law. While not finding resonance amongst

[16] See also draft conclusion 8, ILC, Report of the ILC, 70th the session, 30 April–1 June and 2 July–10 August 2018, Report to the General Assembly, UN Doc. A/73/10, [66].

[17] See, for example, *Gabčíkovo-Nagymaros* case (ICJ 1997) para 53.

his fellow judges at the time, Justice Weeramantry's view could well find greater support in the advisory opinion, given that national courts from all the world's major legal systems have, in recent years, given the concept of intergenerational equity significant substance.[18] Thus, recent national court decisions that make reference to intergenerational equity or responsibilities towards future generations include: the Supreme Court of Columbia 2018 decision in *Demanda Generaciones Futuras v Minambiente* (para 5.2); the Supreme Court of India's decisions in *State of Himachal Pradesh and Others v Ganesh Wood Products* (1996) and in *Goa Foundation v Union of India & Ors* (2014); the National Green Tribunal of Delhi's decision in *In re Court on Its Own Motion v State of Himachal Pradesh* (2016); the National Green Tribunal of India's decision in *Sudiep Shrivastava v Union of India* (2014: para 25); the Lahore High Court's decision in *Ashgar Leghari v Federation of Pakistan* (2015: 5); the Supreme Court of Nepal's decision in *Shrestha v Office of the Prime Minister et al* (2018); the High Court of Kenya's decision in *Waweru v Republic of Kenya* (2006: 677–96); the High Court of South Africa's decision in *Ground International Work Trust & Vukani Environmental Justice Alliance Movement in Action v Minister of Environmental Affairs & Others* (2022: para 82.4); the Federal Constitutional Court of Germany's decision in *Neubauer et al.* (2021: 56); the US Montana First Judicial District Court Lewis and Clark County decision in *Held v Montana* (2023: 95, 97); and, in Australia, the Land Court of Queensland's decision in *Waratah Coal Pty Ltd v Youth Verdict Ltd & Ors* (2022), which has not been appealed.

Decisions of national courts constitute a subsidiary source of international law (ICJ Statute 1945: art. 38(1)(d)), depending on the status of the court and the quality of the reasoning (Roberts & Sivakumarani 2018: 99). It also makes a difference whether the court is interpreting a rule of international law. In many of the national decisions that refer to intergenerational equity, this is not what was happening; rather, the courts were interpreting national constitutional and/or legislative provisions. However, the *international law principle* of intergenerational equity was referred to in the Supreme Court of Columbia's decision in *Demanda Generaciones* (2018), the Lahore High Court's decision in *Ashgar Leghari* (2015), and in the decision of Nepal's Supreme Court in *Shrestha* (2018). Moreover, in all these decisions, intergenerational equity was given operative force, in the sense of substantively impacting the decision made by those courts. This methodology could inspire the ICJ to give the concept of intergenerational equity greater normative force and substantive content.

[18] See survey of cases in Wewerinke-Singh, Garg & Agarwalla (2023: 9–14). In qualitative analysis (currently under review), researchers identified over 100 domestic climate opinions within a subset of the Sabin Center for Climate Change Litigation database (https://climatecasechart.com/) that either explicitly or implicitly reference considerations of intergenerational equity.

Moreover, the burgeoning decisions of national courts referring to intergenerational equity could be used by the ICJ as evidence that it constitutes an emerging 'general principle of law' – a source of law within Article 38(1)(b) of the ICJ Statute. While the ICJ has been cautious in recognising rules found in municipal legal systems as general principles, the reference to intergenerational equity in the *Paris Agreement* implicitly recognises that the principle applies to the international relations between countries and is not limited to the national context (Gaja 2020: para 19). We now turn to this reference to intergenerational equity in the climate regime.

6.7.3 Intergenerational Equity as a Principle of Treaty Interpretation

The principle of intergenerational equity is reflected in the UN climate regime in many ways. The UNFCCC (1992) requires parties to implement it guided by, *inter alia*, the principle that 'the parties should protect the climate system for the benefit of present and future generations of humankind, on the basis of equity' (Article 3). The Preamble of the *Paris Agreement* requires parties to be guided by the UNFCCC Article 3 principles (preambular para 2) and refers to the need 'when taking action to address climate change' to promote various principles, including 'intergenerational equity' (preambular para 11). This would seem to imply that intergenerational equity has some normative force in relation to the climate regime, but specifying exactly what this is proves challenging. But this is not the end of the story. Intergenerational equity is part of the concept of sustainable development (International Law Association (ILA) 2002: para 2.1). Does this provide an alternate source of relevant international legal obligations?

The Brundtland report defines sustainable development as 'development which meets the needs of the present without compromising the of future generations to meet their own needs' (Brundtland Commission 1987: 43). This definition is reflected in the UNFCCC Article 3(1), cited earlier, which states that the parties should protect the climate system for the benefit of present and future generations. A 2014 International Law Association (ILA) report on the international legal principles applicable in addressing climate change concluded that states have an obligation to protect the climate system in a manner that 'equitably balances the needs of present and future generations of humankind', bearing in mind, *inter alia*, that present generations of developing countries have legitimate expectations of equitable access to sustainable development (ILA 2014: 13).

Indeed, given that intergenerational equity is a component of sustainable development, references to sustainable development in the UN climate regime would also incorporate intergenerational equity. Thus, the Article 3(4) of the UNFCCC (1992) states that parties have a 'right to and should, promote sustainable development'. Article 2 of the *Paris Agreement* includes the aim of strengthening global responses to climate change 'in the context of sustainable development', while Article 2(2) states that the Agreement will be implemented to reflect 'equity and the principle of common but differentiated responsibilities considering different national circumstances'.

The ICJ has made scattered pronouncements on the status and scope of sustainable development, which suggest that it is a concept with some normative force, capable of being used in conjunction with other rules of international law, but incapable itself of deciding the outcome of cases (Lawrence 2014: 113). The provisions in the UN climate regime relating to intergenerational equity outlined earlier would provide a basis for the ICJ pronouncing that it is to be applied in interpreting these treaty provisions, and that it has normative force in conjunction with other rules of custom (Lawrence 2014: 115; Bodansky, Brunnée & Rajamani 2017: 54). Further, the Court could decide to interpret the principle of harm prevention along the lines set out above on the grounds that this would be consistent with the principle of 'intergenerational equity' enshrined in the UNFCCC and the *Paris Agreement*.

In addition, the normative framework set out in this book could be used by the court as the basis for concluding that the principle of intergenerational equity requires in the climate context certain minimum elements and that anything short of this would make the principle devoid of meaning. Thus, the Court could pronounce that each state, as a minimum in order to meet the requirements of intergenerational equity, must enact:

(i) mitigation and adaptation policies proportionate to their historic contributions to causing climate change and in light of their national circumstances and respective capabilities, and consistent with the principle of common but differentiated responsibilities (Rajamani 2016) sufficient to ensure that the human rights of current generations and of future generations necessary for a decent life are protected, and
(ii) both interim and long-term targets supported with good faith, credible policies to ensure these targets are met and that these targets are both (a) equitable in terms of the distribution of the mitigation burden, and (b) sufficiently ambitious to ensure that the *Paris Agreement* collective 1.5°C/2°C target will be met.

We offer a few points to clarify the rationale for various elements of this proposal. First, the interim targets are necessary, as without them, the mitigation burden could be pushed on to future generations, necessarily harming their human rights (see *Neubauer et al.* 2021). Second, the above principles, by making mitigation obligations proportionate to historic emissions and capacity, would avoid making developing states responsible for the protection of the future generations of developed states. As mentioned earlier, the ICJ would not seek to resolve the conflict as to whether responsibility should be based on historic emissions or capacity.

As we have seen, the idea of giving the principle of intergenerational equity greater normative force and clearer content finds reflection in several national court decisions over the last few years; the ICJ could even consider the principle an emerging general principle of law.[19]

A criticism of the approach suggested earlier is that, by fleshing out what is required by intergenerational equity, the ICJ would be favouring the interests of developed over developing countries, as the latter have tended to emphasise addressing international and *intra*generational justice before moving to address *inter*generational justice. In the global environment negotiations, developing countries have, at times, argued that *intra*-generational justice issues should be given priority over intergenerational equity (for example, when negotiating the Rio Declaration in 1992) (Atapattu 2021: 193). However, developing countries have also often expressed a concern for both *inter* and *intra*generational justice; for example, in the UN negotiations on the Global Summit on the Future held September 2024 (UNGA 2022: para 3).[20] Developing countries involved in this negotiation process have stated that the UN 'development pillar' and intragenerational justice must be given equal importance to intergenerational justice (Khan 2022: para 26).

In summary, the criterion of intergenerational justice would provide a solid basis for the ICJ to interpret the principle of harm prevention as a rule of due diligence (rather than a rule of result which extends to future generations) and to flesh out the principles of harm prevention and intergenerational equity to give them more substance in the climate context. We now turn to examine how procedural rules of the ICJ could be interpreted to facilitate representation of future generations in a manner that could enable an ICJ advisory opinion along the lines sketched above.

6.8 Proxy Representation and Procedural Reform: NGO/Expert *Amicus* Briefs

Implementing proxy representation could provide a vital mechanism to maximise the likelihood of the ICJ interpreting the international law rules to meet the criteria of justice (including intergenerational justice), democratic legitimacy, and

19 The approach argued for here has strong resonance with the decision of the ECtHR in *Verein Seniorinnen* (2024: paras 549–50), where the Court held that intergenerational equity concerns require parties to the ECHR to give 'due regards' to putting in place specific targets and other measures.

20 As this book went to press, the United Nations Summit of the Future on 22 September 2024 adopted *The Pact for the Future* and *Declaration on Future Generations*. For all outcomes of this summit see United Nations (2024) See also chapter 7.

effectiveness. This would involve the ICJ interpreting its procedural rules in a way that facilitates proxy representation of future generations.

Proxy representation involves representation of interests or persons who cannot speak for themselves (Lawrence & Köhler 2018: 654). We have seen that international climate law is seriously biased against the interests of future generations (see Introduction). Proxy representation is justified as a means for redressing this bias; it is also justified as increasing the likelihood of attaining intergenerational justice (Lawrence 2022: 558–61). Proxy representation can also be justified by democratic values which have been accepted by consensus globally in a range of UN instruments endorsed by the international community (see Section 3.2). As we have pointed out (Section 2.3), representation of future generations may be direct or indirect: 'direct representation' occurs where a representative explicitly claims to act on behalf of future generations; 'indirect representation' occurs where the representative does not purport to act on behalf of future generations but, rather, highlights their interests (Lawrence 2022: 553). While not expressed in the language of proxy representation, the ECtHR decision in *Verein Seniorinnen* (2024: para 489) to allow standing to particular associations purporting to represent vulnerable groups – on the basis that, even in democracies, these groups do not have a voice – was underpinned by democratic values similar to those argued for here, with the Court explicitly noting the representational disadvantage of future generations (*Verein Seniorinnen* 2024: para 484; Letsas 2024).

How do these abstract concepts map onto the advisory opinion? One option is that the Court itself purports to act as a proxy or guardian for future generations. Justice Weeramantry has argued for this in several ICJ judgements, including in the *Nuclear Tests Case* (ICJ 1974: 341). However, as mentioned earlier, this proposal faces the difficulty that it involves the Court taking on a role which is not specified either in the ICJ Statute or in the treaties it is applying. Reflecting this reality, other judges of the ICJ have not taken up this approach (with, as with have seen, the exception of Justice Cançado Trindade, who came close to this view in the *Whaling Case*).

A further possibility is that the ICJ acts to *facilitate* such representation. This would mean that the ICJ interprets its Statute and Rules of Procedure in a manner which allows submissions by states, intergovernmental organisations (IGOs), non-governmental organisations (NGOs) and/or scientists on behalf of future generations, or to highlight their interests. By *facilitating* proxy representation, the Court could help increase the likelihood that, in its substantive decisions, it reflects the requirements of justice (including intergenerational justice), democratic legitimacy, and effectiveness. This is because proxy representation involves factoring in the distinctive interests of future generations.

One possibility for such submissions is *amicus curiae* briefs, which are a vehicle for advocacy in the public interest, allowing legal arguments to be aired that would otherwise not be heard (Chinkin & Mackenzie 2002: 136). While the ICJ Statute does not make any specific provision for *amicus* briefs, Article 66 provides that, when a request for an advisory opinion is received, the Court shall notify, in addition to states entitled to appear before it, any 'international organisation … considered by the Court as likely able to furnish information on the question [being considered]' and that such organisation is entitled to make both oral and written statements (ICJ Statute: art 66(2)). To date, this has been interpreted narrowly by the Court to allow IGOs to make submissions but to exclude NGOs *amicus* briefs in advisory proceedings of the ICJ (Sands & Mackenzie 2008: para 9). Continuing its established practice, the ICJ has generally only permitted states and IGOs (such as the World Meteorological Organisation) to make submissions in the advisory opinion process, although the IUCN (World Conservation Union) World Commission on Environmental Law, which brings together governments and civil society, has been allowed to make a submission.[21] Pursuant to the established practice of the Court, where NGOs make submissions, these will be placed in the library of the Peace Palace and made available for any state, intergovernmental organisational, or judge to consult, but will not form part of the official record of the case (Shelton 2007: 152).

There are strong reasons why the ICJ should reverse its narrow interpretation of Article 66 of its Statute. First, this provision was based on a similar provision in the predecessor court – the Permanent Court of International Justice (PCIJ), and 'Advisory proceedings of the PCIJ support the view that the reference to "international organisations" was intended to include non-governmental organisations' (Shelton 2007: 146).[22] Various elements of the normative framework of this book provide further grounds for an interpretation of Article 66 of the ICJ Statute to allow NGOs to submit *amicus* briefs on behalf of future generations in the advisory opinion. One such element is the value of promoting intergenerational justice through facilitating the representation of future generations by proxies, given that future generations will be affected by the advisory opinion. In addition, such proxy representation can highlight the distinctive interests of future generations and help ensure democratic legitimacy in the process.

Could a move in this direction backfire by enabling fossil fuel industry lobby groups to become involved in a way which undermined potential progress? The

[21] See various orders made by the ICJ available through the Court's Press Releases at www.icj-cij.org/case/187/press-releases.

[22] According to Article 31(1) of the *Vienna Convention on the Law of Treaties* (VCLT) (1969) rules on treaty interpretation, a treaty provision is to be interpreted 'in [its] context and in the light of its object and purpose'. The context in this case includes the practice under the PCIJ. Shelton (2007: 144) notes that the drafting history of Article 66 does not help us, as the article was not discussed in the negotiations of the ICJ Statute.

UN climate negotiations have in place workable mechanisms for regulating NGO and industry association input (Streck 2021), which the ICJ could use as a model. A further practical option would be for the Court to limit submissions to NGOs possessing consultative status at the United Nations (Shelton 2007: 149).

A further option would be for the ICJ to use Article 50 of its Statute, which empowers the Court to entrust any organisation it may select 'with the task of carrying out an enquiry or giving an expert opinion' – this could be interpreted as allowing the Court to request an *amicus* brief from a particular NGO possessing relevant expertise (Shelton 2007: 151). States will no doubt be submitting scientific evidence as part of their submissions, as well as including scientists as part of their teams making oral submissions. In addition, the Court could rely on Article 50 to itself call on scientific or legal experts to provide evidence related to the case. Scientific experts making input to the case through one of these routes – to the extent that they are highlighting the impacts of climate change on future generations – could be considered proxy representatives of future generations, within the definition of indirect representation (Section 2.3). This could provide a crucial vehicle for ensuring that the court is sensitised to the distinctive interests of future generations.

The extent to which this would be effective is interconnected with the question of legitimacy; we now turn to these issues.

6.9 Legitimacy and Effectiveness

As we have already observed, the legitimacy of an international tribunal in a general sense is based on state consent to the treaty which establishes it (Section 4.2.2). Thus, at a general level the legitimacy of an ICJ advisory opinion rests on state consent to the UN General Assembly resolution establishing the mandate of the advisory opinion (Bodansky 2023: 186). Article 38 of the ICJ Statute requires the Court to apply international law. However, it is well recognised that, in practice, the Court's role goes well beyond this, by playing a role in clarifying such rules when they are unclear, and even further developing rules of international law (Section 4.2.2). We argue that, where the Court takes on this role, it should do so through pursuing an overarching objective of promoting justice and, by extension, intergenerational justice – interpreted to mean that, regardless of when and where people are born, they are entitled to enjoy the human rights necessary to lead a decent life.

We further argued (Section 4.2.2) that international tribunals, including the ICJ, ought to be democratically legitimate and that this can help bolster their effectiveness. Democratic legitimacy was defined, following Bogdandy and Venzke (2014), as the Court: (i) acting on behalf of the *demos* extended to include both current and future generations; (ii) ensuring impartiality and independence in terms of procedural fairness in relation to court processes; and (iii) responsiveness to the *demos* involving transparency, deliberation, and participation, including involvement of affected individuals in court processes.

Of course, while future generations cannot be directly involved in ICJ processes, they can be indirectly involved through the Court factoring in their interests when interpreting or further developing particular rules. In addition, proxy representation through expert and *amicus curiae* brief processes is possible (see above). The ECtHR in *Verein Seniorinnen* (2024) recognised that the obstacles faced by marginalised groups (elderly people, children, and future generations) in influencing climate-related decision-making in a democracy provided a strong rationale for the Court to allow associations, subject to certain conditions, to represent these interests in court processes (para 554) and relaxing somewhat the victim requirement for a plaintiff to demonstrate that their individual human rights have been violated (paras 499, 502). While not couched in the language of proxy representation, this approach is, in substance, strikingly similar to the approach we argue for here.

We also introduced the concept of *future legitimacy*, which involves looking at an ICJ decision from the vantage point of future generations to see how it would be potentially responsive to the *demos* alive in the future. To have future legitimacy, an advisory opinion, needs to be considered from a vantage point decades from now, at a time when climate scientists predict that many parts of the Earth will be significantly and negatively impacted by climate change. Only through such an extension of legitimacy into the future can we capture the existential threat climate change poses to humanity – including the entire international community and its institutions. Legitimacy involves meeting the requirements of international and *intra*-generational justice, as well as *inter*generational justice.

In considering the legitimacy of an ICJ advisory opinion, it is important to recognise that state consent remains a constraint. If the ICJ pushes too far in developing rules of international law in a manner which states perceive as exceeding its mandate, this will undermine its legitimacy. However, developing rules of international law by the Court, within certain constraints, is nevertheless possible and desirable.

Legitimacy is linked to effectiveness, which we define (Section 4.4) in terms of the *Paris Agreement* 1.5°/2°C targets, as well as the adaptation, climate resilience and sustainability, and finance elements set out in Article 2 of the *Paris Agreement* (2015). We assess the potential effectiveness of an advisory opinion against this yardstick.

While future generations cannot participate directly in ICJ processes, their interests can, nonetheless, can be factored into an ICJ advisory opinion by the Court interpreting relevant applicable rules in a manner which includes the interests of both people currently living and future generations. The interpretation of the principle of intergenerational equity in the climate context argued for above would help bolster the Court's legitimacy. Giving the principle of intergenerational equity more substance and normative bite would meet the requirements of both traditional and future legitimacy. This, in turn, would enhance the likelihood of the ICJ advisory opinion being effective in terms of increasing the likely attainment of the *Paris Agreement* 1.5°C /2°C target, as well as its resilience and adaptation goals. While it must be recognised that the ICJ's functions, as set out in its Statute, do not include addressing climate change in these terms, the role of the Court at a general level, as argued earlier, is to interpret international law rules in a manner which furthers justice, including intergenerational justice. To the extent that the Court succeeds or fails in this respect, it must be recognised that it is constrained by the quality (or lack of quality) of the rules of international law which it is interpreting.

We have seen in this chapter that the normative framework set out earlier in this book would provide a strong basis for an extension of the 'principle of harm prevention' rule to establish an obligation on states in the climate context to prevent harm to future generations. Such an approach could be criticised on the basis that it involves excessive judicial activism that undermines the legitimacy of the Court. In response, however, it could be pointed out that the ICJ has already shown a willingness to extend the principle of harm prevention by deciding in the *Legality of Nuclear Weapons Advisory Opinion* (ICJ 1996: 242) that the rule extends to environmental harm occurring outside areas of national jurisdiction.[23]

The effectiveness of an ICJ advisory opinion on climate change is difficult to judge, particularly given that advisory opinions are non-binding. However, ICJ advisory opinions are authoritative and capable of transforming international law and impacting behaviour at the grassroots level by being taken up by national courts or incorporated into national legislation. As we pointed out in Chapter 4, equity or fairness is an integral element of the climate regime; therefore, by implementing a concept of justice – extended to include intergenerational justice – the ICJ will enhance its legitimacy and, in turn, the effectiveness of an ICJ advisory opinion on climate change.

In this chapter, we have argued that the ICJ should take a reforming role in further fleshing out the principle of intergenerational equity. Whether this will filter through to behavioural change – in the form of modified state action (and action at the substate and nonstate level) and, in turn, a strengthening of the global climate regime – will depend on a whole range of political-economic factors that are difficult to predict. One of the uncertainties is the extent to which, over the

[23] Note that the ICJ has on many occasions acted to progressively develop international law, particularly where rules were unclear. See Tams and Tzanakopoulos (2010).

coming years, young people (whose interests overlap with future generations) can use political activism to increase pressure on governments to take stronger action on climate change. This group is likely to welcome an ICJ advisory opinion that gives more substance to the principle of intergenerational equity.

6.10 Conclusion

The ICJ, in approaching its Advisory Opinion on Climate Change, faces several tensions. If the Court is overly tentative, it could miss an invaluable opportunity to further clarify important principles of international environmental law which could strengthen the global climate regime. On the other hand, if the Court goes too far in pushing reform, it may suffer in terms of legitimacy – and thereby effectiveness – in pronouncing that particular rules of international law exist where there is no basis in state consent for this.

We have argued that the ICJ should apply the normative framework proposed in this book to: (i) interpret the principle of harm prevention as a rule of due diligence, extending to future generations and entailing a threshold informed by elements of the *Paris Agreement*; (ii) give substance and bite to the principle of intergenerational equity by defining it in terms of requiring states to take climate action sufficient to ensure protection of the human rights of future generations necessary for them to lead a decent life; and (iii) interpret the Court's rules of procedure to allow NGOs to make submissions on behalf of future generations and call scientific experts to inform the Court's decision by highlighting the distinctive interests of future generations.

Crucial benefits would follow from taking these steps, including increased pressure on states to strengthen their NDCs; positive flow-on into national climate litigation – which, in turn, can positively interact with the international legal regime; and important ammunition for civil society pressure on governments to raise their levels of ambition on climate mitigation and adaptation efforts.

By taking the steps we advocate here, the ICJ would indirectly facilitate the proxy representation of future generations consistent with the role of the Court in promoting justice. This would also be consistent with the criteria of *democratic legitimacy* and *future legitimacy* which, as we have seen, include extending the *demos* to encompass future generations who will be impacted by international law-making occurring in the present and considering an ICJ advisory opinion adopted now from the perspective of future generations.

The approach argued for here would allow the ICJ to demonstrate impartiality, in terms of the interests of developing and developed countries, in that the Court could emphasise the common but differentiated responsibility of states in addressing climate change embedded in the *Paris Agreement*, while recognising differentiation in terms of responsibilities of individual or groups of states in accordance with historic emissions and capacity. This approach would help to increase pressure on states to implement and strengthen the *Paris Agreement*, while avoiding undermining the Agreement.

References

Advisory Opinion OC-23/17, Inter-American Court of Human Rights (IACtHR) (2017).

Ashgar Leghari v. Federation of Pakistan, case no. 25501/2015, Lahore High Court, Order of 4 September 2015.

Atapattu, S. (2021). Global South Approaches. In Rajamani, L. & Peel, J., eds., *The Oxford Handbook of International Environmental Law*. Oxford: Oxford University Press, 183–99.

Bodansky, D. (2017). The Role of the International Court of Justice in Addressing Climate Change: Some Preliminary Reflections. *Arizona State Law Journal*, 49, 689–712.

Bodansky, D. (2023). Advisory Opinions on Climate Change: Some Preliminary Questions. *Review of European, Comparative & International Environmental Law*, 32, 185–92.

Bodansky, D. & O'Connor, S. D. (2022). *An ICJ Advisory Opinion on Climate Change: Ten Questions and Answers*, Arlington, VA: Centre for Climate and Energy Solutions.

Bodansky, D., Brunnée, J. & Rajamani, L. (2017). *International Climate Change Law*, Oxford: Oxford University Press.

Bogdandy, A. von & Venzke, I. (2014). *In Whose Name?* Oxford: Oxford University Press.

Brent, K. A. (2017). The Certain Activities Case: What Implications for the No-Harm Rule? *Asia-Pacific Journal of Environmental Law*, 20, 28–56.

Brundtland Commission (1987). *Our Common Future*, Oxford: Oxford University Press.

Certain Activities Carried Out by Nicaragua in the Border Area (*Costa Rica v Nicaragua*) *and Construction of a Road in Costa Rica Along the Santa Juan River* (*Nicaragua v Costa Rica*), Judgment, ICJ Reports (2015), 665 ('Certain Activities Case').

Chinkin, C. & Mackenzie, R. (2002). Intergovernmental Organisations as 'Friends of the Court'. In Boisson de Chazoures, L., Romano, C. & Mackenzie, R., eds., *International Organisations and International Dispute Settlement, Trends and Prospects*. Ardsley, NY: Transnational Publishers, 135–64.

Community Mayagna (Sumo) Awas Tingni, Inter-American Court of Human Rights (IACtHR) Judgment (merits), 31 August 2001.

Convention on the Rights of the Child (CRC) (1989) (adopted 20 November 1989; entered into force 2 September 1990), 1577 UNTS 3.

Demanda Generaciones Futuras v Minambiente (*Future Generations v. Ministry of the environment and others*) *2018* STC4360-2018, Supreme Court of Columbia (2018). English translation available at: www.dejusticia.org/en/climate-change-and-future-generations-lawsuit-in-colombia-key-excerpts-from-the-supreme-courts-decision/.

Duarte Agostinho and Others v Portugal and 32 others, App no. 39371/20 (9 April 2024) European Court of Human Rights (ECtHR).

Dupuy, P.-M. & Viñuales, J. E. (2018). *International Environmental Law*, 2nd ed., Cambridge: Cambridge University Press.

Duvic-Paoli, L.-A. & Gervasi, M. (2022). Harm to the Global Commons on Trial: The Role of the Prevention Principle *International Climate Adjudication. Review of European, Comparative & International Environmental Law*, 32(2), 226–36.

Edenhofer, O., Wallacher, J., Lotze-Campen, H., Reder, M., Knopf, B., & Müller, J. eds. (2012). *Climate Change, Justice and Sustainability: Linking Climate and Development*, Dordrecht, Heidelberg, New York, London: Springer.

Gabčíkovo-Nagymaros Project (*Hungary v. Slovakia*), Judgment, ICJ Reports (1997), 7.

Gaja, G. (2020). General Principles of Law. In Peters, A. & Wolfrum, R., eds., *Max Planck Encyclopedia of Public International Law*, Oxford: Oxford University Press. Available at: www.mpepil.com.

Goa Foundation v. Union of India & Ors, Writ Petition (Civil) no. 435 of 2012, Supreme Court of India (2014), Judgment (21 April 2014).

Ground International Work Trust & Vukani Environmental Justice Alliance Movement in Action v Minister of Environmental Affairs & Others, Case no. 39724/2019, High Court of South Africa, [2022] ZAGPPHC 208 (2022).

Held v Montana, CDV-2020-307, Montana First Judicial District Court Lewis and Clark County (2023), decision of 14 August 2023. Available at: https://climatecasechart.com/wp-content/uploads/case-documents/2023/20230814_docket-CDV-2020-307order.pdf.

Humphreys, S. (2022). Against Future Generations. *European Journal of International Law*, 33(4), 1061–92.

In re Court on Its Own Motion v State of Himachal Pradesh, National Green Tribunal Delhi (2016), Decision of 9 May 2016.

Indigenous Community Sawhoyamaxa, Inter-American Court of Human Rights (IACtHR) Judgment (merits), 29 March 2006.

Indigenous Community Yakye Axa, Inter-American Court of Human Rights (IACtHR) Judgment (merits), 6 February 2006.

InfluenceMap. (2020). *Australian Industry Associations and Their Carbon Policy Footprint, an Influence Map Report*. Available at: https://influencemap.org/report/Australian-Industry-Groups-And-their-Carbon-Policy-Footprint-c0f1578c92f9c6782614da1b5a5ce94f.

Intergovernmental Panel on Climate Change (IPCC). (2023). Summary for Policymakers. In Core Writing Team, H. Lee and J. Romero, eds., *Climate Change 2023: Synthesis Report*. Contribution of Working Groups I, II and III to the Sixth Assessment Report of the Intergovernmental Panel on Climate Change. Geneva, Switzerland: IPCC, 1–34, https://doi.org/10.59327/IPCC/AR6-9789291691647.00.

International Law Association (ILA). (2002). *New Delhi Declaration of Principles of International Law Relating to Sustainable Development*, Resolution 3/2002. Available at: www.ila-hq.org/en_GB/documents/conference-resolution-english-new-delhi-2002-3.

International Law Association (ILA). (2014). *Washington Conference: Legal Principles Relating to Climate Change*, Rajamani L. et al. Available at: https://papers.ssrn.com/sol3/papers.cfm?abstract_id=2461556.

International Law Commission (ILC). (2001). Draft Articles on Prevention of Transboundary Harm from Hazardous Activities. With Commentaries. In *Yearbook of The International Law Commission*, Vol. II Part Two, New York/Geneva: ILC.

Jones, M. W., Peters, G. P., & Gasser, T. et al. (2023). National Contributions to Climate Change Due to Historical Emissions of Carbon Dioxide, Methane, and Nitrous Oxide Since 1850. *Scientific Data*, 10, article 155, 1–23. https://doi.org/10.1038/s41597-023-02041-1.

Khan, M. I. (2022). Statement on Behalf of the Group of 77 and China by Mr Muhammad Imran Khan, Counsellor, Permanent Mission of Pakistan to the United Nations, at the Informal Consultations on the Draft Elements Paper on the 'Declaration for Future Generations' (New York, 7 September 2022). Available at: www.g77.org/statement/getstatement.php?id=220907.

Lawrence, P. (2014). *Justice for Future Generations: Climate Change and International Law*, Cheltenham: Edward Elgar.

Lawrence, P. (2022). Justifying Representation of Future Generations and Nature: Contradictory or Mutually Supporting Values? *Transnational Environmental Law*, 11, 553–79.

Lawrence, P. (2024). The International Court of Justice (ICJ) Advisory Opinion on Climate Change and Future Generations. Practice Note. *Chinese Journal of Environmental Law*, 8, 284–300.

Lawrence, P. & Köhler, L. (2018). Representation of Future Generations through International Climate Litigation: A Normative Framework. *German Yearbook of International Law*, 60, 639–66.

Legality of the Threat or Use of Nuclear Weapons Advisory Opinion, Judgment, ICJ Reports (1996) ICJ 3 (‘*Legality of Nuclear Weapons*’).

Legality of the Threat or Use of Nuclear Weapons. Advisory Opinions. ICJ Reports (1996), 429 (‘*Legality of Nuclear Weapons*’), Separate Opinion of Justice Weeramantry.

Letsas, G. (2024). Did the Court in *Klimaseniorinnen* create an *actio popularis*? *European Journal of International Law: Talk!* (Blog, 13 May 2024). Available at: www.ejiltalk .org/did-the-court-in-klimaseniorinnen-create-an-actio-popularis/.

Maastricht Principles on the Human Rights of Future Generations (2023). Available at: www.rightsoffuturegenerations.org/.

Mayer, B. (2023). International Advisory Proceedings on Climate Change. *Michigan Journal of International Law*, 44(41), 41–115.

Nedeski, N., Sparks, T. & Hernández, G. (2023). The World is Burning, Urgently and Irreparably – A Plea for Interim Protection against Climatic Change at the ICJ. *The Law & Practice of International Courts and Tribunals*, 22(2), 301–37. https://doi .org/10.1163/15718034-bja10095.

Neubauer et al., Case No. BvR 2656/18/1, BvR 78/20/1, BvR 96/20/1, BvR 288/20. *Bundesverfassungsgericht* (BVerfG) [Federal Constitutional Court] (2021). English translation available at: https://climatecasechart.com/wp-content/uploads/non-us-case-documents/2021/20210324_11817_order-1.pdf.

Nolan, A. (2023). General Comment No. 26 on Children and the Environment – A Milestone in International Human Rights Law? *European Journal of International Law: Talk!* (Blog, 13 September 2023). Available at: www.ejiltalk.org/general-comment-no-26-on-children-and-the-environment-a-milestone-in-international-human-rights-law.

Nolan, A. (2024). Inter-generational Equity, Future Generations and Democracy in the European Court of Human Rights' Klimaseniorinnen Decision, *European Journal of International Law: Talk!* (Blog, 5 April 2024). Available at: www.ejiltalk.org/inter-generational-equity-future-generations-and-democracy-in-the-european-court-of-human-rights-klimaseniorinnen-decision/.

North Sea Continental Shelf (*Germany v. Denmark; Germany v. Netherlands*), Judgment, ICJ Reports (1969), 3.

Nuclear Tests Case (New Zealand v France), Judgement, ICJ Reports (1974) 317.

Obligations of States in Respect of Climate Change (Request for Advisory Opinion), Order of 20 April 2023.

Pacific Island Students Fighting Climate Change (2024). *Our Journey*. Available at: www .pisfcc.org/ourjourney.

Paris Agreement (2015) (adopted 12 December 2015; entered into force 4 November 2016) 3156 UNTC 79.

Pulp Mills on the River Uruguay (Argentina v. Uruguay), ICJ Reports (2010), 135 (‘*Pulp Mills* case’), Separate Opinion of Judge Cançado Trindade.

Rajamani, L. (2016). Ambition and Differentiation in the 2015 Paris Agreement: Interpretive Possibilities and Underlying Politics. *International and Comparative Law Quarterly*, 65(2), 493–514.

Request for an Advisory Opinion Submitted by the Commission of Small Island States on Climate Change and International Law, International Tribunal for the Law of the Sea (ITLOS) No 31 (21 May 2024) (‘ITLOS Advisory Opinion on Climate Change’).

Request for an Examination of the Situation in Accordance with Paragraph 63 of the Court's Judgement of 20 December 1974 in the Nuclear Tests (New Zealand v. France), ICJ Reports (1995), 320 ('*Request for an Examination* case'), Dissenting Opinion of Justice Weeramantry.

Roberts, A. & Sivakumarani, S. (2018). The Theory and Reality of The Sources of International Law. In Evans, M., ed., *International Law*. Oxford: Oxford University Press, 89–118.

Sacchi et al Case, Decision adopted by the Committee on the Rights of the Child under the Optional Protocol to the Convention on the Rights of the Child on a Communications Procedure in respect of Communication No. 107/2019, UN Doc. CRC/C/88/D/107/2019. (UNCRC) (2021) ('*Sacchi* case').

Sands, P. (2016). Climate Change and the Rule of Law: Adjudicating the Future in International Law. *Journal of Environmental Law*, 28(1), 19–35.

Sands, P. & Mackenzie, R. (2008). International Courts and Tribunals, Amicus Curiae. *Max Planck Encyclopaedia of Public International Law*. Available at: https://opil.ouplaw.com/display/10.1093/law:epil/9780199231690/law-9780199231690-e8.

Scholtz, W. (2021). Equity. In Rajamani, L. & Peel, J., eds., *The Oxford Handbook of International Environmental Law*. Oxford: Oxford University Press, 335–50.

Seneviratne, K. (2023). 'Frustrated' USP Law Students were Catalyst for Landmark UN Climate Vote. *The University of the South Pacific* (USP) (Web Page, 6 April 2023). Available at: www.usp.ac.fj/wansolwaranews/news/frustrated-usp-law-students-were-catalyst-for-landmark-un-climate-vote/.

Shams, A. (2023). Tempering Great Expectations: The Legitimacy Constraints and the Conflict Function of International Courts in International Climate Litigation. *Review of European Comparative and International Environmental Law*, 32, 193–205.

Shelton, D. (2007). The International Court of Justice and Non-Government Organisations. *International Community Law Review*, 9, 139–55.

Shrestha v. Office of the Prime Minister et al, NKP 2075 Supreme Court of Nepal (2018), 61(3), Decision No. 10210.

Stankovic, T., Hovi, J. & Skodvin, T. (2023). The Paris Agreement's Inherent Tension between Ambition and Compliance. *Humanities & Social Sciences Communication*, 10, article 550. https://doi.org/10.1057/s41599-023-02054-6.

State of Himachal Pradesh and Others v Ganesh Wood Products and Others, Supreme Court of India (1996), A.I.R., Supreme Court 149.

Statute of the International Court of Justice (adopted 29 June 1945; entered into force 24 October 1945), XV UNCIO 355 ('ICJ Statute').

Stephens, T. (2020). See You in Court? A Rising Tide of International Climate Litigation. *The Interpreter*, Lowy Institute. Available at: www.lowyinstitute.org/the-interpreter/see-you-court-rising-tide-international-climate-litigation.

Streck, C. (2021). From Laggards to Leaders. In R. Barnes & R. Long, eds., *Frontiers in International Environmental Law: Oceans and Climate Challenges*. Leiden: Brill, 75–105.

Sudiep Shrivastava v Union of India, National Green Tribunal of India (2014), Appeal No. 73/2012 (2014).

Tams, C. (2005). *Enforcing Obligations Erga Omnes in International Law*, Cambridge: Cambridge University Press.

Tams, C. J. & Tzanakopoulos, A. (2010). *Barcelona Traction* at 40: The ICJ as an Agent of Legal Development. *Leiden Journal of International Law*, 23, 781–800.

The Pact for the Future, contained in UNGA resolution A/RES/79/1 (22 September 2024).

Tørstad, V. & Sælen, H. (2017). Fairness in the Climate Negotiations: What Explains Variation in Parties' Expressed Conceptions? *Climate Policy*, 18(5), 1–13. https://doi.org/10.1080/14693062.2017.1341372.

Tørstad, V. H. (2020). Participation, Ambition and Compliance: Can the Paris Agreement Solve the Effectiveness Trilemma? *Environmental Politics*, 5, 761–80.

UN Committee on the Rights of the Child (UNCRC). (2023). *General Comment No. 26 on Children's Rights and the Environment, with a Special Focus on Climate Change*, 22 August 2023, UN Doc. CRC/C/G C/26, 2.

UN Department for General Assembly and Conference Management. (2021). *Report of the International Law Commission. Seventy-second session. 26 April–4 June and 5 July–6 August 2021*, General Assembly Official Records Seventy-sixth Session Supplement No. 10 (A/76/10) 31.

UN General Assembly (UNGA). (2006). *Transboundary Harm from Hazardous Activities*. Resolution adopted by the General Assembly. UN Doc. A/RES/61/36.

UN General Assembly (UNGA). (2018). *Report of the ILC. 70th the session, 30 April–1 June and 2 July–10 August 2018*, Report to the General Assembly, UN Doc. A/73/10.

UN General Assembly (UNGA). (2022). *Modalities for the Summit of the Future*, Resolution adopted by the General Assembly, UN Doc. A/RES/76/307.

UN General Assembly (UNGA). (2023). *Request for an Advisory Opinion of the International Court of Justice on the Obligations of States in Respect of Climate Change*. Resolution of the General Assembly. UN Doc. A/RES/77/276.

United Nations. (2024). *Summit of the Future*, *Our Common Agenda*. Available at: www.un.org/en/summit-of-the-future/pact-for-the-future.

United Nations Framework Convention on Climate Change (UNFCCC) (adopted 9 May 1992; entered into force 21 March 1994) 1771 UNTS 107.

Vanderheiden, S. (2008). *Atmospheric Justice: A Political Theory of Climate Change*, Oxford: Oxford University Press.

Verein Klimaseniorinnen v Switzerland, App no. 53600/20 European Court of Human Rights (ECtHR) (9 April 2024).

Vienna Convention on the Law of Treaties (VCLT) (1969) (adopted 23 May 1969; entered into force on 27 January 1980) 1155 UNTS 331.

Voigt, C. (2023). The Power of the Paris Agreement in International Climate Litigation. *Review of European, Comparative & International Environmental Law*, 32, 237–49.

Waratah Coal Pty Ltd v Youth Verdict Ltd & Ors (No. 6), Land Court of Queensland [2022] QLC 21.

Waweru v. Republic of Kenya, High Court of Kenya (2006) 1 KLR (E&L).

Wewerinke-Singh, M. & Hinge Salili, D. (2020). Between Negotiations and Litigation: Vanuatu's Perspective on Loss and Damage from Climate Change. *Climate Policy*, 20(6), 681–92.

Wewerinke-Singh, M., Aguon, J. & Hunter, J. (2021). Bringing Climate Change before the International Court of Justice: Prospects for Contentious Cases and Advisory Opinions. In Alogna, I., Bakker, C., & Gauci, J.P. eds., *Climate Change Litigation: Global Perspectives*. Leiden: Brill, 393–414.

Wewerinke-Singh, M., Garg, A. & Agarwalla, S. (2023). In Defence of Future Generations: A Reply to Stephen Humphrey. *European Journal of International Law*, 20, 1–17.

Whaling in the Antarctic (Australia v. Japan: New Zealand intervening), ICJ Reports, (2014), 348, Separate Opinion of Judge Trindade.

Young, O. R. (2014). Does Fairness Matter in International Environmental Governance? Creating an Effective and Equitable Climate Regime. In Cherry, T. L., Hovi, J. & McEvoy, D. M., eds., *Toward a New Climate Agreement: Conflict, Resolution and Governance*. London: Taylor & Francis, 16–28.

Zahar, A. (2014). Mediated versus Cumulative Environmental Damage and the International Law Association's Legal Principles on Climate Change. *Climate Law*, 4, 217–33.

7

A UN Committee on the Rights of the Child Case Study

The Sacchi et al. Case

by Nicky van Dijk

7.1 Introduction

Young people alive now and future generations have overlapping, albeit distinctive interests. In this chapter, we zoom in on a legal case study where young people speak on their own behalf, while also using a framing where they seem to speak on behalf of all children impacted by climate change – now and in the future – thus constituting a striking example of proxy representation that lies squarely within the central theme of this book.[1] We focus on one specific complaint ('communication') brought under the complaints mechanism of the UN *Convention on the Rights of the Child* (CRC) (1989): the communication by 16 children to the UN Committee on the Rights of the Child (Sacchi et al. 2019). This communication argued that Argentina, Brazil, Germany, France, and Turkey violated the children's rights to life, health, and culture by failing to cut greenhouse gas emissions sufficiently or to encourage other high-emitting countries to do so.

This human rights case study in the context of *Representation of Future Generations* is timely because proactive and innovative lawyers, activists, and scholars are now testing opportunities to evolve human rights law to better protect future people in the climate emergency. While there are inherent limitations to using a human rights framing, in that it is inherently anthropocentric, improving or repurposing existing legal frameworks through incremental changes may be more efficient than initiating new frameworks. Moreover, there has arguably been a greening of human rights law, with human rights scholars increasingly acknowledging the inherent interdependence of social-human and ecological systems. Further, some countries have extended rights language to non-human nature (Gellers 2021), and several court cases stress the threat of environmental harm to

[1] An earlier version of this chapter was published as Nicky van Dijk, 'From exacerbating the Anthropocene's problems to intergenerational justice: An analysis of the communication procedure of the human rights treaty system', *Earth System Governance Journal*, 10 (2021) 100123.

human rights (see Peel & Osofsky 2018). Many countries include the right to a safe climate, environment, or future in their constitution or legislation (UN Special Rapporteur on Human Rights and the Environment 2019); the right to a healthy environment is now also recognised by the UN Human Rights Council (UNHRC 2021a) and by the UN Committee on the Rights of the Child Convention (hereafter 'the Committee') in its General Comment 26 (UNCRC 2023). Human rights language focuses public attention on the human consequences of climate change and puts a 'human face' on the climate disaster (Peel & Osofsky 2018: 40).

The global character of human rights institutions is a second key attraction for including a human rights case study. On a national scale, people have already used human rights law successfully to protect their future, such as in the famous *The State of the Netherlands v Urgenda* case decided by The Hague Court of Appeal in 2018, and subsequently upheld by the Supreme Court of the Netherlands on 20 December 2019 in *The State of the Netherlands v Urgenda Foundation.* And increasingly, international courts also speak about the threat climate change poses to future generations, such as in the *Verein Klimaseniorinnen v Switzerland* decision of the European Court of Human Rights (ECtHR 2024: para 420). As seeking justice on a national level is costly, unpredictable, and time consuming to repeat in different national jurisdictions, the communication procedure discussed in this chapter offers another avenue for children to seek justice for a global problem on a global scale, with the possibility of setting global precedents.

Finally, the communication procedure is one of the few international legal mechanisms where children can seek justice directly, offering a powerful voice to people who usually do not even have a seat at the table: it creates public awareness that children – not abstract entities – are harmed by climate change today; and is inherently future looking, since foreseeable harms are also considered by the Committee.

This case study provides an analysis of the complaints system under the CRC, and the Sacchi case in particular, as an example of proxy representation of future generations. An analysis is made of the democratic legitimacy and effectiveness of the communication procedure illustrated by the Sacchi case, using the criteria developed in Chapter 4.

As the impact of this case on substantive justice is inherently uncertain, we focus our analysis mostly on procedural justice. Nevertheless, an analysis is also made of this case in terms of its potential contribution to substantive justice, using a concept of intergenerational justice based in human rights as set out in (Section 3.4.1). It will be recalled that this conception of intergenerational justice entails the idea that, regardless of when a person is born, they are entitled to enjoy the full spectrum of human rights necessary to lead a decent life.

In the remainder of this chapter, I will, first, elaborate on the complaints procedure generally and the children's communication in Sacchi, specifically

(Section 7.2), then assess the democratic legitimacy and effectiveness of the procedure (Section 7.3), before drawing conclusions (Section 7.4), which includes a discussion of reform options.

7.2 The Communication

On 19 December 2011, the UN General Assembly (UNGA) adopted an *Optional Protocol to the Convention on the Rights of the Child on a Communications Procedure* (Third Optional Protocol) (2011). Article 5 of this Protocol allows children to make a communication to the Committee when they believe their rights, as outlined in the CRC, have been violated by the actions or omissions of a state. After a communication is lodged, both the state or states, other stakeholders, and, in turn, the petitioners can set out their response to the complaint by filing additional documents with the Committee; they can also make oral submissions to the Committee. Once all information is in, the Committee decides on whether the communication is admissible and, if so, formulates recommendations to the states about whether the Committee finds that rights were violated and/or the states should change their policies or behaviour. The states are under no obligation to implement the recommendations, but are obliged to submit a written response justifying the extent to which they implemented the recommendations (Third Optional Protocol 2011: art. 11(1)).

While the Committee merely has power to make recommendations, and the influence of the procedure on substantive justice is uncertain and limited, this procedure could nevertheless help build the momentum of climate litigation. For example, by making authoritative recommendations, the Committee can help overcome legal hurdles related to, for example, causation, jurisdiction or standing that are now often faced by young climate litigants. This could help build other legal cases *globally* (Gubbay & Wenzler 2021). More broadly, the procedure gives children a genuine voice – as victims of climate change, and as activists and litigants – holding states accountable (Rogers 2019, 2020). It offers a pathway for groups of young petitioners from around the world to file communications collectively. The perspectives of children in the communication may influence states' laws and policies; it can also influence societal narratives more broadly.

7.2.1 Children Claim Their Future

On 23 September 2019, 16 children from 12 different countries filed a communication under the Third Optional Protocol with the CRC Committee (Sacchi et al. 2019). The children alleged that five countries (Argentina, Brazil, France, Germany, and Turkey) violated their rights to life (Third Optional Protocol 2011: art. 6), health (art. 24), and culture (art. 30), and the requirement to act in the children's best interest (art. 3). While all UN members, except for the United States, are parties to the CRC – making it the most rapidly and widely endorsed treaty to date – only 52 countries have ratified its Third Optional Protocol. So, only these 52 countries are subject to the compliance mechanism of the CRC. The plaintiffs chose to bring their case against these five countries because of their disproportionate emissions. The children argued that these countries violated their rights by insufficiently cutting greenhouse gas emissions, and insufficiently encouraging other high-emitting countries to do so.

The 16 children are from 12 diverse countries. Their communication (Sacchi et al. 2019: paras 96–167) explained in clear and emotive language how each of them had been impacted by climate change related events. For example, 12-year-old Nigerian Debby Adegbile has been hospitalised repeatedly over the past years for her asthma, as hotter temperatures in her city worsen air quality. Marshallese David Ackley III contracted Chikungunya, a new mosquito-borne disease that was not present on his island until global warming. Argentinian Chiara Sacchi's neighbourhood was destroyed during an unprecedented windstorm. Tunisian Raslen Jbeili survived a wildfire approaching his home; his neighbours did not.

These examples demonstrate powerfully the impact of climate change on the children's physical health and safe living conditions. The petition also describes the impact on children's mental health. For example, Swedish well-known climate activist Greta Thunberg was so disturbed by climate change she fell into a depression and stopped eating. It is noteworthy that most of the 16 plaintiffs do not live in one of the five countries, but all children claim to have been impacted by the high emissions of these five countries.

Next to addressing the impacts of climate change on the children's right to health and life, the communication also describes the impact of rising temperatures, extreme weather events, and rising sea levels on Indigenous cultures. Seventeen-year-old Palauan Carlos Manuel witnessed waves breaching sea walls and crashing into homes on his low-lying island in the Pacific. And in Northern Sweden, the reindeer food supply is being destroyed by climate change, preventing Sami Ellen-Anna from learning the subsistence way of life of her Indigenous community – reindeer herding. When climate change substantially alters the living conditions of Indigenous communities – sometimes even making their lands uninhabitable, as in the case of communities living on low-lying islands in the Pacific – this threatens these communities' ability to live with their culture and to pass on their culture to future generations.

The language in the petition can be construed as framing the claim on behalf of *all* children impacted by climate change now and in the future, thus implying that, in this respect, the petitioners are acting as proxy-representatives for future children, in addition to acting on their own behalf. The petition emphasises that the government respondents, by supporting policies that delayed decarbonisation, are 'shifting the enormous burden and cost of climate change on to children and future generations … and in doing so … had breached their duty to ensure the enjoyment of children's rights for posterity, and failed to act in accordance with the principle of intergenerational equity' (Sacchi et al. 2019: para 28). The petition also points to the principle of intergenerational equity as used in the *United Nations Framework Convention on Climate Change* (UNFCCC) (1992), and to the notion that states function as 'stewards of public commons held in trust for the good of future generations' as recognised by several UN human rights treaty bodies (Sacchi et al. 2019: para 194). This concept of stewardship is strikingly similar to the concept of proxy representation elaborated in Chapter 2 of this book.

Needless to say, this well thought through petition was not initiated by the 16 children who happened to run into each other. Rather, a proactive community of public interest lawyers looked for suitable plaintiffs for their case. In this way, children who would otherwise have lacked the resources or knowledge to seek legal representation were now empowered to share their story and seek political and legal change. Also, by selecting the most suitable plaintiffs, the lawyers increased their chances of establishing global precedents and further adding to the momentum of climate change litigation that has exploded over the last years (Setzer & Byrnes 2019).

To minimise future rights violations, the petitioners asked the Committee to *find* that climate change impacts children's rights, that the states knowingly perpetuate the climate crisis, and therefore that the states violated the children's rights. The children also asked that the Committee *recommend* to the five countries that they accelerate climate mitigation and adaptation efforts, initiate cooperative international climate action, and ensure children's political participation in climate policy-making (Sacchi et al. 2019: 96–7). On 1 May 2020, David R. Boyd and John H. Knox (2020), the current and former UN Special Rapporteurs on the Issue of Human Rights and a Healthy Environment, submitted an *amicus curiae* brief to the Committee, arguing in favour of the children's case.

On 20 January 2020 Germany, France, and Brazil replied to the communication, arguing the petition was inadmissible because: (a) the Committee lacked jurisdiction; (b) the petition was ill-founded and unsubstantiated; and (c) that the petitioners had not exhausted domestic remedies. They reiterated these points during the oral hearings in May 2021 (UNCRC 2021a). The petitioners responded to these arguments (see Sacchi et al. 2020). The replies from the states clearly showed that these governments were not willing to take responsibility for the climate crisis under the communication procedure, as they highlighted exclusively procedural obstacles aimed at preventing a consideration of the case on the merits.

In October 2021, the Committee published its decision (UNCRC 2021a, 2021b, 2021c, 2021d, 2021e). It found the communication inadmissible under Article

7(e) of the Third Optional Protocol, stating that the children had failed to exhaust domestic remedies. This was not the result the petitioners had hoped for. In the remainder of this chapter, I highlight both the value and shortcomings of the communication procedure generally, and this decision in particular.

7.3 Democratic Legitimacy and Effectiveness of the Communication Procedure

As explained in Chapter 4, at the most general level, legitimacy of the communication procedure rests on the consent of states, particularly the consent given to the treaty which established it. This consent was clearly present, since the five state respondents voluntarily became parties to the CRC and its Third Optional Protocol. Representatives of all these state parties explicitly consented to recognise the powers of the Committee, pledged to protect the rights outlined in the Convention, and promised to allow citizens to submit petitions to the Committee. The Committee is a well-respected and independent expert body; the CRC is the most rapidly and widely ratified human rights treaty in history. Moreover, as the Committee has merely non-binding powers, it cannot override democratically made decisions at the national level. This means that the source-based legitimacy of any policies – including potential policy changes inspired by the recommendations of the Committees – still lies at a national governmental level of each country.

Questions around the legitimacy of the communication procedure extend much further than this. In Chapter 4, we set out five criteria for analysing the democratic legitimacy of international institutions for future generations. In the following four sections, we analyse the communication procedure – and, specifically, the complaint by Sacchi et al. – following these criteria: procedural legitimacy entailing inclusive and fair representation (Section 7.3.1); accountability, transparency, and deliberation (Section 7.3.2); source-based legitimacy, including discourse, expertise, and resources (Section 7.3.3); and substantial legitimacy or effectiveness and equity (Section 7.3.4). While the Committee is not a judicial body and its findings are non-binding, it nevertheless operates on a quasi-judicial basis, with its decisions influencing interpretation of the CRC and national decisions. It is therefore appropriate to apply the criteria for democratic legitimacy of international tribunals to this case study.

7.3.1 Procedural Legitimacy: Inclusive and Fair Representation

Democratic legitimacy of international tribunals requires that they be responsive to the *demos*/public and that they demonstrate impartiality and fairness in their procedures. In Chapter 4, we argued that this responsiveness should be extended to include a responsiveness to future generations, given the existential threat posed by climate change, and we called this future legitimacy.

At a general level, the communication procedure displays a responsiveness to future generations. Petitions can be made by children purporting to speak on behalf of future generations; the Committee could, consistent with its mandate, have considered the petitions as proxy-style complaints on behalf of future generations. The normative framings of solidarity, vulnerability, and intergenerational justice (set out in Chapter 3) would provide arguments in favour of this approach: by bringing a complaint, children living now express their solidarity with children who will be alive in the future. Children living now are amongst the most vulnerable in terms of climate impacts, and this vulnerability will increase as climate impacts worsen.

The Third Optional Protocol opens the door for petitioners to speak on behalf of others. Article 5(2) provides that 'where a communication is submitted on behalf of an individual or group of individuals, this shall be with their consent unless the author can justify acting on their behalf without such consent'. Following this requirement, the Committee could have taken the view that the petitioners justifiably could not seek consent of future generations (since future generations are not yet born) but were nevertheless legitimate representatives of future generations, given the substantial overlapping interests. The Committee could then have gone on to draw some conclusions about states' obligations towards future generations under the CRC. The Committee's reasoning could have been extended to the responsibility of states for violations of children's human rights into the future, based on the foreseeability of harm and control of harmful activities within the originating states. While one concern here could have been nervousness about recognising the human rights of persons not yet born, this could be addressed by indicating that persons, upon being born, possess human rights and that this is sufficient to ground international legal obligations relating to human rights into the future. An example of this is the 2024 ECtHR judgement in *Verein Klimaseniorinnen v Switzerland*, where the Court acknowledged the increased burden of climate change on future generations, which – combined with the short-term bias of today's policy-making – was found to justify judicial review in light of intergenerational risks (ECtHR 2024: para 420). Nevertheless, the Committee interpreted its role narrowly in terms of focusing on the impact of human rights violations on the children existing now and, in this sense, demonstrated a lack of responsiveness to the interests of future generations.

But while the Committee has not (yet) taken the step of explicitly permitting petitioners to speak on behalf of future generations, there are other ways for this procedure to increase its procedural legitimacy: it can be more inclusive, transparent, impartial, participatory, evidence based, and non-discriminatory.

Many of these characteristics are present in the communication procedure. For example, it allows individuals from marginalised communities and children to file petitions. This gives a formal voice to a wide variety of individuals who might otherwise not have a voice (because, for example, they are undocumented or below voting age). In addition, some inherent characteristics of the procedure make it fairer for individuals seeking to use it. For example, the Committee consists of a wide variety of independent experts from different nationalities, genders, and backgrounds, suggesting that, on the face of it, the decision-making process is impartial. The Committee does not merely consider the petition itself, but also submissions by the respondent countries and a second reply by the petitioners, as well as allowing for *amicus curiae* briefs from other stakeholders, thereby allowing many affected groups (and those speaking on their behalf) to influence the final decision.

As discussed in Chapter 4, inclusiveness is strongly connected to the All Affected Principle (AAP), a foundational principle of democracy, according to which all those affected by a decision should be able to have a say in making it. Children are particularly vulnerable to, and disproportionally affected by, climate change policies, but often do not have a say in shaping these policies. This communication procedure gives children a voice. This is very special, since in most decision-making, children either do not have a voice – they cannot vote, they cannot become politicians – or their input is not very impactful.

The communication procedure also gives a voice to Indigenous children. These children do not only speak about how climate change impacts them now but also about how climate change threatens their cultural practices, traditions, and connection with their country going into the future. Most Indigenous peoples do not have a (Western) linear conception of time, where the past is in the past, the future is still to come, and the present is where we are now. Instead, they conceptualise time as a loop, circle or spiral, where the past and future are integral to the present (Winter 2022: 17–8). This means that, conceptually, protecting Indigenous practices and culture for people who are not yet alive is just as important as protecting it for the current generation: the future is no less than the present or past. In other words, these Indigenous children could be considered proxy representatives for as yet unborn Indigenous peoples.

Furthermore, blurring conceptual binaries – between children and future generations, but also between human and non-human nature, or between one and another jurisdiction – may be essential to fully understand the amorphous complexity of climate change (Earth System Governance; Kotzé 2019). Therefore, offering a platform for stories that counter these dichotomies and creating legal precedents that acknowledge, for example, the validity of a non-linear conception of time, is extremely valuable.

In addition to speaking for themselves – and, as could be argued, also as proxy representatives for future generations who are similar to them – the plaintiffs were aided by their legal team to articulate their stories and present their evidence in the strongest way possible. Further, *amicus curiae* briefs could be submitted by experts to strengthen the petitioners' claims. Thus, the current and previous UN Special Rapporteurs for Human Rights and the Environment, David Boyd and John Knox (2020), filed an expert statement supporting the communication.

Lawyers and other representatives often come from the dominant culture of wealthy countries in the Global North, while most petitioners do not. For this reason, we might expect them to have a bias that could hinder them from adequately representing the needs of vulnerable future persons. While this mismatch in power between the plaintiffs and their proxy representatives should be treated with caution, it also offers opportunities. Since the needs of children and future generations clearly require action to ensure that their rights are protected from the impacts of climate change, representatives working with the children in this case can use their position of power to further the children's cause.

The fairness of any procedure also requires that it be non-discriminatory. At first glance, the communication procedure might appear inherently non-discriminatory because of the CRC's explicit commitment to granting *all* human beings *equal* rights (Preamble para. 1). In the Sacchi case, the children's communication also emphasises that, if countries do not take urgent and serious climate action, 'the devastating effects of climate change will nullify the ability of the Convention to protect the rights of any child, everywhere' (Sacchi et al. 2019: 6). As we have seen, the Committee did not interpret the Protocol as permitting claims to be made by proxy representatives on behalf of future generations of children, so the temporal discrimination against future generations is still present in the procedure. Moreover, no claim can be brought against states that are not a state party to the Convention and its Third Optional Protocol. This excludes many young people from harnessing the communication procedure and perpetuates an asymmetric power imbalance that strongly favours the sovereignty of the state. Additionally, no claim can be made by people outside the jurisdiction of state parties. However, legal precedents that acknowledge a global jurisdiction in cases of harms related to excessive emissions of a state could overcome these hurdles. (This is addressed in Section 7.3.4.1.)

A further limitation of the communication procedure which reflects its state-centric nature is that it cannot be used to bring direct claims against non-state actors (such as fossil fuel companies), thus perpetuating the structural bias of the international law system. Although the findings of the Committee can speak about the responsibility of states for emission-related harms within their territory, many polluting multinationals escape the binding obligations that are needed to curb their emissions.

Finally, overarching shortcomings of the human rights treaty body system also negatively impact the fairness of the communication procedure. For example, as elaborated in the following sections, states often do not engage with the human rights treaty system, or only do so in a superficial way, either due to lack of capacity or political will. At the same time, the wider public (outside specialist circles) is often unaware of the communication procedure; if they are aware, they perceive it as inaccessible and ineffective (Limon 2018). This is particularly true for countries outside Europe: over half of the parties are European countries, while over 90 per cent of communications are brought against European countries (Child Rights Connect 2024). This low level of engagement and belief by individuals and states in the treaty body system as a whole – and the communication procedure, specifically – makes it inherently less accessible and inclusive as a pathway for change. In other words, reforming the communication procedure to ameliorate these shortcomings (for example, by increasing transparency or access) would not only improve its effectiveness, but also its fairness towards currently living and future generations.

7.3.2 Accountability, Transparency, and Deliberation

Accountability to persons not yet born can only occur indirectly. For example, the mandate of a proxy representative can reflect the interests of future generations; independent non-governmental organisations (NGOs) can check whether the proxy representative acts consistently with this mandate (see Chapter 4). Some dimensions of the communications procedure would work in the direction of such accountability, including the possibility of *amicus curiae* briefs by experts, which have the potential to factor into proceedings the interests of future generations; for example, by making explicit projected climate impacts on future generations.

Accountability depends on transparency – and the process could certainly be more transparent. Under the current system, most written documents are not made public until the Committee has made its recommendations, limiting the capacity of those able to engage with a particular case to create awareness or learn from it. Given the overlap of interests between young people living now and future generations, the recent increased level of consultation between the Committee and young people certainly works in favour of increased accountability of the Committee towards future generations.

Deliberation is a key element of any democratic process, but its importance is often only minimally present in international legal institutions. Informed, in-depth discussions between the parties involved under favourable circumstances happen in the communication procedure, mostly through submissions written by lawyers. However, there is a page limit for all written documents, which does not allow plaintiffs to do justice to their case on paper. Similarly, the Committee's recommendations are often brief. This brevity is a limitation for activists, legal scholars, lawyers, policy-makers, and others who wish to use the evidence, arguments or analysis in these documents for future cases. Also, as mentioned earlier, most written documents are not made public until the Committee has made its recommendations, limiting those willing to engage with the case to create awareness or learn from it.

Most importantly, deliberation about the substance of the problem articulated in this communication (the climate emergency and ensuing human rights violations) was completely avoided by the five countries in their responses – the vast majority of which related to the admissibility criteria and was therefore purely procedural and not substantive. The five countries did not need to respond to the substantive legal arguments of the children and were able to avoid in-depth discussion about, and accountability for, their part in causing the possible rights violations of the children.

7.3.3 Source-based Legitimacy: Discourse, Expertise, and Resources

Next to this lack of direct deliberation between the children and the states, it is questionable whether the necessary format and discourse – written documents, often written by lawyers in Western countries, using a human rights discourse – truly represents the heart of the climate debate. This has consequences for the source-based legitimacy of the process. The children's perspectives did get a place in their written submissions, including their personal stories about how climate change has negatively impacted their lives. But these stories were selected and shaped to make a positive legal outcome most likely, and had to be written using a narrative of human rights law. While the human rights instruments were not developed with climate change in mind, in recent years, the discourse of human rights has increasingly been adapted to the climate emergency. The use of a well-established discourse and international legal framework offers significant benefits to climate action and bolstered the legitimacy of the claims being made.

Furthermore, the expertise and resourcing of the Committee potentially enhance its source-based legitimacy. The Committee consists of independent experts from different nationalities, elected by state parties from amongst their nationals and serving in their personal capacities with a range of genders and backgrounds, on the face of it showing impartiality in the decision-making process (OHCHR 2024). We can still question how independent and expertise driven the Committee members are. As the Committee covers such a wide variety of cases, we cannot expect that these members are experts on all (or even some) of the topics strongly relevant to a particular case. They might not, for example, understand climate science or how climate change drastically impacts future people – and might not have time to brush up on this knowledge.

Linked to this, the human rights committees have been criticised for not having adequate resources to handle such a high caseload. There is a major backlog of petitions – active cases doubled between 2018 and 2022 – which delays justice for the petitioners (Child Rights Connect 2022a). Because of this, it can take a very long time to receive a response from the Committee. On average, it takes three and a half years for the Committees to reach its final views; in case of complicated communications, it can take up to seven years (Limon 2018).

7.3.4 Substantial Legitimacy: Effectiveness and Equity

A final way to improve the legitimacy of a person, process, or institution is through its outcomes: that is, whether an institution is seen as doing a good job, such as producing economic growth or promoting social justice (Bodansky 2007). The European Union (EU), for example, is criticised for having a democratic deficit partly due to its high reliance on expert committees and minimal transparency. However, the basis of the EU's legitimacy lies in its success in promoting peace and prosperity in Europe, so not at the level of its transparent and inclusive procedures, but of their outcomes. In this section, we analyse whether the communication procedure is a good vehicle for promoting intergenerational justice (bearing in mind the link between effectiveness and equity or justice), and whether it contributes to addressing causes of short-termism and to the strengthening international law on climate change. (For our definition of effectiveness, see Section 4.2.3.) We do so in two parts: addressing first, whether it is accessible to use (Section 7.3.4.1); and, second, when used, whether it is likely have an impact and be effective (Section 7.3.4.2). Given that greater accessibility will likely increase the chance of effectiveness, these two elements are interconnected.

7.3.4.1 Accessibility

For a communication to have an impact in the real world, there must first be a communication. This raises the question of how feasible and accessible it is for children to file a communication with the Committee, when seeking intergenerational justice. This question is threefold: (i) how easy is it to lodge the communication; (ii) what are the obstacles to writing a communication that the Committee will likely find admissible; and (iii) what are the obstacles and opportunities for the Committee to make recommendations that would promote intergenerational justice? These questions related to the procedures of the communication procedure will be addressed in this section, and the potential impact of 'positive' recommendations by the Committee will be addressed in Section 7.3.4.2.

(1) How accessible is it to make a claim? Individual complaints mechanisms under the UN human rights treaty bodies tend to be 'widely unknown' (see references in Steinert 2024: 4). Those seeking justice are thus unlikely to know that this pathway exists and therefore be unlikely to use it. In the case of the petitions by the children in the Sacchi case, it took a group of proactive lawyers to bring together a group of plaintiffs, to gather information through research and contacting experts, to find evidence of the harms that were done, to write a promising communication, and to manage other correspondence with the Committee. Indeed, a study of the individual complaints mechanisms under the UN human rights thematic and country-specific mandates found that marginalised groups and poorer countries were systematically under-represented, while acknowledging that further research is required to test whether the conclusions of this study would apply to other human rights mechanisms (Steinert 2024: 13–14).

Many people, while not categorically excluded from using the procedure, find the CRC complaints procedure inaccessible (for example, because of the cost, time commitment, knowledge requirements, or legal skills involved) and this disproportionally affects historically oppressed populations and young people. While still costly, the communication procedure does have a major benefit compared with traditional legal pathways. In many countries, plaintiffs run the risk of having to pay all the legal costs of the other party, thus creating a significant barrier to bringing public interest cases. Under the communication procedure, the Committee cannot order this, making this pathway significantly less risky in terms of costs.

(2) What are the obstacles to writing a communication that the Committee will likely find admissible? A very large proportion of communications are found to be inadmissible. As of September 2019, the Committee had received more than 300 individual complaints; only 99 of these were registered, with the rest failing admissibility requirements (Children Rights Connect 2022b). Therefore, it is crucial that those writing a communication receive help from lawyers or NGOs with appropriate expertise.

Article 7 of the Third Optional Protocol sets out when communications are admissible. Most of the conditions we could reasonably expect to be met by the children's communication: the communication must not be anonymous (art. 7(a)); the communication must be in writing (art. 7(b)); all countries must have ratified the CRC and its Third Optional Protocol (arts. 1(3) and 7(c)); the same matter must not already have been examined by the Committee (art. 7(d)); the communication must be timely (art. 7(g)); the communication must be in the children's best interest (art. 3(2)); and the children must have consented to lodge the communication (art. 5(2)).

This leaves three options for why the Committee could find the communication inadmissible, as described by Germany, France, and Brazil in their reply to the children's petition. First, the state parties argued that the petition was unsubstantiated and unfounded. The children argued against this convincingly, and the Committee rejected the States' argumentation. In their decision, the Committee confirms that the children 'have personally experienced real and significant harm in order to justify their victim status' (UNCRC 2021d: para 10.13).

Second, according to France and Germany, the Committee lacked jurisdiction. While some of the 16 children live in one of the 5 countries, the majority does not: they live in countries with lower emissions and/or countries that have not ratified the CRC or its Third Optional Protocol. However, Article 2(1) of the CRC and Article 5(1) of the Protocol do not mention the word 'territory' but refer to 'jurisdiction'. As mentioned by the Committee (UNCRC 2023: para 39), the CRC 'does not limit a State's jurisdiction to "territory".' States have obligations when their domestic acts are causally responsible for an extraterritorial harm that could 'in a direct and foreseeable manner' impact people's rights, and this responsibility remains intact also in the case of a shared contribution to a harm.

To substantiate their claim on jurisdiction, the plaintiffs needed to show the causal link between the behaviour of the countries, climate change impacts, and the harms done to the plaintiffs (Gubbay & Wenzler 2021: 360ff). While showing causation between a state's behaviour and a plaintiff's harms is generally uncomplicated in human rights cases, it would be impossible to relate the specific emissions of one state to a specific human rights violation of a child. However, affirming a test adopted by the Inter-American Court of Human Rights (IACtHR) in its *Advisory Opinion* of 15 November 2017 (*Advisory Opinion OC-23/17* (IACtHR)), the Committee found that:

> when transboundary harm occurs, children are under the jurisdiction of the State on whose territory the emissions originated … if there is a causal link between the acts or omissions of the State in question and the negative impact on the rights of children located outside its territory, when the State of origin exercises effective control over the sources of the emissions in question (UNCRC 2021d: para 10.7).

This is hopeful, but since then the European Court of Human Rights (ECtHR) in the 2024 *Duarte Agostinho and Others* case (ECtHR 2024: paras 181–213) rejected arguments asserting responsibility for extraterritorial climate change related harms.

Following this, there are three causal relationships that the plaintiffs had to address. First, anthropogenic greenhouse emissions must be shown to have been responsible for climate change. This has been shown extensively by climate science (Intergovernmental Panel on Climate Change [IPCC] 2023), so it was not an obstacle. Second, the causes of the rights violations of the children, such as extreme weather events or temperature change, had to be a result of anthropogenic climate change and not merely a natural occurrence. While attribution science – the science linking specific changes in the Earth's climate to emissions – is evolving rapidly, it is not conclusive (Burger Wentz, & Horton, 2021). For the Committee to find this causal link sufficiently substantiated, it needed to accept minor scientific uncertainty with regard to some of the causes of the children's (future) rights violations; for example, based on the precautionary principle (UNFCCC 1992: art. 3(3)). However, the causes of the children's alleged rights violations were likely linked to climate change, and without drastic mitigation, further emissions would unavoidably – directly and foreseeably – impact future people's rights. The plaintiffs had to show that these impacts were the result of the behaviour or omissions of the states. As all five states were high emitters, their emissions were causally responsible for the climate change impacts that harmed the children, albeit only a proportion of the cause. The Committee found that, since a state can regulate the high-emitting sectors within its territory, it has effective control over the emissions within its territory. The Committee also found that, despite the collective nature of climate change, each state party had: 'individual responsibility that may derive from the harm that the emissions originating within its territory may cause to children, whatever their location' (UNCRC 2021d: para 10.10). In short, the decision set another global precedent acknowledging the global character of climate change and the corresponding need to understand jurisdiction in a more global way.

Finally, the responding countries argued that the petitioners had not exhausted all domestic remedies. And this is true; they had not. However, Article 7(3) of the Third Optional Protocol states that this does not impact the admissibility of the communication if 'the application of the [domestic] remedies is unreasonably prolonged or unlikely to bring effective relief'. The children argued that filing separate domestic lawsuits would have been futile, as it would have been very costly and would have caused unreasonable delays (Sacchi et al. 2019: 91ff). Moreover, independent domestic lawsuits would not have provided the type of far-reaching international relief needed to combat climate change. However, since the petitioners did not clarify well enough why they believed the available national remedies would not lead to effective relief, or that they would lead to an unreasonably long timeframe, the Committee concluded that the communication was inadmissible on the ground that the petitioners had failed to exhaust domestic remedies.

In summary, the Committee found that the plaintiffs had not exhausted all domestic remedies but found in their favour in terms of causation and jurisdiction, thus paving the way for successful similar cases in the future. So that while some of the overarching obstacles to accessibility to this procedure remain, the legal obstacles are by no means insurmountable.

(3) What are the obstacles and opportunities for the Committee to make recommendations that would promote intergenerational justice? Even though the

Committee did not find the communication admissible, and therefore did not analyse the communication on its merits, the Committee could (and, to some extent, did) still speak about an intertemporal and intergenerational dimension. For example, when discussing the victim status of the plaintiffs, the Committee confirmed that each plaintiff suffered 'real and significant harm' (UNCRC 2021d: para 10.14). As children, the plaintiffs are particularly impacted by climate change, not just now but 'throughout their lifetimes, in particular if immediate action is not taken' (UNCRC 2021d: para 10.13). Because of this foreseeable harm, children are entitled to 'special safeguards' and states have a 'heightened obligation' to protect children from future harm (UNCRC 2021d: para 10.13).

The decision of the Committee in the Sacchi case needs to be seen in the context of a trend of mounting pressure on the UN human rights committee system to respond to the climate change emergency. In September 2019, two years before the Sacchi decision, five human rights committees, including the Committee on the Rights of the Child, issued a joint statement on human rights and climate change (United Nations Office of the High Commissioner of Human Rights (OHCHR) 2019). In this statement, they argued that 'climate change poses significant risks to the enjoyment of the human rights … among others, the right to life, … the right to health … and cultural rights' (OHCHR 2019: para 1.3). Children are especially 'at heightened risk of harm to their health, due to the immaturity of their body systems' (para 1.3). They also acknowledged that human rights mechanisms are important to prevent climate inaction, that states should 'dedicate the maximum available resources' to mitigation measures, and that states 'must guarantee [children and other persons the] human right to participate in climate policy-making' (paras 1.7–2.1). Further, states must prevent discrimination in their mitigation and adaptation efforts. The five committees gave an assurance that, in their future work, they would keep a close watch on the influence of climate change on human rights and 'provide States parties with guidance on how they can meet their obligations' (para 18). In other words, the Committee had – prior to Sacchi – generally acknowledged that climate change impacts the human rights of people, and had offered recommendations on how states should prevent further rights violations and give young people a voice in climate law-making. In October 2021, this was further strengthened by the Human Rights Council's recognition of the right to a safe, clean, healthy and sustainable environment (UNHRC 2021a), and the establishment of a Special Rapporteur on the promotion and protection of human rights in the context of climate change (UNHRC 2021b).

Since the Sacchi decision in 2021, the link between human rights and climate change has been further substantiated. In 2023, the Committee issued a 'General Comment No. 26 on children's rights and the environment, with a special focus on climate change' (UNCRC 2023). This General Comment was the result of an extensive consultation procedure, involving an advisory team comprising 12 advisers aged between 11 and 17 years, with more than 16,000 contributions from children from 121 countries (UNCRC 2023: para 2). On the positive side, this General Comment clarified that children have the right to a clean, healthy, and sustainable environment (UNCRC 2023: para 63). It also clarified states' due diligence obligations to take appropriate preventive measures to protect children against reasonably foreseeable environmental harm (UNCRC 2023: para 69), and that states must ensure mechanisms are in place for children's views to be heard at all stages of environment decision-making processes at all levels (para 27).

However, in terms of intergenerational justice and the rights of children, the General Comment was a missed opportunity (Nolan 2023). The Committee recognised 'the principle of intergenerational equity and the interests of future generations', but no attempt was made to define intergenerational equity, nor was any attempt made to address the relationship between future generations' interests and those of current generations, including children (Nolan 2023). The General Comment states that, 'While the rights of children who are present on Earth require immediate urgent attention, the children constantly arriving are also entitled to the realisation of the human rights to the maximum extent' – yet, no attempt was made to link this to the responsibility of states, beyond a vague statement that 'States bear the responsibility for foreseeable environment-related threats arising as a result of their acts or omissions now, the full implications of which may not manifest for years or even decades' (UNCRC 2023: para 11). The General Comment pleads for increased access to justice to enable children to access the legal system (UNCRC 2023: paras 82–86), but makes no mention of possible standing for children to bring claims on behalf of future generations.

These recent developments give hope that the Committee's decisions in response to communications such as those of the children in the Sacchi case – if found admissible – could include at least a partial finding of a human rights violation and a (non-specific) recommendation on how to remedy this. That said, it is also clear that there are some practical and legal limitations to accessing the communication procedure and using it as an avenue of representation, both for children who are currently living, and even more so for children of future generations.

7.3.4.2 *Impact/Effectiveness*

This section analyses the potential impact of the Sacchi decision and the communication system more generally on climate politics, future litigation, and the wider public. First, if the Committee had proceeded to make a decision on the merits in response to this petition, the decision would have merely been advisory. States do not have an obligation to implement the Committee's recommendations:

while they do have an obligation to respond to the recommendations and justify why they choose to (not) implement them, there is no compliance mechanism to enforce this. Overall, states' implementation of the Committee's recommendations appears to be very poor. While precise information on this question is scarce, existing studies suggest that only one-quarter to one-third of decisions by human rights treaty bodies have been effectively implemented (Principi 2017; Limon 2018). One might wonder, then, if a high-emitting state has not changed its behaviour after the joint statement of the committees, its commitments made under the *Paris Agreement*, numerous IPCC reports, and massive bottom-up activism addressing its inadequate climate policies, can we really expect another non-binding recommendation to have any impact?

On top of the poor implementation rate, states often do not justify *why* they choose to not remedy the rights violations. While there is a high response rate of states to the recommendations of the committees, the quality of the responses from states varies considerably. In an analysis of 100 communications, researchers showed that, in nearly half of the cases, states either rejected the recommendations without offering any substantive justification or failed to address the recommendations at all (Limon 2018). This failure even to justify why a state does not change its policies after being called out on a human rights violation shows that the communication procedure leaves the current power imbalance intact. The power to initiate climate action, for example, remains with national-level governments – which are influenced by many causes of harmful short-termism (MacKenzie 2016). A UN Committee calling out a human rights violation will not be the silver bullet to change this. On the other hand, a positive recommendation from the Committee could contribute to a tipping point. It might not drive the change, but it could help build momentum to hold governments accountable.

What is promising about the communication procedure is that it helps lawyers, activists, legal scholars, and others *globally* with their future climate litigation. The procedure creates official documents with evidence and arguments supporting climate change related rights violations, which is available for *all* future communication procedures and other litigation. Especially in states with national human rights frameworks, a decision by a Committee about causality and jurisdiction (as occurred in this case) is regarded as authoritative and can be used by litigants in national and international tribunals globally.

Finally, it is essential to acknowledge that, even without ambitious recommendations of the Committees – and even if the petitions are not found admissible – the communication already has an influence on policy-makers and the wider public, simply by being lodged. Communications are often accompanied by media campaigns, and every step of the communication – lodging it, states replying, plaintiffs replying, Committees recommending, states responding – can serve as a hook for proactive NGOs, activists, scholars, and others to spread the message. The media coverage of these communications, in which children from all over the world are portrayed as victims of climate change, as well as litigants and activists keeping adults accountable (Rogers 2020), can change the hearts and minds of the wider public.

7.4 Conclusion

Throughout this chapter, we have mentioned limitations and opportunities of the complaints system generally and, specifically, in relation to the children's communication in Sacchi et al. The communication procedure offers a pathway for children's interests to be recognised and represented, and for children's voices to be heard. This procedure is one of the few pathways accessible to children to take international legal action related to climate change. However, future generations cannot participate (as they are not yet born) and the Committee has not been responsive to the idea that they be represented by proxies. While there is room to explicitly consider the interests of future generations – for example, in the Committee's decision, or in the proposed mandate of the newly established Special Rapporteur on the issue of human rights and a healthy environment – they are currently left out. On the one hand, we might argue that explicitly including the needs of future generations is not needed, as their needs largely overlap with those of children currently alive: these children are already suffering serious impacts from climate change now, making children the preferred plaintiffs. On the other hand, finding a way to grapple with human rights violations in the long-term future, especially where the needs of children might be different from those of future generations, might be needed for future cases.

Interestingly, the Committee seems to be lagging behind the thinking of young people on this point. A recent global survey of climate litigation brought by young people found that, in the vast majority of cases, the claimants purported to speak on behalf of future generations – demonstrating solidarity with them and emphasising the importance of intergenerational equity (Donger 2022). Indeed, in national court decisions, intergenerational equity has increasingly been given weight (see Section 6.7).

When focusing on the potential substantive justice impact of the communication procedure, the analysis is grimmer. Even if the communication of the children had been found to be admissible, and even if the decision of the Committee had advised states to change their behaviour, it is unlikely to have had a large impact on states' behaviour directly. The asymmetry in power, where the interests of adults in national governments tend to overpower those of young people and future generations, is hard to overcome in international human rights law.

However, the Committee's decision with regard to causation and jurisdiction constitutes a modest but significant step forward. Human rights law has the potential to better deal with the uncertain global and intergenerational character of climate change; precedents, such as the one discussed in this chapter, help to build momentum for future climate litigation globally and for minimising state-centrism.

References

Advisory Opinion OC-23/17, Inter-American Court of Human Rights (IACtHR) (15 November 2017).

Bodansky, D. (2007). Legitimacy. In Bodansky, D., Brunnée, J. & Hey, E., eds., *The Oxford Handbook of International Environmental Law*. Oxford: Oxford University Press, 704–26.

Boyd, D. R. & Knox, J. H. (2020). *Before the United Nations Committee on the Rights of the Child, C.S. et al v. Argentina, Brazil, France, Germany and Turkey: Amici Curiae Brief on Special Rapporteurs on Human Rights and the Environment in Support of Admissibility*. United Nations Special Rapporteur on Human Rights and the Environment and former UN Special Rapporteur on the Issue of Human Rights Obligations relating to the Enjoyment of a Safe, Clean, Healthy and Sustainable Environment.

Burger, M., Wentz, J. & Horton, R. (2021). The Law and Science of Climate Change Attribution. 51 *Columbia Journal of Environmental Law*, 10646. Available at: https://scholarship.law.columbia.edu/sabin_climate_change/32.

Burgers, L. (2020). Should Judges Make Climate Change Law? *Transnational Environmental Law*, 9, 55–75.

Child Rights Connect. (2022a). *Mid Year OPIC Trends 2022* (June 2022). Available at: https://opic.childrightsconnect.org/read-about-opics-latest-trends-through-our-2022-mid-year-opic-trends-report/.

Child Rights Connect. (2022b). *The Mechanisms, The Communications Procedure, OPIC, Optional Protocol on a Communications Procedure*. Available at: https://opic.childrightsconnect.org/what-is-opic/the-mechanisms/.

Child Rights Connect. (2024). *Ratification Status, OPIC, Optional Protocol on a Communications Procedure*. Available at: https://opic.childrightsconnect.org/ratification-status/.

Convention on the Rights of the Child (CRC) (1989) (adopted 20 November 1989; entered into force 2 September 1990), 1577 UNTS 3.

Donger, E. (2022). Children and Youth in Strategic Climate Litigation: Advancing Rights through Legal Argument and Legal Mobilization. *Transnational Environmental Law*, 11(2), 263–89.

Duarte Agostinho and Others v. Portugal and 32 Others, App no. 39371/20 European Court of Human Rights (ECtHR) (9 April 2024).

Earth System Governance Project. (2018). *Earth System Governance. Science and Implementation Plan of The Earth System Governance Project*. Utrecht: ESGP.

Fox Principi, K. (2017). United Nations Individual Complaint Procedures – How Do States Comply? *Human Rights Law Journal*, 37, 1–31.

Gellers, J. C. (2021). Earth System Law and the Legal Status of Non-Humans in the Anthropocene. *Earth System Government*, 7, 100083. https://doi.org/10.1016/j.esg.2020.100083.

Gilabert, P. & Lawford-Smith, H. (2012). Political Feasibility: A Conceptual Exploration. *Political Studies*, 60, 809–25. https://doi.org/10.1111/j.1467-9248.2011.00936.x.

Gubbay, I. & Wenzler, C. (2021). Intergenerational Climate Change Litigation: The First Climate Communication to the UN Committee on the Rights of the Child. In Alogna, I., Bakker, C. & Gauci, J.-P., eds., *Climate Change Litigation: Global Perspectives*. Leiden: Brill, 343–65. https://doi.org/10.1163/9789004447615_016.

Intergovernmental Panel on Climate Change (IPCC). (2023). Summary for Policy Makers. In *AR6 Synthesis Report*. Climate Change. Geneva: IPCC, 1–34.

Kotzé, L. J. (2019). Earth System Law for the Anthropocene. *Sustainability*, 11(23), 6796. https://doi.org/10.3390/su11236796.

Limon, M. (2018). *Reform of the UN Human Rights Petitions System*. Geneva: Universal Rights Group.

MacKenzie, M. K. (2016). Institutional Design and Sources of Short-Termism. In González-Ricoy, I. & Gosseries, A., eds., *Institutions for Future Generations*. Oxford: Oxford University Press, 24–46. https://doi.org/10.1093/acprof:oso/9780198746959.003.0002.

Nolan, A. (2023). General Comment No. 26 on Children and the Environment – A Milestone in International Human Rights Law? *European Journal of International Law: Talk!* (Blog, 11 September 2023). Available at: www.ejiltalk.org/general-comment-no-26-on-children-and-the-environment-a-milestone-in-international-human-rights-law/.

Optional Protocol to the Convention on the Rights of the Child on a Communications Procedure (adopted 19 December 2011; entered into force 14 April 2014) 2983 UNTS 135. Contained in a resolution adopted by the UN General Assembly, UN Doc. A/RES/66/138. ('Third Optional Protocol'.)

Peel, J. & Osofsky, H. M. (2018). A Rights Turn in Climate Change Litigation? *Transnational Environmental Law*, 7, 37–67.

Rogers, N. (2019). *Law, Fiction and Activism in a Time of Climate Change*, Abingdon/New York: Routledge.

Rogers, N. (2020). Victim, Litigant, Activist, Messiah: The Child in a Time of Climate Change. In Richardson, B. J., ed., *From Student Strikes to the Extinction Rebellion. New Protest Movements Shaping our Future*. Cheltenham: Edward Elgar, 103–21.

Sacchi, C. et al. (2020). *Petitioners' Reply to Admissibility Objections of Brazil, France, and Germany, in Sacchi et al v Argentina, Brazil, France, Germany and Turke*y (4 May 2020).

Sacchi, C., Lorenzo, C., Ivanova, R., Ackley, D., Anjain, R., Kabua, L., Islands, M., Adegbile, D., Manuel, C., Melithafa, A., Thunberg, G., Smith, C., Villaseñor, A., (Sacchi et al. decision) (2019). *Communication to the Committee on the Rights of the Child, in Sacchi et al v. Argentina, Brazil, France, Germany and Turke*y (23 September 2019).

Setzer, J. & Byrnes, R. (2019). *Global Trends in Climate Change Litigation: 2019 Snapshot*. Grantham Research Institute on Climate Change and the Environment. London: Centre for Climate Change Economics and Policy.

Steinert, C. V. (2024). Elitist Remedies? Complaint Resources and Representation in International Human Rights Bodies. *International Studies Quarterly*, 68, 1–16.

The State of the Netherlands (Ministry for Infrastructure and the Environment) v Urgenda Foundation, Decision of the Hague Court of Appeal, Case no. ECLI:NL:GHDHA:2018:2610 (in Dutch) 200.178.245/01 (English translation) (9 October 2018).

The State of the Netherlands (Ministry of Economic Affairs and Climate Policy) v Urgenda Foundation, Decision of the Supreme Court of the Netherlands, Case no. ECLI:NL:HR:2019:2006 (in Dutch) 19/00135 (English translation) (20 December 2019).

United Nations Committee on the Rights of the Child (UNCRC). (2021a). *Decision adopted by the Committee on the Rights of the Child under the Optional Protocol to the Convention on the Rights of the Child on a communications procedure in respect of Communication No. 107/2019*, UN Doc. CRC/C/88/D/107/2019.

United Nations Committee on the Rights of the Child (UNCRC). (2021b). *Decision adopted by the Committee on the Rights of the Child under the Optional Protocol to the Convention on the Rights of the Child on a Communications Procedure in Respect of Communication No. 108/2019*, UN Doc. CRC/C/88/D/108/2019.

United Nations Committee on the Rights of the Child (UNCRC). (2021c). *Decision adopted by the Committee on the Rights of the Child under the Optional Protocol to the Convention on the Rights of the Child on a Communications Procedure in Respect of Communication No. 106/2019*, UN Doc. CRC/C/88/D/106/2019.

United Nations Committee on the Rights of the Child (UNCRC). (2021d). *Decision adopted by the Committee on the Rights of the Child under the Optional Protocol to the Convention on the Rights of the Child on a Communications Procedure in Respect of Communication No. 104/2019*, UN Doc. CRC/C/88/D/104/2019.

United Nations Committee on the Rights of the Child (UNCRC). (2021e). *Decision adopted by the Committee on the Rights of the Child under the Optional Protocol to the Convention on the Rights of the Child on a Communications Procedure in Respect of Communication No. 105/2019*, UN Doc. CRC/C/88/D/105/2019.

United Nations Committee on the Rights of the Child (UNCRC). (2023). *General Comment no. 26 (2023) on Children's Rights and the Environment, with a Special Focus on Climate Change*, UN Doc. CRC/C/G C/26 (22 August 2023).

United Nations Framework Convention on Climate Change (UNFCCC) (1992) (adopted 9 May 1992; entered into force 21 March 1994), 1771 UNTS 107.

United Nations Human Rights Council (UNHRC). (2021a). *The Human Right to a Safe, Clean, Healthy and Sustainable Environment*. Resolution adopted by the Human Rights Council. UN Doc. A/HRC/RES/48/13.

United Nations Human Rights Council (UNHRC). (2021b). *Mandate of the Special Rapporteur on the Promotion and Protection of Human Rights in the Context of Climate Change*. Resolution adopted by the Human Rights Council, UN Doc. A/HRC/48/L.27.

United Nations Office of the High Commissioner (OHCHR). (2024). *Membership, Committee on the Rights of the Child*. Available at: www.ohchr.org/en/treaty-bodies/crc/membership.

United Nations Office of the High Commissioner of Human Rights (OHCHR). (2019). *Statement on Human Rights and Climate Change* (9 September 2019). Joint statement by five UN Human Rights Treaty Bodies, UN Doc. HRI/2019/1. Available at: www.ohchr.org/en/statements-and-speeches/2019/09/five-un-human-rights-treaty-bodies-issue-joint-statement-human.

United Nations Special Rapporteur on Human Rights and the Environment. (2019). *Report of the Special Rapporteur on the Issue of Human Rights Obligations Relating to the Enjoyment of a Safe, Clean, Healthy and Sustainable Environment*, Annual Report to the UN General Assembly, UN Doc. No. A/74/161. UN General Assembly.

Verein Klimaseniorinnen v Switzerland, App no. 53600/20 European Court of Human Rights (ECtHR) (9 April 2024).

Winter, C. J. (2022). *Subjects of Intergenerational Justice*, Abington/New York: Routledge.

8

A UN Special Envoy for Future Generations

8.1 Introduction

The United Nations held a Summit of the Future on 22 September 2024 and adopted a *Pact for the Future*, including a non-binding *Declaration on Future Generations*. The Declaration in para 32 noted the proposal by the UN Secretary General to appoint a Special Envoy for Future Generations but did not agree to create one (UNGA 2022a: para 3).[1] However, in October 2024 it was reported that a senior UN official had announced at a major international conference that the Secretary-General was intending to proceed to create such an envoy (Day 2024).

This chapter makes a preliminary assessment of the proposed UN Special Envoy for Future Generations (hereafter, UN Special Envoy) by examining it through the lens of three frameworks. These frameworks provide both the rationale or normative basis for such a proposal and a basis for evaluating or critiquing such an institution (Section 8.2). The three frameworks involve the principles of intergenerational justice, solidarity, and vulnerability (set out in Section 3.2). The UN Special Envoy proposal is then evaluated (Section 8.3) in terms of its legitimacy and effectiveness using the criteria elaborated in Chapter 4. Legitimacy is crucial here, given that previous attempts to establish bodies of this nature – including a proposed UN Commissioner for Future Generations made at the 2014 Rio +20 summit – failed due to lack of support from developing countries (Lawrence 2014: 17). Garnering such support will be essential for any such mechanism to succeed. Thus, likely effectiveness is inexorably connected to legitimacy. This

[1] For all outcomes of the UN Summit for the Future, including the *Pact for the Future* and *Declaration for Future Generations*, see United Nations (2024). For the mandate of the Summit see UNGA (2022a: para 4). The mandate included considering the appointment of a UN Special Envoy for Future Generations contained in the Secretary-General's report (UNSG 2022). Other elements considered in the lead up to the summit included establishment of a revamped Trusteeship Council, repurposed to focus on intergenerational justice issues and global public good issues, such as those relating to outer space (debris and peaceful use) (UNSG 2021, 2023).

chapter then examines the UN Special Envoy proposal by considering lessons that can be learned from the establishment of UN mechanisms to further the interests of other vulnerable groups (Section 8.4.1), and institutions purporting to represent future generations at the national level, such as ombudsperson or commissioners for future generations (Section 8.4.2). In Section 8.5 the possible functions of a UN Special Envoy are examined and recommendations made as to what mandate the Envoy should have applying the matrix of proxy functions elaborated earlier in this book (Chapter 2, Section 2.5). Finally, an overarching framework for measuring the potential effectiveness of the UN Special Envoy which incorporates both frameworks – proxy representation functions and democratic legitimacy – is proposed (Section 8.6).

8.2 Justifying a UN Special Envoy for Future Generations

A starting point for this book is that current institutions, policy, and law-making at both national and international levels are biased against the interests of future generations. Evidence for this bias is ubiquitous, including the inadequate response to climate change and biodiversity, just to mention two areas. The best response to this crisis is to incorporate the interests of future generations and nature in decision-making, a process called 'mainstreaming' (Dryzek). A second-best – but still worthwhile – parallel strategy involves proxy-style representation of both nature and future generations to increase the weight given to these interests in law-making processes (Lawrence 2022). A third approach involves the use of so-called commitment devices which bind decision-makers to a particular course of action (see Section 8.4.2). Such devices come in a range of forms: they can be legal, institutional, soft, or hard. They also require policy-makers to consider long-term interests – including the interests of their future selves – as an integral part of the decision-making. A UN Special Envoy would constitute both a commitment device and an advocate for other – more effective – commitment devices.[2]

A further justification for a UN Special Envoy rests in the democratic ideal. We saw earlier (Chapter 3) that a common thread running through theories of democracy is the 'all affected principle', whereby those affected by a decision should have a say in the making of that decision. A UN Special Envoy or similar type of institution is justifiable as a mechanism by which future generations can be given a voice. Currently, no UN mechanisms are assigned this task.

Further normative justification is grounded in the three key normative principles elaborated in Chapter 3, namely, the concepts of intergenerational justice, solidarity, and vulnerability. The three normative pillars set out in Chapter 3 provide a

[2] Thank you to Jonathan Boston for pointing this out.

strong rationale for proxy representation of future generations in the form of a UN Special Envoy or similar type of institution. The strands of the argument are interconnected. For example, future generations are, in many ways, akin to other vulnerable groups which are disproportionately impacted by climate change because of their vulnerability. These include the young, elderly, people with disabilities, people living in poverty, and women (more so than men). Proxy representation can help address these vulnerabilities by putting pressure on decision-makers to factor in the interests of future generations in law and policy-making aimed at ensuring that their human rights are protected. Given human dependency on functioning ecosystems, these rights include the right to a healthy environment. This, in turn, is an expression of solidarity. Solidarity is important: without some notion of being connected to future generations, there is no basis for action benefiting them.

But proxy-style institutions, such as a UN Special Envoy, need to meet criteria of democratic legitimacy, which (as argued in Chapter 4) is inexorably intertwined with their effectiveness.

8.3 Democratic Legitimacy of a UN Special Envoy

In Chapter 4 (Section 4.2.1), we set out criteria for the democratic legitimacy of international institutions based on an amalgam of criteria from Klaus Dingwerth (2007, 2014), Sylvia Karlsson-Vinkhuyzen and Antto Vihma (2009), and Daniel Bodansky (1999), adapted to the context of institutions for future generations. We also introduced the concept of future legitimacy (Section 4.2.1).[3]

These criteria can be summarised as follows.

(A) Procedural (input legitimacy): inclusive/fair representation, accountability, transparency, and deliberation.
(B) Source based (input legitimacy): expertise, legal legitimacy, tradition, and discourse.
(C) Substantive (output legitimacy): effectiveness, and equity.

We now turn to examine each criterion separately.

Procedural or input legitimacy involves **inclusive and fair representation** and, in particular, the idea that, for a decision to be democratically legitimate, those affected by the decision should have a say in the making of the decision – the 'all affected principle' (Goodin 2007). Future generations cannot directly have a say in decisions taken now but can indirectly have a say through proxy representatives. Importantly, 'representation' does not just include acting on behalf of somebody as an agent. Rather, as Hannah Pitkin points out, it also includes

[3] This section draws upon Lawrence (2021).

'substantive acting for others' interests' (Pitkin 1967: 209). This opens the possibility of a proxy representative of future generations on the basis that future generations possess interests (Goodin 1996: 835; Ball 2006: 137). The proxy can make reasonable assumptions as to the interests of future generations, including the need for a stable climate and functioning ecosystems upon which their welfare will depend (Vanderheiden 2008: 129).

In the context of proxy representation of future generations, youth representation of future generations can enhance legitimacy. While empirical research suggests that young people do not necessarily accord more weight to future generations than do older people,[4] the interests of young people overlap significantly more with the interests of persons not yet born than those of older people in the sense that climate change will threaten the interests of younger people over a longer span of their lives. Reflecting both this truth and altruism, young people have initiated school strikes around the world, as well as launching climate litigation where they have not only purported to speak for their own interests, but also on behalf of future generations (Donger 2022). Thus, as argued in Section 4.2.1, appointing a young person as a UN Special Envoy would increase the legitimacy of this office as it performs the important function of acting as an advocate for the welfare of future generations. Interestingly, the Mary Robinson Foundation's 2018 proposal for Global Guardians for Future Generations – which no doubt helped lay the groundwork for the recent push for a UN Special Envoy – proposed appointing three individuals as Global Guardians for Future Generations, one of whom would be under 30 years of age (Mary Robinson Foundation 2018: 10).

Accountability and Transparency are potentially problematic in the context we are discussing because it would seem impossible to make a proxy for future generations accountable to persons not yet born. Nevertheless, accountability can be achieved, at least indirectly, by ensuring that the proxy operates consistently with a mandate which reflects the interests of future generations. Moreover, the proxy could be held to account by non-governmental organisations (NGOs) having a role in monitoring the proxy's performance. Transparency of the proxy's activities is an important precondition for this monitoring to take place (Hale 2008).

Deliberation is a vital element in many theories of democracy and is often seen as the vehicle by which citizen's views are conveyed to representative institutions (Saward 2008). As argued in Chapter 3, deliberative democracy provides a strong justification for a proxy to represent the interests of future generations in the deliberative process.[5] Thus, if we consider the role of proxies for future generations as

[4] The empirical evidence as to whether young people are more concerned about the future than older people is mixed. See discussion of the literature in Gonzalez-Ricoy and Rey (2019: 7).

[5] Inclusion in deliberative processes through incorporation of discourses which encapsulate the interests of future generations is a further possibility (Niemeyer & Jennstål 2017). See discussion at Section 2.5.2.

articulating the interests of persons not yet born (rather than representing them), this would open the possibility of a UN Special Envoy meeting this criterion.

Expertise can feed into legitimacy if, for example, a proxy can provide expert advice to government on best practices in representing future generations' interests in policy-making.

Legal legitimacy involves authority based on being in accordance with law. At the international level, this involves institutions acting in a manner consistent with the treaty that established them; the treaty, in turn, derives its legitimacy from states' consent (Bodansky 1999: 604–605).

Tradition as a source of legitimacy can include, for example, the legitimacy of the United Nations *Framework Convention on Climate Change* (1992) (UNFCCC)/*Paris Agreement* (2015) regime as the legitimate form of intergovernmental governance to address climate change (Karlsson-Vinkhuyzen & Vihma 2009: 410). A UN Special Envoy may derive legitimacy from the status of similar types of UN Special Envoy created in the past.

Discourse refers to legitimacy, which can be derived from an institution being linked to a dominant ideology; for example, sustainable development. This issue is taken up (Section 8.5) in terms of the appropriate mandate for a UN Special Envoy.

Output legitimacy includes the effectiveness and equity of outcomes. Given this book's focus on climate change, we define effectiveness (see Section 4.4) in terms of the extent to which an international mechanism promotes: (i) intergenerational justice and the values of inclusiveness, solidarity, and addressing vulnerability; and (ii) the *Paris Agreement* objectives, including both the 1.5/2°C overarching target and the ability to ensure adaptation for future generations, as well as climate resilience, low greenhouse gas emission development, and adequate financing. A further important criterion is the extent to which the institution addresses the cause of wrongful short-termism.

Effectiveness is strongly linked to the concept of future legitimacy (see Section 4.2.3), which involves an institution looking at the present from the perspective of future generations. Examining a UN Special Envoy from this perspective would lead us to favour an institutional mechanism with strong powers and the capacity to exert maximum pressure on law and policy-makers in the direction of redressing the bias against the interests of future generations. We argue (see Section 4.2.1) that, to avoid the concept of 'future legitimacy' pushing too far in the direction of emphasising intergenerational justice at the expense of intragenerational justice and the needs of a person alive now, legitimacy would comprise the overlap between current and future legitimacy.

In the context of a UN Special Envoy, the concept of 'future legitimacy' provides an additional dimension to accountability in the sense that we must consider accountability from the perspective of future generations. Accountability through adherence to a mandate involving intergenerational equity (as discussed earlier) and accountability to persons alive in the future would push in the same direction. Given that a UN Special Envoy is likely to be limited to making non-binding recommendations – and unlikely to be given any powers to override states – the risk of such a mechanism pushing too far in the direction of the interests of future generations would seem negligible.

Equity reflects the idea that substantive legitimacy involves both contributing to solving a particular problem and furthering justice. Given the context of extreme global inequality, mechanisms need to not only just change behaviour or solve a particular problem but also enhance justice. The link to effectiveness is that norms or mechanisms perceived to be both legitimate and fair are more likely to be complied with (see literature referred to in Section 4.2.1).

Table 8.1 summarises the application of the legitimacy criteria to the proposed UN Special Envoy outlined in the earlier discussion. The left-hand column sets

Table 8.1 *Legitimacy criteria for a UN Special Envoy for future generations*

Legitimacy criteria	Design features which maximise achievement of the particular criterion	Design features which would minimise achievement of the particular criterion
i. Inclusive/fair representation (procedural – input legitimacy)	• Inclusion of youth in design • Appointment of youth	• Exclusion of youth in design • No appointment of youth
ii. Democratic control (accountability and transparency) (input legitimacy)	• Accountability through strong mandate • NGO monitoring role	• Weak mandate • No NGO role
iii. Deliberation (input legitimacy)	• Mandate allows participation in UN processes	• Mandate precludes participation in UN processes
iv. Source based (input legitimacy – expertise, legal legitimacy, tradition, discourse)	• Expert staff • Well resourced • Mandate contained in treaty consented to by states • Mandate linked to sustainability discourse	• Lack of expert staff • Poorly resourced • Mandate does not mesh with existing discourses
v. Substantial (output legitimacy), effectiveness, equity	• Achieves stronger consideration of future generations' interests in international law-making and furthering of intergenerational equity	• Fails to achieve stronger consideration of future generations' interests in international law-making

out the legitimacy criteria. The middle column includes the design features which would maximise achieving the criterion. And the far right-hand column sets out the features which would minimise achieving the criterion.

8.4 Lessons from Existing International Institutions to Protect Other Vulnerable Groups and National Institutions for Future Generations

8.4.1 Existing International Institutions for the Vulnerable

A further strand of the argument for a UN Special Envoy is to examine existing UN mechanisms which protect and give some representation to vulnerable groups. This will help us to assess which normative arguments have gained political traction in campaigns to establish such mechanisms. In Chapter 5, we made such an assessment, when we looked at the history of the UN mechanisms relating to children, people with disabilities, people living in poverty, and women. To use the proxy representation *functions* language outlined in Chapter 5 (and discussed at Section 8.5), these mechanisms involve a combination of compliance and representation functions, with the particular mechanism aiming to enhance compliance with the obligations in the particular treaty involved, while also indirectly providing a form of representation for the particular vulnerable group. Understanding which normative arguments have gained traction in these areas will provide insights into which types of normative arguments are also likely to gain traction in efforts to justify establishing a UN Special Envoy and other related mechanisms.

A preliminary finding in relation to these case studies is that vulnerability linked to human rights and human dignity is a strong theme, but the concept of development has also been crucial in terms of developing countries coming on board. For example, in the campaign to establish the UN *Convention on the Rights of the Child* (CRC 1989), protecting children to become good citizens of the future and contribute to nation-building was a key discourse (Holzscheiter 2010: 166). The upshot of these case studies is that arguments for justifying the establishment of institutions for future generations need to be linked to concepts of development to gain global political traction. A further critical point is that recognition of the development aspirations of developing countries, their need to address poverty, and intragenerational justice issues should be reflected in both the normative arguments justifying institutions for future generations and whatever mandate is agreed for a UN Special Envoy (see the following).

An additional crucial point is that the process of appointing a UN Special Envoy, and the functions of such an envoy (including accountability mechanisms), must involve the participation and support of all countries, particularly developing countries. As mentioned earlier, lack of support from developing countries was a key reason for the failure of the 2014 push to establish a commissioner for future generations.

To maximise the likelihood of developing countries' support, the Mary Robinson Foundation has made several helpful proposals. These include a proposal that the UN establish a Commission for Future Generations involving two persons – one from a developing and one from a developed country (Mary Robinson Foundation 2015: 3). The Foundation's proposal for Global Guardians for Future Generations involves appointing three individuals on a basis that would ensure 'representation for developed and developing countries, gender balance and diversity of age' (Mary Robinson Foundation 2018). Certainly, a larger, Commission-type structure would allow for a wider range of interests, spanning geopolitics, age, gender, and so on, to be represented – a theme we return to later.

8.4.2 Lessons from National Institutions for Future Generations

So-called 'commitment devices … seek to bind a person, organisation, or government to an agreed course of action or norms or rules' (Boston 2021a: 87; 2017; Boston, Bagnall & Barry 2019). The idea is – through such devices – to rebalance the scales in the direction of protecting long-term interests (Boston 2021a: 87). National institutions representing future generations in the form of Commissioners or Ombudspersons constitute just some of the possible 'commitment devices' open to governments to foster long-term policy-making (Boston 2021a: 89–95).

An important lesson from experience at the national level is Jonathan Boston's observation that, to be effective, such institutions 'depend on certain ethical norms being widely shared and actively supported' and on developing a political culture that 'values the future and exercises prudence and foresight' (Boston 2021a: 107). A threshold level of support within a society that current generations have minimal core responsibilities towards future generations – that is, a conviction that intergenerational justice is required – is thus imperative. The same is true at the international level. The UN Secretary-General, in both the 2013 report (UN SG 2013) and the 2021 report, *Our Common Agenda* (UN SG 2021), points to support for intergenerational solidarity as being reflected in all the world religions and belief systems (UN SG 2021: 18).

Interestingly, the concept of intergenerational equity has been used in the vast majority of climate litigation cases initiated by youth plaintiffs in recent years (Donger 2022: 272). While most of these cases have been heard in developed states (for example, United States, Canada, Western Europe, and Australia), a substantial number have also occurred in developing countries, such as in South

America and Asia (Donger 2022: 272). While it is possible to point to some strong formal endorsement of intergenerational equity and human rights applying into the future, the acute pressure on governments caused by the COVID-19 pandemic and the energy and food supply crises created by the ongoing war in Ukraine are pushing long-term thinking into the background.

A further lesson from national institutions for future generations is that, to be successful, they require bipartisan or multi-party support. Comparing this to the international system, bipartisan support is equivalent to develop/developing country support – which, of course, glosses over significant differences between groups of countries. The most effective of all such national institutions of this nature, the New Zealand Parliamentary Commissioner for the Environment, has enjoyed bipartisan support since its establishment; this has clearly been significant in its success, albeit without delivering transformative change (Boston 2021b: 455). In addition, the New Zealand Commissioner has been well resourced (Boston 2021b: 444). Any UN Special Envoy would clearly require adequate resources to be effective. A poorly resourced Special Envoy would be worse than no Special Envoy at all, as it would result in tokenism.

8.5 Proxy Functions of a UN Special Envoy

A UN Special Envoy did not emerge from the 2024 Futures Summit, but the Secretary-General could nevertheless proceed to appoint a Special Envoy. The Secretary-General's *Our Common Agenda* report suggests that a function of the UN Special Envoy would be to make recommendations on the best institutional form a mechanism to represent future generations might take (with options including regional guardians of future generations or a UN Commissioner) (UN SG 2021: 45).[6] Combining a 2013 report of the previous Secretary-General (UN SG 2013: 17) with the UN Secretary-General's 2023 report gives some indication of what functions a UN Special Envoy could have (UN SG 2023: 13). These functions might include a mandate to:

1. act as a 'global independent advocate for intergenerational solidarity, with a particular concern for the welfare of future generations';
2. 'promote … best practices in policy-making at all levels';
3. 'promote … engagement and full participation of all stakeholders in United Nations processes related to intergenerational solidarity';
4. 'conduct public advocacy to raise awareness of the measures needed at the global level';

[6] This section draws on Lawrence (2019: 88–99).

5. facilitate long-term thinking and better use of foresight mechanisms;
6. report annually to the General Assembly and upon request to the high-level political forum; and
7. act pursuant to a mandate that would extend beyond today's youth to include the 'needs of future generations'.

As set out in Section 2.5, proxy representation can be broken down in accordance with the functions it performs, as follows:

- **'Proxy representative function'** occurs when the proxy purports to speak or act on behalf of future generations ('direct representation'), with 'indirect representation' occurring where the proxy highlights the interests of future generations without purporting to speak on their behalf.
- **Proxy compliance function** occurs where the proxy operates to help ensure compliance with existing international rules that factor in future generations' interests. This in turn leads to:
- **Proxy law reform function**, where the proxy advocates for reform of international law rules and institutions, including other types of commitment devices. Such a function is likely to be included in the mandate of the new UN Special Envoy for Future Generations (see further).
- **Proxy norm-entrepreneurial function** occurs where the proxy plays a leadership role in persuading others to adopt a particular norm; for example, a UN Special Envoy could advocate for the norm of *intergenerational equity* (entailing an assessment of the impacts of current policies on future generations) to be incorporated across all UN programmes. The concept of 'norm entrepreneurs' is linked to constructivist concepts of international relations (see, for example, Wendt 2001). Intuitively, it would seem likely that there is a strong relationship between the legitimacy of the norm being advocated and the legitimacy of the leadership of the particular proxy representative. In other words, if the norm being advocated is not seen as being in the interests of all countries, then a proxy representative advocating for this norm will have an uphill battle. Conversely, if the norm is perceived as being in the interest of all states, this may facilitate the norm-entrepreneurial function.

A proxy representative of future generations may perform some or all these functions, to varying degrees. A central argument of this chapter is that the most effective proxy representative will maximise the performance of all these functions. By breaking down proxy representation into these elements, a more nuanced analysis can be made as to exactly what a proxy representative is and should be doing. As we shall see, this breakdown also allows a more nuanced analysis of the democratic legitimacy of proxy representatives – to which we now turn.

To ensure the legitimacy and effectiveness of a UN Special Envoy, its mandate should be linked to principles or discourses that already enjoy strong support in the international system. Such principles could include:

- Human rights necessary to lead a decent life (Caney 2010) and including a healthy environment extending into the future[7] aimed at protecting human beings' underlying core needs and interests.
- Intergenerational equity and solidarity between generations interpreted as ensuring that future generations enjoy – as a minimum – human rights necessary for a decent life and a healthy environment, including a functioning climate system.
- Strong sustainability including an obligation to preserve the irreplaceable elements of the global ecological systems upon which human beings depend (Dryzek & Pickering 2018: 89–92).

It is important to note that the concept of intergenerational equity is a component of sustainable development which has received broad international endorsement since the oft-cited formulation in the Brundtland 1987 report, *Our Common Future*. This report defined sustainable development as 'development that meets the needs of the present without compromising the ability of future generations to meet their own needs' (UN SG 1987: 43). Strong support for the principle of intergenerational equity and solidarity in securing the interests of future generations was identified in the initial consultations on elements to be included in a Declaration for Future Generations to be adopted at the Summit for the Future by the UN General Assembly in September 2024 (see United Nations 2023; see Issues Paper 2023). In the Declaration on Future Generations ultimately adopted by the Summit (United Nations 2024), while there were references to the promotion of intergenerational solidarity (para 4), and the principles of equity and solidarity (para 5), there were no references to 'intergenerational equity' but rather the (weaker reference) to taking into account the 'needs and interests of present and future generations' (para 20).

While the Declaration on Future Generations made reference to sustainable development (para 20) this concept has become tarnished in that it has been interpreted as justifying unfettered economic development at the expense of the environment (Dryzek & Pickering 2018: 85–6). When interpreted as 'weak sustainability', the concept allows natural capital – including biodiversity, forests, fauna, and flora – to be substituted by artificial capital (Ott 2017: 24; Neumayer 2003). This is problematic, as the multi-functionality of many ecological systems limits their substitutability (Harte 1995). The upshot is that weak sustainability can

[7] The UNGA on 26 July 2022 recognised 'the right to a clean, healthy and sustainable environment' (UNGA 2022b: para 1).

involve not protecting future generations' human rights as the ecological systems upon which they will depend are degraded. This suggests that a strong version of sustainability should be incorporated in the mandate of the UN Special Envoy, entailing the principle that the irreplaceable elements of global ecological systems should not be degraded. While, undoubtedly, this would be difficult to negotiate, it would clearly strengthen the mandate of the UN Special Envoy. Absent such a clear principle, a UN Special Envoy would necessarily have to fall back on less direct principles, such as arguments about the dependence of human beings on global ecological systems.

Whether the mandate of the UN Special Envoy should seek to incorporate a right to development is a complicated issue, which touches on the tension between the rights of contemporaries and future generations (Spijkers 2018: 7). In the past, there have been attempts to combine the right to development with intergenerational equity. Thus, the 1972 Stockholm Declaration Principle 3 states that 'the right to development must be fulfilled to equitably meet developmental and environmental needs of present and future generations'. In the drafting, this principle initially referred only to the 'right to development'; a reference to 'future generations' was added at the insistence of the Nordic countries, ensuring that the final text refers to both current and future generations. Interestingly, however, the provision is now interpreted as referring only to intergenerational rights and not the right to development (Spijkers 2018: 6–7).

The breadth of the mandate would be a key issue here. A broad mandate allowing the UN Special Envoy to operate guided by the principles set out earlier would allow the Envoy to represent future generations across the UN system. A UN Special Envoy with a broad mandate to represent future generations based on these principles could be given discretion as to how it performs its functions. However, a broad mandate would entail potential risks of overlap with existing UN regimes or agencies, including the *Framework Convention on Climate Change* (UNFCCC), the UN Environment Programme (UNEP), the UN Development Programme (UNDP), the World Health Organization (WHO), and the UN Educational, Scientific and Cultural Organisation (UNESCO), to name some of them.

One way of reducing this risk would be to design the UN Special Envoy to ensure that it had a strong *proxy compliance function*, with its mandate linked to specific intergovernmental norms, processes, or treaties. One such candidate here would be the 2030 Agenda for Sustainable Development (adopted in 2015): this comprises 17 Sustainable Development Goals (SDGs) (UNGA 2015), which require a commitment to future generations and long-term policy-making as part and parcel of their implementation (Soltau 2021; cf. Spijkers 2018). The Group of 77 at the United Nations (G77), representing developing countries and China, indicated in the lead up to the Summit for the Future that it would support a focus in the Declaration on Future Generations on implementing existing commitments including the 2030 agenda (G77 and China 2022: para 26). The G77 and China also indicated that eradicating poverty, the 'development pillar' (included in the Preamble of the United Nations Charter), and intragenerational justice should be given equal importance to intergenerational justice in the intergovernmental process leading to the Declaration on Future Generations (G77 and China 2022; paras 7, 18, and 25), and that any new mechanisms would need to be established through the intergovernmental process related to the declaration (G77 and China 2022). They ruled out the possibility of any amendment of the UN Charter (G77 and China 2022: para 31), which would be a prerequisite for repurposing the existing Trusteeship Council. It may, however, be possible to repurpose the Trusteeship Council through a UN General assembly resolution without amending the Charter. In any event, the UN Secretary-General has indicated that UN members do not favour this proposal (UNSG 2023: 17). The G77 and China implicitly accepted that 'intergenerational equity' and 'solidarity' were appropriate principles for inclusion in the Declaration but argued, in addition, that there should be reference to 'the principles of multilateralism, equity and Common but Differentiated Responsibilities' (UNSG 2023: para 17).[8]

Indeed, the Declaration on Future Generations adopted at the Summit (United Nations 2024) reflected the G77 and China position with most of its content comprising the repetition of existing commitments already made by countries in, for example, the SDGs.

In terms of functions of a UN Special Envoy, a further possibility that has been discussed over recent years is the idea that it play a role in international judicial processes. In the lead-up to the 2014 Rio +20 conference, some NGOs argued that a UN Commissioner for Future Generations should have standing to bring cases on behalf of future generations in the International Court of Justice (ICJ) (Ward 2012). This idea has never been pursued and is a 'bridge too far' for states zealous of their sovereignty. Nevertheless, the normative principles reflected in the proposed mandate for a UN Special Envoy set out earlier – particularly the concept of intergenerational equity – could provide a basis for the ICJ to interpret its rules of procedure flexibly to allow NGOs to represent future generations in *amicus curiae* briefs, which could operate to bring to the Court's attention the interests of future generations in particular proceedings (Lawrence & Köhler 2018). Such a function would be enhanced if states explicitly granted a UN Special Envoy this right in the rules of procedure of the ICJ.

[8] The principle of Common but Differentiated Responsibilities involves the idea that all countries have a responsibility to address environmental challenges, but that it is necessary to take into account the differing capacity and responsibility for causing environmental problems in assigning responsibilities to take action in response. See Rajamani (2006).

Similarly, a UN Special Envoy could exercise compliance functions and law reform functions more effectively, if it were given explicit standing in the UN climate negotiations. This seems unlikely given that the Declaration on Future Generations only contains broad-brush, rather than precise, obligations.[9] Nevertheless, even the Declaration with its general obligations could provide sufficient leverage for a UN Special Envoy to exert pressure on governments to factor in the interests of future generations in policy and law-making. A declaration could have important political and normative effects, even if it did not create new legal obligations (Hale et al. 2023: 23–4). It could, for example, serve as a reference point for future more specific rulemaking, as did the UN Universal Declaration on Human Rights in relation to the development of the global human rights regime (Hale et al. 2023: 24).

As mentioned, the UN Secretary-General's *Our Common Agenda* report envisages that the UN Special Envoy would develop proposals on the ultimate governance structure adopted by the UN, with possibilities listed including regional guardians for future generations, a global commissioner for future generations, or a revamped Trusteeship Council. Interestingly, a wide spectrum of mechanisms is envisaged, ranging from formal through to softer peer-review type mechanisms. The experience in other areas of international law demonstrates that success can often be achieved by starting with informal mechanisms that require exchanges of views and confidence building, which then provide the basis for moving to more formal mechanisms.

While space precludes discussion here, a longer-term proposal worth pursuing could be establishing a new *Optional Protocol to the UN Convention on Economic, Social and Cultural Rights* that would require parties to establish national institutions to represent future generations and to report on long-term impacts of policy-making.[10] Such an instrument could be linked to an existing human rights instrument.

8.6 Synthesis: Strategic Alignment for Future Generations

Table 8.2 combines the democratic legitimacy of Table 8.1 with the proxy representation functions outlined earlier to demonstrate what is likely to be most effective in terms of the design of a UN Special Envoy for Future Generations.

[9] This is in accordance with the proposals made earlier in the negotiation process. See Elements Paper, Declaration for Future Generations, prepared by The Republic of Fiji and Kingdom of the Netherlands. Available at: www.un.org/pga/76/wp-content/uploads/sites/101/2022/09/Elements-Paper-Declaration-for-Future-Generations-09092022.pdf.

[10] See requirements introduced in New Zealand to require Departmental heads every three years to produce 'Long-term Insights Briefings' which set out future trends and policy options in response (February 2024); available at: https://dpmc.govt.nz/our-programmes/policy-project/long-term-insights-briefings.

Table 8.2 *Strategic alignment for future generations*

Legitimacy criteria	Strong	Weak
i. Inclusive/fair representation (procedural – input legitimacy)	• Inclusion of youth in design • Appointment of youth	• Exclusion of youth in design • No appointment of youth
ii. Democratic control (accountability and transparency) (input legitimacy)	• Accountability through strong mandate • NGO monitoring role	• Weak mandate • No NGO role
iii. Deliberation (input legitimacy)	• Mandate allows participation in UN processes	• Mandate precludes participation in UN processes
iv. Source-based (input legitimacy) expertise, discourse	• Expert staff • Well resourced • Mandate linked to sustainability	• Lack of expert staff • Poorly resourced • Mandate does not mesh with existing discourses
v. Substantial (output legitimacy), effectiveness, equity.	• Achieves stronger consideration of future generations' interests in international law-making and furthering of intergenerational equity	• Fails to achieve stronger consideration of future generations interests in international law-making
Legal form	• Hard law	• Soft law peer review
Proxy functions	Strong	Weak
Representative	• Appointment of youth special envoy and both developing country and developed country envoys	• Special envoy appointed who is not young and no developing country envoy
Compliance	• Standing in ICJ and UN climate negotiations	• No standing in ICJ or UN climate negotiations
Law reform	• Mandate to propose mechanisms to represent future generations, and • Advise governments on best practice re national institutions for future generations	• No mandate to propose mechanisms to represent future generations • Limited or no mandate to advise on best practice re national institutions for future generations
Norm-entrepreneurial	• Mandate includes leadership in advocating support for norm of intergenerational equity through the public, working with NGOs and industry	• No mandate or limited mandate to advocate for norm of intergenerational equity.

The argument is that effectiveness will be optimised where the UN Special Envoy maximises its various legitimacy criteria and proxy functions (left-hand column of Table 8.2) with the features of 'Strong' strategic alignment set out in the centre column. When this occurs, this is described as 'strategic alignment for future generations', meaning that the UN Special Envoy is most likely to be effective and operate in a way that maximises intergenerational justice; in other words, its functions align with the interests of future generations. When this occurs, the UN Special Envoy is most likely to function in a way which helps transform policy and international law-making to balance intergenerational and intragenerational justice (see Chapter 4). Conversely, where the UN Special Envoy's functions are aligned with the features of 'Weak' strategic alignment (set out in the right-hand column of Table 8.2), it is more likely to be ineffective and poorly aligned with the interests of future generations.

It is important to note (as discussed in Section 4.2.3) that effectiveness is linked to: (i) how a particular institution promotes intergenerational justice and the values of inclusiveness, solidarity, and addressing vulnerability; (ii) the Paris goals; and (iii) the extent to which a particular mechanism addresses causes of harmful short-termism. As we have seen, one important cause of short-termism is the lack of awareness of long-term policy impacts. A UN Special Envoy could not only help to address this deficiency by authoring high-quality reports on long-term trends and impacts of policy but also through sharing best practices and strengthening national mechanisms for future generations. From a practical point of view, a UN Special Envoy would focus on climate impacts which are short- or medium term, as these are more certain and easier to document. As mentioned in the Conclusion of Chapter 4, there is a lack of research on the structural causes of short-termism in terms of international law-making and international institutions more generally. Appointing a UN Special Envoy could be a trigger for quickly redressing this research deficit.

It is important to recognise an important lesson from the design of such mechanisms at the national level. The stronger the mandate such institutions have had in terms of their powers, the more likely governments are to become nervous and clip the wings of such institutions by reducing their powers.[11] This demonstrates a difficult dilemma in designing a global UN Special Envoy. A UN Special Envoy with a strong mandate is likely to generate concerns amongst states zealous of their sovereignty – particularly developing countries concerned about interference with their economic development. On the other hand, a UN

[11] An example of this phenomenon is the Hungarian Parliamentary Commissioner for Future Generations created in 2007 with a strong mandate including investigating complaints. In 2012, the office was subsumed into the functions of the main Hungarian ombudsman and its status considerably reduced. See Beckman and Uggla (2016: 117, 121).

Special Envoy with a weak mandate may struggle to have an impact, particularly if the UN Special Envoy is poorly resourced. A weak UN Special Envoy may be worse than none at all.

Finally, it should be noted that, since 2020, there has been a significant shift in improving the extent of consultation with young people in UN processes. Evidence for this is the extensive consultation with youth undertaken by the UN Secretary-General in producing the *Our Common Agenda* report (UN SG 2021: 39). Further examples include the extensive consultations undertaken by the UN Human Rights Committee in the drafting of a General Comment on children, human rights, and the environment (particularly climate change), with consultation taking place in regions across the world with youth groups (UNOHCHR 2021). In addition, the 2024 UN Summit for the Future included youth representatives selected by the President of the General Assembly in consultation with member states (UN GA 2022a: para 4). As mentioned earlier, engagement with youth in these processes is indispensable to their legitimacy. This engagement with young people needs to be across both the age and developing–developed country spectrum. Addressing both these dimensions of legitimacy is likely to be a key factor in building legitimacy and support for a UN Special Envoy and implementing the various elements agreed at the 2024 Summit of the Future.

References

Ball, T. T. (2006). Democracy. In Dobson, A. & Eckersely, R., eds., *Political Theory and the Ecological Challenge*, Cambridge: Cambridge University Press, 131–47.

Beckman, L. & Uggla, F. (2016). An Ombudsman for Future Generations, Legitimate and Effective? In González-Ricoy, I. & Gosseries, A., eds., *Institutions for Future Generations*. Oxford: Oxford University Press, 117–34.

Bodansky, D. (1999). The Legitimacy of International Governance: A Coming Challenge for International Environmental Law? *American Journal of International Law*, 93(3), 596–624.

Boston, J. (2017). *Governing for the Future: Designing Democratic Institutions for a Better Tomorrow*, Bingley: Emerald.

Boston, J. (2021a). Protecting Long-term Interests: The Role of Institutions as Commitment Devices. In Linehan, J. & Lawrence, P., eds., *Giving Future Generations A Voice, Normative Frameworks, Institutions and Practice*. Cheltenham: Edward Elgar, 86–107.

Boston, J. (2021b). Parliamentary Commissioner for the Environment, New Zealand. In Cordonier Segger, M.C., Szabó, M. & Harrington, A. R., eds., *Intergenerational Justice in Sustainable Development Treaty Implementation: Advancing Future Generations Rights through National Institutions*. Cambridge: Cambridge University Press, 434–60.

Boston, J., Bagnall, D. & Barry, A. (2019). *Foresight, Insight and Oversight, Enhancing Long-Term Governance through Better Parliamentary Scrutiny*, Victoria University, Wellington: Institute for Governance and Policy Studies.

Caney, S. (2010). Climate Change, Human Rights and Moral Thresholds. In Humphreys, S. ed., *Human Rights and Climate Change*. Cambridge: Cambridge University Press; reprinted in Gardiner, S. et al., eds., *Climate Ethics Essential Readings*. Oxford: Oxford University Press, 163–77.

Coalition for the UN We Need (C4UN). (2023). *Interim Peoples Pact for the Future: 2023 Civil Society Perspectives on the Summit of the Future*. Available at: https://c4unwn.org/wp-content/uploads/2023/05/Interim-Peoples-Pact-for-the-Future-Compressed.pdf.

Convention on the Rights of the Child (CRC) (1989) (adopted 20 November 1989; entered into force 2 September 1990), 1577 UNTS 3.

Day, R. (2024). Coming Soon A UN Envoy for Future Generations, United Nations University (October 9, 2024). Available at: https://unu.edu/cpr/blog-post/coming-soon-un-envoy-future-generations.

Dingwerth, K. (2007). *The New Transnationalism: Transnational Governance and Its Democratic Legitimacy*, London: Palgrave Macmillan.

Dingwerth, K. (2014). Global Democracy and the Democratic Minimum: Why a Procedural Account Alone Is Insufficient. *European Journal of International Relations*, 20(4), 1124–47.

Donger, E. (2022). Children and Youth in Strategic Climate Litigation: Advancing Rights through Legal Argument and Legal Mobilization. *Transnational Environmental Law*, 1(2), 263–89.

Dryzek, J. & Pickering, J. (2018). *The Politics of the Anthropocene*, Oxford: Oxford University Press.

Gonzalez-Ricoy, I. & Rey, F. (2019). Enfranchising the Future: Climate Justice and the Representation of Future Generations. *WIREs Climate Change*, 10(4), e598. https://doi.org/10.1002/wcc.598.

Goodin, R. E. (1996). Enfranchising the Earth, and Its Alternatives. *Political Studies*, 44(5), 835–49.

Goodin, R. E. (2007). Enfranchising All Affected Interests, and Its Alternatives. *Philosophy and Public Affairs*, 35(1), 40–68.

Group of 77 and China. (2022). *Statement on behalf of the Group of 77 and China by Mr Muhammad Imran Khan, Counsellor, Permanent Mission of Pakistan to the United Nations, At the informal consultations on the draft elements paper on the 'Declaration for Future Generations'* (New York, 7 September 2022). Available at: www.g77.org/statement/getstatement.php?id=220907.

Hale, T. N. (2008). Transparency, Accountability, and Global Governance. *Global Governance*, 14(1), 73–94.

Hale, T., Moorhouse, F., Ord, T. & Slaughter, A. (2023). *Towards a Declaration on Future Generations*, Blavatnik School of Government, Policy Brief.

Harte, M. J. (1995). Ecology, Sustainability, and Environmental Capital. *Ecological Economics*, 15(2), 157–64.

Holzscheiter, A. (2010). *Children's Rights in International Politics, The Transformative Power of Discourse*, Houndmills: Palgrave Macmillan.

Issues Paper on the Intergovernmental Process for the Declaration on Future Generations prepared by the Co-facilitators (Issues Paper 2023), 27 June 2023. Available at: www.un.org/sites/un2.un.org/files/sof-dfg_-_issues_paper.pdf.

Karlsson-Vinkhuyzen, S. I. and Vihma, A. (2009). Comparing the Legitimacy and Effectiveness of Global Hard and Soft Law: An Analytical Framework. *Regulation & Governance*, 3(4), 400–20.

Lawrence, P. (2014). *Justice for Future Generations: Climate Change and International Law*, Cheltenham: Edward Elgar.

Lawrence, P. (2019). Representation of Future Generations. In Kalfagianni, A., Fuchs, D. & Hayden, A., eds., *Routledge Handbook of Global Sustainability Governance*. London: Routledge, 88–99.

Lawrence, P. (2021). International Institutions for Future Generations and Democratic Legitimacy. In Cordonier Segger, M. C., Szabó, M. & Harrington, A. R., eds., *Intergenerational Justice in Sustainable Development Treaty Implementation: Advancing Future Generations Rights through National Institutions*. Cambridge: Cambridge University Press, 597–614.

Lawrence, P. (2022). Justifying Representation of Future Generations and Nature: Contradictory or Mutually Supporting Values? *Transnational Environmental Law*, 11(3), 1–27.

Lawrence, P. & Köhler, L. (2018). Representation of Future Generations through International Climate Litigation: A Normative Framework. *German Yearbook of International Law*, 60(1), 639–66.

Mary Robinson Foundation Climate Justice. (2015). *Meeting the needs of Future Generations: Applying the Principle of Intergenerational Equity to the 2015 Processes on Climate Change and Sustainable Development*. Available at: www.mrfcj.org/wp-content/uploads/2015/09/MRFCJPositionPaper_MeetingtheNeedsofFutureGenerations_12August2015.pdf.

Mary Robinson Foundation Climate Justice. (2018). *Global Guardians: A Voice for Future Generations*, Policy Brief. Available at: www.mrfcj.org/wp-content/uploads/2018/02/Global-Guardians-A-Voice-for-Future-Generations-Position-Paper-2018.pdf.

Neumayer, E. (2003). *Weak versus Strong Sustainability: Exploring the Limits of Two Opposing Paradigms*, Cheltenham: Edward Elgar.

Niemeyer, S. & Jennstål, J. (2017). The Deliberative Democratic Inclusion of Future Generations. In González-Ricoy, I. & Gosseries, A., eds., *Institutions for Future Generations*. Oxford: Oxford University Press, 247–65.

Ott, K. (2017). Sustainability: Theory and policy. In Klauer, B., Manstetten, R., Petersen T. & Schiller, J., eds., *Sustainability and the Art of Long-Term Thinking*. London: Routledge, 16–30.

Paris Agreement (2015) (adopted 12 December 2015; entered into force 4 November 2016), 3156 UNTC 79.

Pitkin, H. (1967). *The Concept of Representation*, Berkeley: University of California Press.

Rajamani, L. (2006). *Differential Treatment in International Environmental Law*, Oxford: Oxford University Press.

Saward, M. (2008). Representation and Democracy: Revisions and Possibilities. *Sociology Compass*, 2(3), 1000–13.

Soltau, F. (2021). The 2030 Agenda the Sustainable Development: What are its Implications for Future Generations? In Linehan, J. & Lawrence, P., eds., *Giving Future Generations a Voice: Normative Frameworks, Institutions and Practice*. Cheltenham: Edward Elgar, 108–27.

Spijkers, O. (2018). Intergenerational Equity and the Sustainable Development Goals. *Sustainability*, 10, 1–12.

The Pact for the Future, contained in UNGA resolution A/RES/79/1 (22 September 2024).

United Nations. (2023). Issues Paper on the Intergovernmental Process for the Declaration on Future Generations, Prepared by the Co-facilitators, 27 June 2023. Available at: www.un.org/sites/un2.un.org/files/sof-dfg_-_issues_paper.pdf.

United Nations. (2024). *Summit of the Future, Our Common Agenda*. Available at: www.un.org/en/summit-of-the-future/pact-for-the-future.

United Nations Framework Convention on Climate Change (UNFCCC) (1992) (adopted 9 May 1992; entered into force 21 March 1994), 1771 UNTS 107.

United Nations General Assembly (UNGA). (2015). *Transforming our World: The 2030 Agenda for Sustainable Development*, UN Doc. A/RES/70/1.

United Nations General Assembly (UNGA). (2022a). *Modalities for the Summit of the Future*. Resolution adopted by the General Assembly, UN Doc. A/RES/76/307.

United Nations General Assembly (UNGA). (2022b). *The Human Right to a Clean, Healthy and Sustainable Environment*. Resolution adopted by the General Assembly, UN Doc. A/76/L.75.

United Nations Human Rights, Office of the High Commissioner (UNOHCHR). (2021). *General Comment No. 26 on Children's Rights and the Environment with a Special Focus on Climate Change*. Available at: www.ohchr.org/en/documents/general-comments-and-recommendations/draft-general-comment-no-26-childrens-rights-and.

United Nations Secretary-General (UNSG). (1987). *Report of the World Commission on Environment and Development: Our Common Future*, UN Doc. A/42/427.

United Nations Secretary-General (UNSG). (2013). *Intergenerational Solidarity and the Needs of Future Generations: Report of the Secretary-General*, UN Doc. A/68/322.

United Nations Secretary-General (UNSG). (2021). *Our Common Agenda*.

United Nations Secretary-General (UNSG). (2022). *Press Release*, UN Doc. SG/SM/21399.

United Nations Secretary-General (UNSG). (2023). *Our Common Agenda Policy Brief 1, To Think and Act for Future Generations*.

Vanderheiden, S. (2008). *Atmospheric Justice*, Oxford: Oxford University Press.

Ward, H. (2012). Committing to the Future We Want: A High Commissioner for Future Generations at Rio+20, Foundation for Democracy and Sustainable Development, World Future Council. Available at: www.fdsd.org/wordpress/wp-content/uploads/Committing-to-the-future-we-want-main-report.pdf.

Wendt, A. (2001). Driving with a Rearview Mirror: On the Rational Science of Institutional Design. *International Organization*, 55(4), 1019–49.

9
Conclusion

9.1 Introduction

The failure of existing forms of international law-making and global governance to adequately respond to the climate change crisis means that there is an urgent need to explore new forms of governance. Mechanisms involving proxy representation of future generations are one such form that can play a modest role in helping to ensure the long-term consequences of political action are incorporated in law- and policy-making. If this does not happen, the ecological consequences of inadequate action on climate change are at risk of becoming so dramatic that future generations will suffer massively from these effects. The current political and legal debates on how best to respond to the ongoing and worsening consequences of climate change can be understood as an attempt to address this question.

Representing Future Generations contributes to this discourse on possible theoretical and practical pathways. Our main argument is that the search for – and collective experimentation with – new forms of representation are immensely important elements of sustainable climate policy. Through proxy representation, future generations can be practically and institutionally involved in climate law and policy-making, considering both the vulnerability of future generations and their distinctive interests. By having a proxy reflect their concerns in the present, the medium- and long-term consequences of climate change can become politically manageable, leading to better climate policy.

Representation is a meaningful form of political governance because it is based in democratic theory. In this book, we have presented different understandings and practices of democracy and demonstrated that all consider representation as a central method of democracy. Some construe it narrowly, others more broadly; in all traditions, it plays an important role. Moreover, while recognising that the value of the democratic ideal at the international level remains controversial, we argue that the normative ideal of democracy has received formal endorsement from the international community in a raft of international instruments (Chapter 2) and remains a valid ideal for the same reason it is justified at the national level, namely to avoid tyranny and abuse of power and also to maximise the likelihood of just outcomes in decision-making.

This concluding chapter is structured as follows. We first set out how the pragmatist approach has shaped the various elements of this book (Section 9.2). We then make an assessment of the book's value in relation to real-world international political processes (Section 9.3), before concluding with some suggestions as to fruitful directions for future research (Section 9.4).

9.2 Proxy Representation through a Pragmatist Lense

Consistent with the pragmatist approach of the book, we have not developed an ideal-theoretical justification of representation. Instead, we have identified representation as a central, inherent value of democratic practice and have explored how it can evolve in the face of ecological issues. This does not mean that representation only plays a role in democracies. It also does not mean that all countries and global politics must adopt a specific type of democracy as the basis for political governance. This would be an unrealistic proposal. Our goal is not to democratise the world but, rather, to utilise the idea of representation, which has its origins in various democracies (understood in a very broad sense). We propose reconstructing existing forms of proxy representation at the global level. We also consider how they can be convincingly further developed to facilitate representation of future generations as a means for addressing the climate crisis.

The question of who can (and may) be understood as a proxy is contentious. Some approaches suggest a narrow, actor-centred understanding. In this view, only individuals or clearly defined institutions, established through specific procedures and deriving legitimacy from them, can be understood as proxies. In current debates, the ombudsperson in the national parliamentary system is often mentioned: with clear legal foundations, an ombudsman can have, for example, an auditing or even a veto right over the legislative branch. The proxy then has a very clearly defined task and is, in turn, accountable to Parliament. Expressed broadly, the proxy is tasked with deciding as to whether a piece of legislation is problematic for reasons of intergenerational justice.

At the international level, there is no Parliament, although the United Nations General Assembly plays some of the roles of a global parliament, albeit with very limited powers. At the international level, the proposed UN Special Envoy for Future Generations (discussed in Chapter 8) is the international version of the ombudsman-style proxy mechanisms.

The theoretical considerations of this book, as well as the case studies, show that it is meaningful to broaden such a narrow understanding of proxy representation. In the political and legal fields, proxies for future generations need not only be individuals or narrowly defined (institutional) actors but can also comprise (open) networks, such as social movements, laws themselves, and even social or legal discourses that reflect the interests of the future in the present. Of course, these forms of proxy representation are underpinned by varying degrees of legitimacy: an elected ombudsman has higher legitimacy concerning traditional legal categories than does a social movement or a legal discourse. However, they can all have a significant impact on current political processes. If representation – as we have argued – depends on identifying a sufficiently large audience that shares and implements these concerns, various forms of proxy representation can be justified, even if their legitimacy in the strict sense is lower.

We have argued that, in terms of their future legitimacy, all the proxies mentioned earlier can integrate the needs or interests of future generations in current political and legal mechanisms and have an impact in law- and policy-making. Our argument is: political decisions gain legitimacy only when they represent currently living people and their concerns *and* those of future generations. Legitimacy, therefore, needs to be expanded to include future legitimacy.

Our case studies demonstrate how proxies have already emerged, or are currently emerging, in the field of international law. In some areas, they have already had a pronounced impact, while in others, their impact remains diffuse. Difficulties in delineation arise in certain instances (e.g., between young persons currently living and future generations) which stem from the fact that human beings are temporal beings; thus, the relationship between present and future generations is constantly changing. The case studies show that, despite such challenges, a clear trend is discernible: many legal discourses, actors, and institutions are increasingly taking the concerns of future generations seriously, thereby becoming new forms of proxy representation.

The pragmatist approach underlying this book, inspired by John Dewey, interprets this constant change and expansion of forms of representation not as a problem but as potential. In contrast to other political-philosophical approaches that aim for the generalisability and extensive immutability of political and legal institutions, pragmatist approaches view political processes as ongoing processes. There is no ideal concept that could be deduced in advance for theoretical reasons. Instead, faced with complex problem situations, people have no choice but to experimentally adapt and improve their responses continuously. Politics and law are not fixed and ideal: they are not immutable. Rather, ideals, politics, and law must be tested – not just through ideas but also implemented in the real world to test the extent to which they ameliorate the human condition.

In this sense, the development of new forms of proxy representation can be understood: there is no final blueprint, no ultimate framework. Instead, there are normative heuristics, such as the acknowledgment that it is good and meaningful to take the vulnerability of future generations seriously and thus expand our understanding of justice based on solidarity with these future individuals. How this can be achieved politically or legally must be tested. These are new steps that require political courage and endurance because some developments may lead to dead ends and not be productive.

This does not mean that anything goes or that there are no criteria for evaluating how proposed new political or legal mechanisms or processes should be developed. In a fallibilistic sense, their legitimacy can be analysed and discussed for effectiveness. Both the development of the three normative principles (Chapter 4) and, correspondingly, the justification of proxy institutions in terms of legitimacy and effectiveness (Chapter 5) should be understood as involving criteria for evaluating the experimental process. It is through this constant readjustment and development that stable and effective institutions in the field of international law are possible.

This pragmatist approach seems to contradict some current interpretations of law in theory and practice. Does the law not stand for (timeless) stability and resist constant evaluations and transformations? This appears to us to be a truncated understanding of the law. The law also has no blueprint: it is not an absolute, timeless ideal. Instead, the law is to be further developed with a focus on both accepted procedures and normative considerations. This understanding does not imply a naïve legal positivism that struggles to adequately process normatively the perspectives of vulnerable groups and those without a voice. On the contrary, giving a voice to such groups through proxy forms of representation serves the goal of integrating future generations into the logic of law.

Our argument is that law-making is always an experimental process; the law needs to be further developed in response to important values, changing societal conditions, and global crisis phenomena. International law should not be conceived of from the perspective of rules made by all-powerful sovereign legal subjects but, rather, from the perspective of the vulnerable individual. Only then can it meet its own normative claim for justice and, in a compelling sense, meaningfully consider the interests of future generations by integrating them into legal institutions at all levels.

In this sense, international law is clearly not an absolute and timeless ideal. Rather, because global dynamics and problems are so complex and change rapidly, international law must constantly adapt to global circumstances to provide appropriate and reality bound responses to the crises of the time. In *Representations of Future Generations*, we demonstrate ways in which the concerns of future generations can be understood not as an 'external disruptor' to international law but, rather – through the highlighted discourses, practices, and institutional developments – as an integral part of international law. Our goal is to mainstream the interests of future generations in international law. The forms of proxy representation outlined in the case studies, and their ongoing development, are crucial steps towards achieving this goal.

9.3 Real-World International Political Processes

One initial value of our approach will be evident from the previous discussion: namely a perspective that connects climate change and development issues. Through proxy representation, the concerns of future generations should not be pitted against those of currently living individuals and vice versa. Politically formulated, climate and development policies need to be thought of together. The impacts of climate change affect both people living today and in the future, particularly those who are poor and vulnerable. Therefore, connecting these two perspectives is necessary – including in the design of representation mechanisms, which can involve a fresh perspective on sustainable development, of which intergenerational equity has always comprised a key component.

This is well illustrated with the example of human rights as international legal practice. The consequences of climate change need to be addressed, especially where climate impacts restrict, or make impossible, a decent life. Studies on climate change clearly show that, even with an immediate halt to all greenhouse gas emissions, there will be massive negative consequences that continue into the future. The consequences of climate change already complicate access to basic food and clean water in developing countries. Therefore, climate change already poses a serious threat to human rights. Both climate mitigation and adaptation are thus two necessary conditions to uphold the human right to a decent life. This entails securing basic needs in developing countries, rather than luxury needs in industrialised nations (Shue 1993).

The question of the conditions influencing the satisfaction of basic needs is also central to development policy. Aligning climate policy with human rights, therefore, brings a closer connection between climate and development policy (see Comim 2008). United Nations' institutions have been intensively addressing this intertwining for two decades. Against the backdrop of ever worsening climate change, such integration of development and climate policy is only possible if we strengthen the potential for people living in poverty to exercise agency. This is the foundation of the idea of self-determined development and, at the same time, the most effective means to reduce vulnerability to climate change and increase the ability of vulnerable groups to cope with its inevitable consequences in a dignified manner. Conflicts of interest may arise between the interests of current and future generations, for example, when developing countries have an increasing need for energy. Politically, strategies must be sought that allow for climate protection and sustainable development, while also respecting the needs of future generations and the imperatives of freedom. To ensure the enactment of climate-friendly energy policy, transfers of low-carbon energy technologies will play a crucial role.

Despite our best efforts, conflicts can still arise – including between different dimensions of human rights themselves. Freedom and equality, for example, may lead to different (political) demands in shaping climate policy. For instance, the right to independent development includes a right to energy for emerging and developing countries, which can, in turn, have a negative impact on climate protection goals and the interests of future generations. Politically, a wise combination of various strategies (technology transfer, adaptation support, and linkage with development measures) is needed to allow developing and emerging countries to actively participate in climate protection without diminishing their chances of widespread economic development and poverty reduction. In resolving such conflicts, one dimension of human rights should not be given exclusive priority – as is the case in the approaches outlined earlier. The strength of human rights lies in their ability to establish a legal and ethically meaningful practice that can bring together different beliefs into a coherent framework. Justice, solidarity, and the overcoming of vulnerability form the starting point.

As we have seen earlier, these principles provide a powerful rationale for developing proxy-style mechanisms to represent future generations. Such institutions can be seen as integral to the promotion of sustainable development, which in its classic Brundtland (1987: 43) formulation involves 'development that meets the needs of the present without compromising the ability of future generations to meet their own needs'. This close connection between sustainability and intergenerational justice provides a further rationale for proxy representation of future generations as a means for ensuring that their interests are properly factored into policy-making. As we have seen (Chapter 5), UN mechanisms developed to protect particularly vulnerable groups (such as children, disabled persons, and women) have, to date, been justified using normative arguments that have always included elements relating to development. Similarly, for new proxy-style mechanisms to represent future generations (such as a UN Special Envoy for Future Generations), normative arguments that gain the support of developing countries will be an important precondition of their success. Moreover, such arguments will need to include international, intragenerational, and intergenerational dimensions interacting constructively – not being traded off against one another.

It is also important to remember that, as we have demonstrated (Chapter 5), proxy-style mechanisms already find expression in several areas of international law, including in relation to the European Convention on Human Rights (ECHR). This is important because it means that further development of new proxy-style mechanisms involves incremental reform rather than a radical revolution in terms of international legal mechanisms and institutions.

9.4 Further Research

Our train of thought up to this point indicates that the representation of future generations in international law and institutions constitutes a meaningful political pathway to implement intergenerational justice and solidarity, both politically and legally. At the same time, theoretical considerations, combined with our case studies, show that, from this standpoint, there are still some open questions that require further research. We suggest some key areas of research desiderata below.

We based our *effectiveness criteria* on the objectives of the *Paris Agreement* (2015) and included as a criterion the extent to which mechanisms address sources of harmful short-termism (Chapter 4). This is clearly an area where further research is needed. One obstacle in tackling such research is the extent to which it is feasible to measure the effectiveness of institutions designed to make a difference over the long term. Yet, this challenge can be overstated. For example, if we consider the effectiveness of a UN Special Envoy for Future Generations, we can analyse the effectiveness of comparable institutions, such as the UN High Commissioners for human rights or refugees or special envoys created in the past in relation to other subject areas (Boston 2016). This is not to understate the significant challenges of untangling the causes of short-termism, then analysing the potential impact of new international mechanisms. Assessing the latter may pose challenges because of the way such international institutions operate in conjunction with national institutions. Future research projects will need to be designed in ways that recognise these complexities. In designing such research projects, the theory of proxy representation elaborated in Chapter 3 – which breaks proxy representation down according to its representational, compliance, and norm-entrepreneurial functions – provides a valuable framework to help ensure that such research will be nuanced in terms of the context in which proxy representation takes place.

Another field where further research is needed is the *proxy representation of nature* and the international legal order. Many of the arguments justifying representation of future generations are synergistic with the arguments justifying representation of nature (Lawrence 2022). Nevertheless, there are significant differences, with a range of complex questions to be addressed, including whether all of nature should be represented, or species, or ecosystems. A further challenge is whether a consensus can be developed to support global institutions to represent nature, given the range of world views concerning the relationship between human beings and non-human nature. Despite these challenges, this is a crucial area of research and reform, given the dependence of all human beings on nature and the strong bias in existing international institutions against the interests of non-human nature.

The *case studies* incorporated in this book are necessarily limited. Further case studies that could usefully test the normative framings proposed here include examining the possibility of representation of future generations through the processes and procedures of the Inter-American Court of Human Rights. As we have already observed, there is also a need to closely examine UN climate treaty processes, as well as non-state and substate climate law-making processes, as a vehicle for proxy representation of future generations.

A further serious gap in the existing research is the interaction between global mechanisms to represent future generations and Indigenous approaches. With other scholars, we suggest that such approaches could be a valuable source for the ICJ's forthcoming Advisory Opinion on Climate Change (see Chapter 6; Wewerinke-Singh et al. 2023).

Legitimacy not only plays a central role in democracies but also in global politics in general and in international law. We have also seen that the question of legitimacy is answered differently, depending on whether one looks at decisions from an input or output perspective. In terms of input legitimacy, we can ask, 'Who must consent to or acknowledge a decision for it to be considered legitimate?'. If the decision implies long-term consequences, it seems logical to inquire about the – at least hypothetical – consent of those affected by these decisions in the future. Various strands of democratic theory explicitly develop this argument, such as deliberative democratic theory, which conceptualises future generations as discourse partners in democratic settings. The concept of 'future legitimacy' (Chapter 4) would encompass this situation under the concept of legitimacy, thus requiring the consideration of future generations within this fundamental concept for politics and law.

The same applies to output legitimacy. This is because the ecological consequences of political decisions, including long-term consequences for future generations, are currently not given sufficient attention. In this context, a modification or extension of the concept of output legitimacy is necessary in order to take the long-term ecological consequences of climate change for future generations into account. The concept of 'future legitimacy' implies a critique of such short-term thinking. Regarding output, decisions can only be considered legitimate if decision makers recognise the interests of future generations and take these into account in current decisions.

Researching future legitimacy would mean theoretically expanding the concept of legitimacy. It would require consideration of the narratives and argumentative figures through which this could happen, as well as the specific legal or political practices to which such an expansion could be applicable. An interdisciplinary perspective for such research is essential, as are connections to best practices in this field. *Representing Future Generations* contributes to this task. How this concept can be further developed in theory and practice, and thus politically and legally implemented, undoubtedly requires further research.

Science plays a central role in the current climate debate. Over recent decades, scientists (as individuals), scientific entities in the form of journals, institutions (such as universities and funding organisations), and organisations at the intersection of science and politics (such as the Intergovernmental Panel on Climate Change (IPCC) have all had an important impact on the climate debate. Scientists and their academic discourse have increasingly included links between the physical processes of climate change and its ecological impacts and impacts on human societies (Beck 2018). Combining both the natural and social sciences, a distinct transdisciplinary field of 'climate science' has emerged. In this field, researchers from various disciplinary backgrounds research the impacts of rising greenhouse gas emissions, their causes, and fair forms of burden-sharing and adaptation in sustainable climate policy.

Science has, in many ways, become a proxy for future generations in that scientists, by analysing and bringing the effects of climate change on future generations into the political discourse, have brought the distinctive interests of this group into focus. There has also been increasing research on the political role of science, especially climate sciences. Jürgen Habermas, in the 1970s, engaged with John Dewey and philosophical pragmatism, raising questions about how to conceptualise the relationship between science and politics. Dewey was sceptical of the idea that politics dictates both goals and means for scientific research and vice versa. Instead, he advocated for a deliberative experimental practice in which science and politics jointly agree on publicly meaningful steps. Such Dewey-inspired perspectives also play a significant role in public discourse and the self-perception of scientists and politicians. Others, such as Kowarsch and Edenhofer (2015), emphasise the distinctiveness of politics and science and argue for cooperative understanding between the two from a pluralistic perspective.

Behind the question of the relationship between politics and science in the face of climate change is also the question of whether, and to what extent, science can be understood as a form of proxy representation: who, exactly, is the proxy, and how does representation work? Science gains legitimacy, for example, not so much through law and morality, but by producing true or evidence-based insights.

Must the criteria of legitimacy, therefore, be expanded? And in what forms does representation take place?

These important questions are only just beginning to be explored. Their urgency lies in the fact that climate discourse and the question of long-term consequences for future generations are undoubtedly heavily influenced by science – and will continue to be so in the future. Therefore, the crucial question of science as a proxy for future generations warrants further exploration.

After the fall of the Berlin Wall in 1989, political science entered a new phase of globalisation. This has posed challenges for various disciplines to rethink relationships between national and supranational actors. In the 1970s and 1980s, theories were often developed that did not adequately consider the relativity of social reality. Global structures were described as a rigid system of individual elements and primarily seen as the creation of nation-states. These theories are now outdated because the globalised world consists of different relations on various levels (Rosenau 2003), including subnational and non-state actors, such as, cities, intergovernmental organisations (IGOs), non-governmental organisations (NGOs), industry, and industry associations.

In response to this insight, the concept of *global governance* emerged, in an attempt to develop new ways of understanding world politics in the era of globalisation. Since the 1990s, global governance has become an important paradigm in both theory and practice, aiming to describe and explain global structures and dynamics in an appropriate manner. Scholars such as Dirk Messner (2000) and Michael Zürn (2018) explicitly place their research within this paradigm. Global governance theories typically first provide a description of global relationships and their resulting structures using various disciplines. In a second step, they inquire whether and how this complex structure can be controlled. A governance understanding is thus developed which departs from the nation-state concept of governance and emphasises dynamic mutual influence. 'Governance without Government' has become the central message of this newly developed paradigm.

The background of this theoretical development is the observation that the process of globalisation is changing traditional forms of national governance. Governance is increasingly taking on a transnational character (Reder 2009), altering the conditions for (transnational) governance in terms of both its origins and legitimacy. Three characteristics play a particularly significant role. First, there is a significant proliferation of actors at the global level involved in this governance action (Rosenau 2003). With this increase in actors, debate about the legitimacy of transnational forms of governance also expands because legitimacy is generated through the involvement of diverse actors and not limited to the realm of formal political institutionalisation. Secondly, the forms of control have also multiplied. Transnational governance action is therefore referred to as governance, rather than government. This means that numerous actors (private and public institutions, as well as individuals) exert influence, resulting in control structures that aim for a balance of influencing factors. This has been evident in the global climate regime which features not just governments but also industry and industry associations, NGOs, and subnational actors, such as cities (Kuyper et al. 2018). These structures cannot be captured by the traditional concept of government.

In the face of this analysis, global governance implies less a direct control of political processes by institutions and more a complex system of influence and regulation arising from the plural interaction of different actors: 'Governance is the totality of the numerous ways in which individuals as well as public and private institutions regulate their common affairs. It is a continuous process through which controversial or different interests are balanced, and cooperative action can be initiated' (Commission on Global Governance 1995). World politics can only be interpreted as a multilevel system, with special consideration given to the multitude of actors and mechanisms.

Earth Systems Governance emerged as an interdisciplinary project in the early 2000s, in an effort to bring together physical scientists working on the science of earth systems with social scientists to examine how global governance (and, indeed, governance at every level) could be brought into line with the needs of the ecosystem (Biermann 2007). The idea was to bring together social sciences analysing how human beings respond to Earth system transformation, with the aim of steering human development in a way that ensured 'safe' co-evolution with natural processes (Biermann 2007). From the start, inclusiveness – including the participation of non-state actors – was an essential element of this project (see Bierman et al. 2019; Earth System Governance, ESG 2024).

The impact of environmentally harmful behaviour on future generations provides a good example to illustrate the global dimension of politics and the multiplication of actors beyond the nation-state (Kuyper et al. 2018; Kuyper & Bäckstrand 2016; Angstadt & Betsill 2021). From this perspective, the representation of future generations can be understood as one element of a sustainable global governance strategy. Proxy representation of future generations can both be a counterbalance to state governance and take forms constituted by states (such as a UN Special Envoy) and also be outside the state, such as NGOs or the IPCC (science as representation of future generations). More research is clearly needed on the potential interactions between proxy representation of future generations at different levels of governance, and also proxy representation of non-human elements of nature.

The *multilateralism* expressed in these theories, both in theory and practice, has come under significant pressure in recent years. Inward-looking nationalist-oriented political forms are on the increase worldwide. This has been accompanied by a rise in authoritarian states that seek to act more hegemonically than multilaterally. In many deliberatively oriented forms of multilateral cooperation, this trend continues to be clearly felt, with a political retreat to national issues. However, the considerations outlined in this book clearly show that sustainable attention to future interests should – and, indeed, can only – be globally oriented in tackling the global ecological crisis of which climate change is a part.

The interests of future generations should, in theory, be incorporated in decision-making by the state. But where this 'mainstreaming' does not happen, the interests of future generations can be taken up by a range of non-state or substate actors, including IGOs, NGOs, and scientists. *Representing Future Generations* has only begun to scratch the surface of the full range of possibilities here. Recent scholarship on the involvement of non-state actors in the global climate regime demonstrates that there can be both advantages and serious difficulties in terms of climate action taken by substate or non-state actors, for example, in ensuring accountability for pledged action on climate change (Kuyper & Bäckstrand 2016).

Unfortunately, multilateralism is also under pressure in the research sphere. Although international law as a research discipline stands against this in terms of its subject and spirit, this narrowing is felt in philosophy, for example. For years, publications on explicitly global issues have been declining, which is highly problematic. How multilateralism can be conceived of and justified in the face of complex global crises, how political science, law, and philosophical arguments about the future design of the multilateral order can be connected and strengthened, especially against the backdrop of a surging inward nationalism, is an urgent and important field of research. We envisage this book as a partial response. There is still much work ahead in designing and implementing mechanisms to represent future generations in the global legal order. Future generations deserve nothing less.

References

Angstadt, M. & Betsill, M. (2021). Non-state Actors. In Rajamani, L. & Peel, J., eds., *Oxford Handbook of International Environmental Law*. Oxford: Oxford University Press, 666–83.

Beck, S. & Mahony, M. (2018). The IPCC and the New Map of Science and Politics. *WIREs Climate Change*, 9(6), e547. https://doi.org/10.1002/wcc.547

Biermann, F. (2007). 'Earth System Governance' as a Crosscutting Theme of Global Change Research. *Global Environmental Change*, 17(3–4), 326–37.

Biermann, F. et al. (2019). The Earth System Governance Project as a Network Organization: A Critical Assessment after Ten Years. *Current Opinion in Environmental Sustainability*, 39, 17–23.

Boston, J. (2016). *Governing for the Future: Designing Democratic Institutions for a Better Tomorrow*, Bingley: Emerald.

Brundtland, G. (1987). *Our Common Future*, Oxford: Oxford University Press.

Comim, F. (2008). Climate Injustice and Development: A Capability Perspective. *Development*, 51, 344–49.

Commission on Global Governance. (1995). *Our Global Neighbourhood, The Report of the Commission on Global Governance*, Oxford: Oxford University Press.

Earth System Governance. *Research Agenda and Science Plan*, ESG (2024). Available at: www.earthsystemgovernance.org/research-agenda-science-plan/.

Kowarsch, M. & Edenhofer, O. (2015). Cartography of Pathways: A New Model for Environmental Policy Assessments. *Environmental Science & Policy*, 51, 56–64.

Lawrence, P. (2022). Justifying Representation of Future Generations and Nature: Contradictory or Mutually Supporting Values? *Transnational Environmental Law*, 11(3), 1–27.

Messner, D. (2000). Globalisierung und Global Governance – Entwicklungstrends am Ende des 20. Jahrhunderts. In Siegelberg, J., & Schlichte, K., eds., *Strukturwandel internationaler Beziehungen*. Wiesbaden: VS Verlag für Sozialwissenschaften.

Reder, M. (2009). *Globalisierung und Philosophie. Eine Einführung*, Darmstadt: Wissenschaftliche Buchgesellschaft.

Rosenau, J. N. (2003). *Distant Proximities: Dynamics beyond Globalization*, Princeton, NJ: Princeton University Press.

Shue, H. (1993). Subsistence Emissions and Luxury Emissions. *Law and Policy*, 15(1), 39–60.

Wewerinke-Singh, A., Garg, M. & Agarwalla, S. (2023). In Defence of Future Generations: A Reply to Stephen Humphreys. *European Journal of International Law*, 34(3), 651–68.

Zürn, M. (2018). *A Theory of Global Governance*, Oxford: Oxford University Press.

Index

Printed by Integrated Books International,
United States of America